Father Sheedy's
Ask Me A Question

Father Sheedy's
Ask Me A Question

Our Sunday Visitor Publishing Division
Our Sunday Visitor, Inc.
Huntington, Indiana 46750

ACKNOWLEDGMENTS: The contents of this work originally appeared in various issues of *Our Sunday Visitor* newsmagazine. Except for minor changes (stylistic consistency, clarifications, and the like), the material is substantially the same.

Our Sunday Visitor Publishing Division
Our Sunday Visitor, Inc.
200 Noll Plaza
Huntington, Indiana 46750

INTERNATIONAL STANDARD BOOK NUMBER: 0-87973-426-4
LIBRARY OF CONGRESS CATALOG CARD NUMBER: 89-60270

PRINTED IN THE UNITED STATES OF AMERICA

Cover design by Rodney Needler

426

Contents

Introduction 11

Abortion 12
Abstinence 15
Adam and Eve 16
Adultery 17
Alcohol 17
Angels 18
Annulment 19
Anointing of the Sick 21
Antichrist 22
Apostles 23
Apostles' Creed 24
Ash Wednesday 24
Astrology 25

Baptism 25
Benediction 29
Bible 31
Birth Control 35
Black Priests 38
Blessed Articles 39
Blessings 39
Blind 40
Blue Army 40
Born Again 40

Capital Punishment 42
Catholic Church 43
Celibacy 45
Chain Letters 47
Chalice 48
Charismatics 48
Children 50
Christ 51
Christmas 52
Church and State 52
Church of Christ 52
Cloning 53
Commandments 54
Communion, Holy 55
Communion of Saints 56
Confession (Reconciliation) 58
Confirmation 60
                                                          63

Conscience 63
Cooperation in Evil 65
Cosmetic Surgery 66
Creation 67
Creed 67
Cremation 68
Crucifix 68
Crucifixion 69

Deaconesses 69
Dead 70
Death Penalty 72
Depression 73
Deuterocanonical Books 74
Devil 75
Divine Office (Liturgy of the Hours) 76
Dogma and Doctrine 78
Dogmatism 78

Easter 79
Ecumenical Councils 80
Ecumenism 81
Episcopal Orders 83
Equality of Religions 83
Eucharist 84
Eucharistic Ministers 85
Evolution 86
Excommunication 87
Exorcism 89

Faith and Morals 90
Fátima 90
Father 91
Fear 92
Final Repentance 92
First Fridays 93
First Saturdays 94
Flags in Church 94
Flying Saucers 96
Forgiveness of Sin 96
Forty Hours 96
Free Will 97
Freedom of Religion 98
Funerals 99
Fundamentalism 99

Gambling 102
General Absolution 102
Gifts of the Holy Spirit 103
Gideons 104
Girl Altar Servers 104
God 105
Good Friday 106
Good Works 106
Gospels 106
Grace 108

Heaven 109
Hell 110
Holy Spirit 111
Home Best Teacher 112
Homosexuality 113
Hypnosis 115

Icons 115
Impotency 116
Indulgences 118
Infallibility 119
Infant Death 119
Inheritance 120
Inquisition 120
Insurance 122
Intercommunion 122
Investments 124
Israel 124

Jehovah's Witnesses 125
Jesus 127
Jews 127
Judgment 129
Justice and Peace 130

Killing 131

Laicization 132
Lazarus 133
Legion of Decency 134
Legion of Mary 135
Limbo 135
Living Will 136
Lord's Prayer 137
Lutherans 137

Magnificat 138
March of Dimes 138
Marionite Rite 139
Marriage 140
Martyrs 147
Mary 147
Masons 151
Mass 152
Masturbation 159
Medjugorje 160
Mexico 161
Miracles 162
Morality 162
Mormons 163
Mystical Body 164

Novenas 165

Occasion of Sin 165
Occult 166
Organ Donations 166
Original Sin 167
Orthodox 167
Our Father 168

Papacy 169
Parish 171
Passion 172
Peace Greeting 172
Peer Pressure 173
Penance 173
Permanent Deacons 174
Place of Honor 175
Porno Phones 175
Possession 176
Prayer 176
Predestination 178
Prisons 178
Problem of Evil 179
Protestants 180
Purgatory 181

Race 183
Rape 185
Rapture 186
Reincarnation 186

Religious 187
Restitution 188
Right to Die 188
Rosary 189

Sabbath 190
Sacred Vessels 191
Saints 192
Salvation 201
Satan 202
Scapular 203
Scripture 204
Scruples 208
Seal of Confession 209
Secular Humanism 209
Servile Work 210
Sex 210
Sign of the Cross 211
Sign of Peace 212
Sin 213
Soul 214
Stations of the Cross 215
Statues 215
Suffering 216
Suicide 217
Sunday Obligation 217
Sunday Work 218

Tithing 219
Tradition 220
Transfiguration 220
Transubstantiation 221
Tubal Ligation 222

Ukrainians 223

Virginity 223
Vocations 225

War 226
Wealth 227
Worship 228

Introduction

This book contains a selection of actual questions submitted by readers of *Our Sunday Visitor* and the answers as they essentially appeared in the paper. They are the puzzlements and problems of real people and not made up. It is recognized that brief answers may not completely satisfy theologians and philosophers who are taught to make distinctions and sub-distinctions, but space in a weekly column is limited and treatises are for books. What the column attempts to do is provide brief but accurate answers to problems or confusion some people have about the Catholic faith. When applicable, Church documents, regulations, and laws are cited as authority. This may give a legalistic sound, but rules are made to be followed. We may disagree with a rule or law, and we are free to work to change it. However, to flagrantly ignore authority gives scandal to some and unease to others, as so many of these questions show.

There was a previous volume to this present book, now out of print, which was largely concerned with changes brought about by Vatican II. Now that liturgical renewal is completed and the new Code of Canon Law published, much of the earlier confusion and uncertainty has subsided. Some of this is due to parish catechesis, but most of it can be credited to pastors who did not impose change unilaterally but explained reasons for it.

These questions show that people are hungry to know more about their religion and for answers to their problems. Perhaps this book will suggest to some that more could be done with adult education on a parish level. This book is not intended to be encyclopedic; rather, it answers frequently asked questions, and its aim is solely to give Catholics a better understanding of their beliefs and customs.

Abortion

In *Roe vs. Wade*, the Supreme Court said: "The Aristotelian theory of 'mediate animation' that held sway throughout the Middle Ages continued to be Roman Catholic dogma until the nineteenth century, despite opposition to the 'ensoulment' theory from those in the Church who would recognize the existence of life from the moment of conception." Is this true? Was "mediate animation" the official Roman Catholic dogma until the nineteenth century? — *Edward N. Haas, Pearl River, La.*

The above is not exact. A dogma is a truth of faith or morals authoritatively put forth by the Church as revealed by God and requiring belief by the faithful. The beginning of life was never defined by the Church. However, following the Greek philosophers, most Christian theologians, philosophers, and scientists held to "mediate animation." St. Thomas Aquinas taught that the soul (form) was created when the body (matter) resembled a human being. Aristotle had taught that this occurred on the fortieth day for males, the ninetieth day for females. But it must be remembered that several hundred years ago the sciences of genetics and embryology were unknown, and the teaching of Church theologians was based on limited and faulty knowledge. Modern biological discoveries now give scientific basis for Church teaching, not philosophical supposition. In our own day these sciences have made great leaps forward to genetic engineering. The discovery of the existence of the DNA molecule advanced genetics further in a moment than all the speculation of preceding centuries. We know that when the male sperm fertilizes the female ovum, the full chromosome number of twenty-three pairs is established. At the moment of conception the color of the skin, eyes, hair, body structure, facial appearance, etc., are established. Moreover, at that moment, if there is a defect in the genes of either parent, that defect is passed on. Thus the Church's position today that life begins at conception is rooted in science and not in eighteenth-century guessing. Those of that time who taught that life begins at the point when conception takes place (everything present that the new life needs) have now been proven correct.

ABETTING ABORTION • I understand that Canon 1398 refers only to a person who procures an abortion. What is the official teaching of the Roman Catholic Church concerning the role of the doctor who performs the abortion, the person counseling the abortion, the individuals who fail to stand up against abortion, and the individuals who vote for abortion funding or vote for persons who vote for abortion funding? — *Marilyn M. Prouty, Acampo, Calif.*

Canon 1398 states: "A person who actually procures an abortion incurs a *latae sententiae* excommunication." (A *latae sententiae* penalty is one automatically incurred by committing the crime and does not require the sentence of a judge.) The word "procures" is interpreted in the sense of "causes" and applies to the consenting mother and the necessary physical and moral cooperators (doctor, counselor). However, beyond the Code of Canon Law is the moral law of the Fifth Commandment: "Thou shalt not kill." To cause the death of an unborn child is equivalent to murder and is a grave (that is, mortal) sin. There is no canonical penalty against those who vote for abortion funding, but there is a moral dereliction in cooperation in the evil of another. This also applies to people who give any support to abortion. The position taken by some Catholic politicians that they personally oppose abortion but do not wish to impose their views on another is not logically justifiable. They are saying, in essence, "I won't commit murder, but it is okay for you to do it." Those who vote for abortion funding are, in effect, providing the means for murder, and this cannot be reconciled with Catholic morality.

INDUCED BIRTH • In a recent operation in our hospital the doctor in charge decided to induce premature birth because the physical structure of the mother was such that she could not deliver at the regular time. The doctor said that this was not an abortion, since no one desired the death of the fetus. Will you comment? — *Name withheld, Boston, Mass.*

This seems to be a case of both bad morality and bad medicine. The doctor may call it what he wishes, but it is still an abortion, since the fetus could not be viable outside the womb. The normal procedure is to allow the fetus to experience its normal course and then be born by Caesarean section. No acceleration of birth is permitted unless it takes into consideration the life of the fetus as well as the mother.

WHY EXCOMMUNICATION? • You said in *Our Sunday Visitor* that those who procure an abortion are excommunicated if they are Catholics. An abortion is the taking of a human life. Why does the Church not excommunicate Catholic British soldiers who shot innocent children in Northern Ireland or Christian soldiers in Lebanon who shot Muslims? — *Stuart B. Maguire, Wrentham, Mass.*

The Church has spoken in defense of noncombatants in times of war. Pope John Paul II has condemned the violence in Northern Ireland and in Lebanon and called for peace. God himself in the Fifth Commandment condemns murder: "Thou shalt not kill." It is obvious to Christians and Jews that the unjust taking of life is seriously wrong. Not so obvious, however, is the matter of abortion, since the human being as yet does not live apart from the mother. People argue that the fetus is not yet human life. In order to emphasize its teaching that human life begins at conception, the Church places an extraordinary punishment on this act to dramatize its evil. Yet, in the final analysis, the effects on the individual are the same. Murder is a most grave sin that cuts one off from God's grace and deprives one of the right to the sacraments until the sin is healed through pardon. While many people have been killed in Northern Ireland and Lebanon, the number pales when compared to the millions killed through abortion. In many cities in the United States abortions now outnumber live births. This is a most grievous problem that needs extraordinary measures.

COOPERATION • I am a Catholic hospital administrator currently seeking a new job opportunity. The hospitals where I have previously served did not perform abortions. My question is, since it is not the administrator that establishes policy but the boards of the institutions, what is the administrator's role in a hospital that does perform abortions? — *Name withheld, Denver, Colo.*

Although an administrator may not set policy, he does carry it out and it thus becomes a matter of cooperation with evil. I suggest you read a good moral text on cooperation, such as that found in Father Charles McFadden's *Medical Ethics.* Briefly, one can never directly (formally) cooperate in the sin of another. For a sufficient reason indirect (material) cooperation is sometimes permitted. Material cooperation is defined by Father McFadden as "unwilling aid given to another in the commission of an immoral act; that is, the one cooperating neither agrees with the sinful intentions of the principal agent nor desires the sinful act to take place, but actually does render some aid because of some personal benefit that will be

derived or because of some loss that will thereby be averted."
A nurse or an anesthetist can easily be faced with the problem
of material assistance as something immoral. Your case, however, is somewhat different in that you are not in such a situation now but are asking if you can place yourself in a situation
of material cooperation. Rather than play with legalism, I
would think that a conscientious administrator would seek only
employment in a hospital that obeys divine and natural law and
avoid environments that create serious moral problems.

ABORTION PARDON • I am very much against abortion. I
read an article by Ann Landers which states that a priest
will give absolution to a woman who had an abortion. I
heard that a priest could not give absolution for a marriage annulment or an abortion. This had to come from
the pope. If this is true, when did the Church start con-
doning abortion? — *Fred Kury, Custer, S. Dak.*

The Church does not condone abortion. Canon 1398 imposes the
penalty of excommunication on anyone who procures an abortion. However, this excommunication is not reserved to the
pope but can be removed in confession when the person shows
repentance and purpose of amendment. Abortion is a very serious sin, the sin of the murder of innocent life. Thus the excommunication takes effect immediately upon committing it without the need of judicial sentence. There are certain excommunications reserved to the pope: sacrilege against the Sacred
Species, violence to the pope, giving absolution to a partner in
a sin against the Sixth Commandment, direct violation of the
seal of confession, and the illegal consecration of a bishop. Other excommunications can be removed by a bishop or confessor, and abortion is one of these. So Ann Landers is right in this
instance and her encouragement for women who have committed an abortion to seek forgiveness in the sacrament of
penance was good advice.

Abstinence

I would like to know when it was decreed that Roman
Catholics were not to eat meat on Friday and why meat
rather than fish, bread, or other food. — *P. Steinwachs,
Floral City, Fla.*

Fasting and abstinence extend back into the Old Testament.
The Jews had many dietary laws and some of these were car-

ried over into the early Church. The theological reason was that chastising the body brought it under control of the spirit and it was a way of atoning for sin. Abstinence is first mentioned in a Church document in a decree of the Council of Toledo in the year 447. It was the custom to abstain primarily from meat on Fridays and days of penance. However, people began abstaining from other things as well. In 1666 Pope Alexander VII issued a decree revoking a custom of not eating eggs and cheese during Lent, thus permitting these items of food on days of abstinence. When the Code of Canon Law was issued in 1917, it confirmed the custom and banned the eating of flesh meat and of broth made from meat but did not ban the use of eggs or milk products (cheese and butter) or any seasoning for food, even though it included meat fat. In 1966 Pope Paul VI issued the apostolic constitution *Poenitemini* (*On Penance*), which confirmed this practice of the Church and whose decrees were included in the new Code of Canon Law issued in 1983. Canon 1251 of this code prescribes abstinence from meat or some other food decided upon by a conference of bishops on Fridays throughout the year (unless they are solemnities) and on Ash Wednesday. The National Conference of Catholic Bishops of the United States made abstinence from meat mandatory on Ash Wednesday and all Fridays of Lent and recommended that it be observed on all Fridays of the year but allowed individual Catholics to substitute another penance on Fridays if they could not abstain from meat. Meat was chosen because it was the primary food of Europe at the time. However, with the expansion of the Church into the Third World, meat is not always the primary food there. Under the new regulations the local bishops can adapt the law of abstinence to a more pertinent food.

Adam and Eve

EVOLUTION • Where does Adam and Eve fit in on the theory of man coming from apes? Are they the missing link? This has been puzzling me a long time. — *Name withheld, Valencia, Pa.*

As Catholics we must believe that at some point in history God created the first man and woman, infusing in them the human soul. The Bible names them as Adam and Eve, our first parents. You are correct in stating that evolution is a theory — that is, an unproven supposition. Those who do not believe in

God must of necessity deny creation. They are forced to seek some logical explanation for the universe and thus adopt the theory of evolution. Yet even the evolutionist is stumped when pinned down about the first cause or the origin of primal matter. In the end the theory of evolution leaves far more questions unanswered than answered. Materialistic evolution in my opinion is unscientific because it accepts too many unproven hypotheses. However, for the believer in God, creation is a reasonable explanation. We must distinguish between the evolution of man and the development of man. The first is unproven, but the second can be demonstrated. The Bible and its account of creation, however, is a theological and not a scientific statement and we should not do injustice to the word of God by forcing conclusions from it that were not intended.

Adultery

Why should a wife be branded an adulteress (Matthew 5:32) because her husband divorced her for some reason other than unchastity? How could she be an adulteress if she never again had sexual relations with a man? — A. P. McElroy, Atlanta, Ga.

In interpreting this verse we must be mindful of Luke 16:18 and 1 Corinthians 7:11. Our Lord's words in Luke make the condition that another marriage has taken place. Paul in his letter states that when a woman separates from her husband, she must remain single or be reconciled to her husband. Jesus is condemning divorce and saying that those who remarry after divorce (this is presumed in Matthew) commit adultery. If there is no remarriage, there is no adultery.

Alcohol

What is the Church rule or code of ethics about selling alcoholic beverages on church grounds? — Name withheld, Williams, Ariz.

The Church has no rule on this matter but leaves it up to the discretion of the pastor and local custom. Alcoholic beverages are not evil in themselves; it is their abuse that becomes wrong. Jesus never condemned drinking. His first miracle was to change water into wine, and wine was present at the Last Supper. St. Paul counseled one of his disciples to take a little wine for his stomach's sake. However, eating or drinking is to be done in moderation. To eat or drink to excess becomes the sin of gluttony, one of the capital sins. If there are abuses, the pastor would have to consider this factor.

ALCOHOLIC FATHER • As a true Catholic isn't it wrong to overindulge? I'm with my dad a lot in his work and he drinks a great deal of the time. He even drinks while driving and says it's okay if you don't get caught. Our family gets so disgusted seeing him this way. It's almost like he's encouraging us kids to drink. He even drinks before Mass. I say he's a bad example and I don't want to be like him. What do you think? — *Name withheld, Lansing, Mich.*

From the drinking pattern you describe, I'd say your father is sick with a disease called alcoholism. He needs help to see himself for what he is and to understand what he is doing. The place for him to get help is AA (Alcoholics Anonymous). While I care what is happening to him, I care more what is happening to you and the other members of your family, since you are not responsible. First, I urge you not to get in a car with your father when he is drinking. Half the fatal accidents in this country are caused by drinking drivers. Although he won't admit it, the fact is his driving skills and reflexes are impaired by drinking. Second, AA has a branch called Al-Anon, for families of those with a drinking problem. Like AA it is completely anonymous. There you will learn to understand what is happening to your father, what you can do about it, and learn how not to let your father's drinking habits destroy you. Find out where the nearest Al-Anon meeting is and ask your mother to go with you. AA usually has a telephone number in the directory. It is a sin to drink to excess and it is also a sin to drive while drinking, since one becomes a threat to others.

Angels

Why do we believe that angels have wings and can fly? — *Name withheld, Temple, Tex.*

Angels do not have wings. They are pure spirits of a wholly immaterial nature. As such, they rank ahead of human beings in creation, who are composed of spirit and matter (soul and body). Thus the psalmist describing man says, "Thou hast made him a little less than an angel." While the Old Testament does speak of wings on angels, this is not to be taken literally. The Old Testament also depicts angels as handsome young men (see the Books of Daniel and Tobit). Thus God allows them to assume visible form in order to communicate with people. Artists have adopted the use of wings to differentiate angels from humans and to suggest that they can move about quickly. Angels do not really fly, but being pure spirits they can move instantly from one place to another. However, they can only be in one place at a time. We do not know the number of angels, but Scripture suggests that they are many. A good book on angels is Father Pascal Parente's *Beyond Space* (Tan Books).

GUARDIAN ANGELS • This is the question that was put to me: "What is the basis of the Catholic belief in guardian angels? No other religions speak of them." — *Mary F. Geers, Quincy, Ill.*

The Church teaching comes from Old and New Testaments where belief in such angels is frequent. The prime example is in the Book of Tobit where St. Raphael is assigned to Tobias to guide him and keep him from harm. Jesus spoke of guardian angels (see Matthew 18:10) when he warned his hearers not to give scandal to children: "See that you never despise one of these little ones. I assure you their angels in heaven constantly behold my heavenly Father's face." Also, see Acts 12:7-10 where an angel leads Peter from prison. The Church interprets this angel as a guardian angel who watches over Peter. One of the difficulties in some of these teachings of the Church is that people do not find the exact term that we use in Scripture (for example, guardian angels, purgatory, etc.) and hence deny the teaching itself. But the Church's teachings on these subjects are rooted in Scripture, and it is only time that has given a name to these teachings. The very people who object to this will use such a term as "the Rapture" to describe an event at the Second Coming, even though this term is not used in Scripture.

Annulment

Is a marriage in the Catholic Church possible between a baptized Catholic (single) and a divorced Episcopalian?

Could the Protestant marriage somehow be annulled? What are the grounds for annulment? — *Name withheld, Clarkson, Nebr.*

An annulment, or decree of nullity, is a finding by a Church tribunal that no valid marriage existed in the first place and that the partners are free to marry. The marriage is declared invalid because of a defect in form or the existence of some impediment at the time the contract was made. Among these impediments are impotency, affinity, defect in form, age, preexisting bond, psychological immaturity, prior crimes, and defect in contract. An annulment can be sought by either party and does not need the consent of one's spouse. Asking for an annulment is no guarantee it will be granted; the defect must be established in Church court. The Church recognizes the validity of Protestant marriages but can also rule on the validity. Thus a Protestant wishing to marry a Catholic can have his or her first marriage examined as to validity, and a finding of nullity can be given, leaving the Protestant free to marry the Catholic.

SOURCE OF ANNULMENT • Before our two young co-pastors came to our parish, a marriage annulment was almost impossible to get. Now a record number have been granted. In almost all cases, each party was a Catholic and after an annulment another marriage was contracted. Has the power of the local pastor become that strong? — *Name withheld, Mt. Carmel, Ill.*

No local pastor can grant an annulment. Ordinarily, the local pastor initiates the process. The pastor is approached by both parties seeking an annulment. He takes all the information and forwards it to the diocesan marriage tribunal. Your tribunal is at the chancery in Belleville. Here, set canonical procedures must be followed before the judges render a decision. It is possible that a pastor might hinder people from seeking an annulment, but they have the right to apply directly to their tribunal. It is true that in recent years annulment cases move more rapidly because of procedures Rome allows American courts to compress. It is also true that greater numbers of annulments have been granted because of a new emphasis on psychological reasons invalidating the first marriage. But it is the diocesan court and not the pastor who makes the decision on whether or not to grant the annulment.

LEGITIMATE CHILDREN • A non-Catholic friend of mine at work stated that when the Church annuls a marriage and there are children involved, then that makes bastards of the children. There was nothing I could reply to him and I wonder what your reply is. — *Name withheld, Thorp, Wis.*

Your friend is wrong. Canon 1137 covers this situation. It states: "Children who are born of a valid or a putative marriage are legitimate." A putative marriage is one assumed at the time it was entered to be valid, even though it was shown later that all the conditions necessary for a valid marriage were not present.

Anointing of the Sick

As an emergency medical technician, I am often called to the scene involving a fatality. If the person who was killed is a Catholic, what does the Church teach regarding the last rites? Should a priest be called and, if so, how soon after death? If a priest is not available, what role does a eucharistic minister play in a situation like this? — *Name withheld, Barnesville, Ohio*

The sacrament of anointing of the sick is a sacrament for the living and not the dead. If death has occurred, there is nothing that the priest can do but bless the body. If the person's pastor is known, it might be courteous to call him, as he may want to go where the body is being taken to console the survivors. If the accident victim is in danger of death, then a priest should be notified and the sacrament given. A eucharistic minister is installed for the sole purpose of assisting the priest in the distribution of the Eucharist. In the case you describe, his only role would be that of any Christian: to pray for the deceased that he or she might be received by God into heaven. If death is not certain (an example might be a child who falls through ice and is pulled from the water after being submerged for a time), a priest should be notified who can give the sacrament conditionally. The only valid minister of anointing of the sick is a priest. The true sacrament to be given in the face of death is Viaticum (final Holy Communion), but for this to be received the person must be conscious.

DEGREE OF ILLNESS NEEDED • How ill must one be to receive the sacrament of the sick? I'd presume an unstable heart, angina pectoris, should suffice. How about high blood pressure? Since 1969, I've had three heart attacks, five operations, and as yet can't seem to get any priests to give me the sacrament of the sick. — *Stephen L. Easson, Amesbury, Mass.*

Vatican II's *Constitution on the Sacred Liturgy* has this to say: "Extreme Unction, which may also and more fittingly be called Anointing of the Sick, is not a sacrament for those only who are at the point of death. Hence, as soon as any one of the faithful begins to be in danger of death from sickness or old age, the fitting time for that person to receive the sacrament has already arrived." In the *Decree on the Ministry and Life of Priests*, the council reminds priests that "by Anointing of the Sick they relieve those who are ill." Unfortunately, in some areas the decrees of the council are not being fully implemented, not from any bad will but simply because priests have not been trained in them. This may not be fully corrected until we have a generation of seminarians trained in conciliar practice. Some still think of the sacrament in terms of extreme unction or "one foot in the grave." You are certainly a candidate for the sacrament and I believe if you sat down with a priest and explained all this, he would administer the sacrament to you. In many parishes today the sacrament is administered at Mass once or twice a year to the aged or those who are chronically ill.

Antichrist

My question concerns the Antichrist. Most of us are aware that the Bible is allegorical in many instances. But I am confused by the many interpretations given by theologians. Does the Church have an official teaching? — *Mrs. Virginia Haynes, Amesbury, Mass.*

The Church has no "doctrine" on the Antichrist. The term only appears in the Bible in the two epistles of St. John. Many interpreters hold that the beast of the Apocalypse refers to the Antichrist, as does St. Paul's man of lawlessness and son of perdition (2 Thessalonians 2:3). The epistles of St. John seem to indicate that the author thinks the Antichrist is already present in the world and ever since that time there have been people who see the last days and the Antichrist present in their worlds. As Rudolf Pesch observes, "Ever since the coming of Christ into history the 'Antichrist alert' has been constantly in force." We have no way of knowing whether the Antichrist is apocalyptic or not. We do not know if the Antichrist will be an anti-messiah or a pseudo-messiah. We cannot be sure whether an individual is expected or a spirit of the times. There are always people attracted to the odd and the bizarre. Our Lord's advice is the most practical — namely, that since we do not know the day or the hour of his coming, we should always be ready. The Christian should live each day as if it were his or her last day. Trying to plumb the future or even figuring out the Book of Revelation is wasted time. The whole point of the biblical Antichrist and the last days is that the Christian community should stand in preparedness.

Apostles

I have never read anything about the families of the apostles. What can you tell us? — *Name withheld, Farmington Hills, Mich.*

The focus of the New Testament is on Jesus, hence the apostles are treated rather casually. Moreover, the sacred writers were not as biography-minded as we are today. Even the story of Jesus leaves out much detail that we would like to have. We do know a few things about the apostles but not much. Simon Peter had a brother, Andrew, who was also an apostle. They were natives of Bethsaida and their father was named Jona. Simon lived with his mother-in-law at Capernaum, but we do not know if his wife was alive or whether or not he had children. The apostles James and John were brothers. They were born in Galilee, sons of Zebedee, who was also a fisherman. Their mother was named Salome. James the Less was the son of Alpheus and probably a relative of Jesus. Bartholomew was from Cana and his father was Tolomai. He is also known as Nathanael. Thomas, according to some Scripture scholars, was a twin. Thaddeus, also called Jude, could be the author of the Epistle of Jude. If so, he was the brother of James the Less. Finally, Simeon (Simon) the Zealot is identified in the *Roman Martyrology* as a cousin of Jesus, son of Cleophas, brother of St. Joseph.

APOSTLES AND DISCIPLES • I would like to know the difference between an apostle and a disciple and where in the Bible is the difference designated. — *M. E. Goebel, Denver, Colo.*

23

In Jewish life it was the practice for a rabbi (teacher) to have a group of students to whom he taught the law and its interpretation. Jesus used the same method. He was the teacher and the one who followed him as a pupil was called a disciple (from *disciplus*, Latin for *pupil*). Luke 10:1 tells us Jesus appointed seventy-two disciples and assigned them a mission. Out of the group of disciples, Jesus selected a core band who would be his closest associates. In Luke 6:12-13 we read: "Then he went out into the mountain to pray, spending the night in communion with God. At daybreak he called his disciples and selected twelve of them to be his apostles." Luke then names the Twelve. The number was selected probably as representative of the twelve tribes of Israel. The term "apostle" is from a Greek word meaning "One sent out." Sometimes the Gospel writers use the word "disciples" when apostles are meant (since they were also disciples), but the Twelve played a special role and had a special relationship with Jesus.

Apostles' Creed

I say that the foundation of the Catholic Church is the Ten Commandments. A Catholic nun says I am wrong, that it is the Apostles' Creed. This I cannot swallow at all. Who is right? — *Albert L. Kirch, Phoenix, Ariz.*

The basis of Jewish and Christian morality is the Ten Commandments. They are the fundamentals of moral law. However, what makes the difference between a Jew and a Catholic? It is that the latter believes in the Apostles' Creed, which the former does not. Thus in speaking of morality, you are correct. However, in speaking of adherence to a particular faith, Sister is correct. Therefore, you are both right.

Ash Wednesday

My husband is studying Catholicism. He would like to know about the significance of Ash Wednesday. — *Mrs. Max T. Moore, Kearney, Nebr.*

Ash Wednesday is the first day of Lent, a holy and penitential liturgical season of the Catholic Church. Lent is forty days long, in commemoration of Christ's fast in the desert as preparation for his public life. The day takes its name from the fact that ashes from burned palms are blessed and placed on the heads of the faithful as signs of penance and mortality. In ancient times sackcloth and ashes were symbols of penance and humiliation. They were also used by public penitents in the early Church, surviving today in our Ash Wednesday ceremony. On Ash Wednesday, Catholics who intend to practice Lenten penance come to church and the priest places ashes on their foreheads in the sign of the cross, saying: "Remember you are dust and to dust you will return" or "Turn away from sin and be faithful to the Gospel."

Astrology

In the course of talking to a priest, I remember him saying, "Follow your star." What do you suppose he meant? What is the Church's stand concerning astrology? I would refer you to Isaiah 47:12-15. — Mrs. Mary Del Plato, Batavia, N.Y.

I do not know what the priest meant. I would suppose that his remark is one of those general and meaningless phrases like "Follow your instincts." Astrology is a pseudoscience that is condemned by the Church as superstition. Astrology suggests that a person's life is influenced by the placement of stars. Because it makes scientific pretensions it influences many people to accept its superstition. Astrology is a type of fortunetelling the Church condemns. The future is known only to God, and a man or woman, no matter the position of the stars, has free will to determine his or her own fate. Chapter 47 of Isaiah concerns the fall of Babylon. The prophet condemns Babylon for its false counsels, its superstitions (of which astrology was one), its pride, and its abuse of power. In the verses you quote, Isaiah is using irony which, like satire, many people fail to grasp. Astrology is to be distinguished from astronomy, which is a true science and not given to horoscopes and predictions.

Baptism

In your column you said that immersion is not prescribed in Scripture baptism. But doesn't the word "baptism" derive its origin from the Greek word meaning "immersion"? Therefore, every time the word baptism is used in the Bible, it is reinforcing the method to be used for the sacrament. — *Tom Bivin, Orlando, Fla.*

Someone has given you a bum steer if you have been told that baptism derives from a Greek word meaning solely "immersion." It derives from the Greek verb *baptizo*, which basically means "to wash." The Greek word is used in different senses in the New Testament. It is sometimes used to refer to ritual washing of Jews, as in Mark 7:4 and Luke 11:38. The word is used to refer to the baptism of John (John 1:25, 28), which was a type of ritual washing, signifying death to the old life and resurrection to the new. Paul sometimes uses *baptizo* to denote a person's movement to Christ (1 Corinthians 10:2, Galatians 3:27). While the ritual washings of the Jews (*baptizo*) were by sprinkling or washing as we know it, John added the symbolism of going under and coming up out of the water. It is not clear from historical records whether immersion was the preferred form of baptism in the early Church. It wasn't until fifteen hundred years later that it became a matter of controversy when some Protestant sects insisted that immersion was the only legitimate form of baptism, and to accomplish this some individuals distorted Scripture by taking words out of context. It cannot be proven from Scripture that the baptism described in Acts 8:38, 9:18, 10:48, etc., were by immersion, and to insist that they were is to violate Scripture. While I believe immersion is the most meaningful form of baptism and liturgical instructions seem to prefer it, it is wrong to insist that it is the only way to be "washed" of the past.

INFANT BAPTISM • I am a Protestant but attend Mass regularly. I share Catholic beliefs to a large extent and would like to understand more fully Catholic belief regarding infant baptism, limbo, etc. If it is still a Catholic belief that an unbaptized child, in case of death, is in limbo, why do Catholics wait until a baby is several months old to have it christened? — *Sally R. Greer, Cottontown, Tenn.*

The necessity of baptism is derived from the teaching of Jesus Christ (John 3:5), as stated to Nicodemus: "Unless a man be born again of water and the Holy Spirit, he cannot enter the kingdom of God." Since baptism is necessary for salvation, it is Church teaching that an infant should be baptized as soon after birth as conveniently possible, and in some areas this is even done within hours of birth. Catholics are taught that in danger of death, anyone may baptize, and, if the child survives, the baptismal ceremonies should be later supplied, although the child is not rebaptized. In the early Church, baptism was seen as a sign of regeneration. One descended into water, which washed away old mortality (sin), and ascended from the water, passing from death to life. The sacrament gave the believer participation in the life of Christ and service in the Church. Over the years the teaching on baptism became more systematic and it was seen as a sign of faith (*sacramentum fidei*). Modern theology also stresses the entrance into the Christian community and community obligations incurred in baptism. It is considered the first of the sacraments of initiation, along with the Eucharist and confirmation. Because many Catholics are not instructed in baptismal theology, nor understand the community obligations baptism creates, many dioceses are now insisting that parents and godparents take prebaptismal courses of instruction, which in turn delays baptism. What happens to an unbaptized child has been a source of debate over the centuries among theologians. St. Augustine was of the opinion that such children were condemned to the real (but mitigated) pains of hell. St. Anselm and the Scholastics after him agreed with Augustine that such infants were denied the beatific vision but held that they went to a place of their own, limbo (from the Latin word meaning hem or edge). Modern theology is far from unified and extends from the strict opinion of separation to a more liberal interpretation that places such children in heaven as a result of God's universal salvific will. Some explain this as a baptism of desire exercised by the parents on behalf of the child. While the Church has no defined doctrine on this matter that Catholics are compelled to believe, and hence one is not held to any specific teaching, one should not uncritically dismiss the teaching of past generations of theologians. In pastoral theology one should tell the bereaved parents of such a child that they must entrust it to a kindly and loving God whose grace and power have no limits.

PURPOSE OF BAPTISM • I was told recently that the baptismal rite has been changed and that baptism is to welcome a baby or person into the Catholic community. There is no mention of removing the "stain of original sin" nor the infusion of sanctifying grace. In fact, being born with original sin is no longer believed. — *Marie Ryanczak, Elephant Butte, N. Mex.*

First, let me assure you that the Church still teaches the doctrine of original sin. Genesis 3 details man's original failure and its inheritance in humankind. As St. Paul reminds us in Romans 5:12: "Therefore as sin came into the world through one man and death through sin, and so death spread to all men because all men sinned." Vatican Council II referred to this revelation in its first chapter of its *Pastoral Constitution on the Church in the Modern World*, stating how man failed God at the very start of history and how our inheritance of this fact can be recognized in our own experience. Vatican II also ordered a revision of the sacraments with two purposes: to restore usage of the early Church and more clearly bring out their meaning. The new rite of baptism is the first sacrament of Christian initiation. While the new rite freed the baptized from the powers of darkness (original sin) and gave the baptized new life through water and the Holy Spirit, making the baptized a child of God through the life of sanctifying grace, it also was to be an initiation into the Christian community with all the obligations such membership entails. What the council Fathers were saying is that over the centuries the focus of baptism became centered on original sin, and the life in and obligations to the Church community were forgotten. What you were taught in the past about this sacrament is still valid, but what the Church is asking now is that you also see what it means to be a member of the Christian family of God.

JOHN'S BAPTISM • What is the origin of baptizing by John the Baptist? Did John the Baptist have a mandate from God to baptize? We realize his age is close to that of Jesus and we wonder when his ministry began. — *Mrs. Mary Dolansky, St. Louis, Mo.*

First, it must be remembered that the baptism of John was not a sacramental baptism as we know baptism today. It was a baptism of repentance by which one went down in the water and rose up cleansed of attachment to sin and rededicated to life with God. Sacramental baptism was instituted by Jesus. There are analogies to baptism in the Old Testament (Exodus 40:12, for instance). In all of these the use of water was an act of purification. By the time of Jesus, such washings were common practice and the Essenes made use of them, as the Dead Sea Scrolls show. Many believe that John the Baptist was an Essene, or at least strongly influenced by them. John had been chosen by God for his role of precursor even before his birth. He was to prepare the way for Christ by preaching repentance and using his baptism as a sign of that repentance. As he himself said, he was preparing those he baptized for a nobler baptism that was to come. While others purified (baptized) themselves, John was unique in that he baptized others, as did his disciples. Instead of sprinkling, he used a baptism of immersion as being more symbolic of what he was teaching. John was six months older than Jesus. We do not know when he began his ministry; most think that it was only a short time before Jesus started his. Prior to that John led a hermit's existence in the desert, teaching those who came out to him and gradually acquiring disciples. Although he had been dedicated to God from his birth, we do not know when he left home. It is possible he joined the Essenes, found community life too "soft," and so retired to the desert, but this is only speculation.

BAPTISM BY LAITY • Is it wrong for a Catholic layman (me) to baptize a baby when it is not an emergency? The child's mother was a Catholic but is excommunicated. She married a divorced man with two children. They talked to our parish priest, but he would not marry them. Her husband had been married by a Protestant minister. Would it be wrong in God's eyes to baptize this one-year-old child? — *Name withheld, Greenville, Ohio*

Yes, it would be wrong to baptize this child in the manner you suggest. Baptism is the door to life and the kingdom of God, but it is also the sacrament of initiation into the Church. The ordinary ministers of baptism are bishops, priests, and deacons who act in the name of the Church and who must have moral certitude that the person being baptized must be able to lead a Christian (Catholic) life. Even when emergency baptism takes place, the remaining baptismal ceremony must be performed by an authorized minister later. However, it may be possible to have the child baptized in the Church. First, the mother is not excommunicated. That penalty is no longer applied to those who marry outside the Church. Second, if a priest can be assured by the mother and a godparent that the child will be given a Catholic upbringing, he can baptize the child even though the parents may not be properly married in the Church. You and your friend should discuss this matter with a priest in whom you have confidence.

Benediction

Will you please explain the devotion of Benediction of the Blessed Sacrament in the Catholic Church? Who is qualified and authorized to administer Benediction? What are the primary preparations and rules for administering Benediction? What significance does the Catholic Church attach to Benediction? — *Paul G. KoPack, Woodruff, Wis.*

The revised rites place emphasis on the Mass as the most suitable form of eucharistic worship because Christ instituted this sacrament "to be near us, to feed, to heal, and to comfort us." For this reason the Eucharist may not be exposed while Mass is going on. However, eucharistic worship outside of Mass is also permitted but not solely to give a blessing with the sacrament to the people. Benediction today is properly placed within the context of eucharistic devotion and exposition. The structure of the celebration of eucharistic exposition is as follows: 1. Exposition. 2. Adoration, which includes readings from Scripture, prayers and song, a homily, and a period (or several periods) of silence. 3. Benediction (blessing with the monstrance or ciborium). 4. Reposition. To carry out this ceremony, the altar is prepared with four to six candles (at least two if only the ciborium is used). The minister, wearing a humeral veil, goes to the place of reservation and returns with the Blessed Sacrament, which is then exposed. The Sacrament is then incensed. Adoration follows and, when this is ended, a eucharistic song is sung and the minister incenses the Sacrament. One of the ritual prayers is said to which the people respond "Amen." Then, wearing the humeral veil, the minister genuflects, takes the Sacrament and blesses the people (this can only be done by a priest or deacon), making the sign of the cross. After the blessing the minister returns the Blessed Sacrament to its place of reservation while an acclamation is sung by all as the minister leaves. The new ritual does not mention the Divine Praises, but they may be sung or recited as a recessional, or may be used during the Adoration rite as a prayer. The ordinary minister of this rite is a priest or deacon. However, in their absence, with consent and appointment by the Ordinary (bishop), an acolyte, a special minister of the Eucharist, or a member of a religious community (using the vesture approved for their ministry) may expose and repose the Sacrament but, as noted, may not give a blessing. The purpose of the new rite is to give honor and worship to our sacramental Lord.

Bible

I bought a Bible marked "Catholic" on the cover from our parish church. It didn't seem right to me, so I checked with a Catholic Bible published in 1958 and discovered my Bible was a Protestant Bible. I tried to buy one at our religious bookstore in town and learned that the Catholic Bible is no longer published but that I could get one in the library. When I questioned my pastor, he said my Bible was okay, since it was approved by Vatican II. — *Helen Yonke, Toledo, Ohio*

There is some confusion here because of terminology. For some centuries the accepted Catholic English edition of the Bible was called the *Douay-Rheims Version*, and the Protestant, the *King James Version*. Because of scriptural discoveries and the new availability of ancient texts, this century saw a great advance in biblical scholarship. New Catholic versions began appearing — Knox, the Confraternity, Spencer, etc. — culminating in many years of scholarly work in the *New American Bible*. However, there are other new works that have approved Catholic forms: the *Revised Standard Version (Catholic Edition)*, the *Jerusalem Bible*, etc. Two versions of the Bible are approved for use at Mass, the *New American Bible* and the *Jerusalem Bible*. You are probably referring to the *Douay-Rheims* translation when you speak of a "Catholic" Bible. This was first published in 1609 and its scholarship has been vastly improved upon in the newer translations that appeared concurrently with Vatican II. It is still available from Bible houses, but few stores carry it anymore. The best way to tell a Catholic Bible is to look for the imprimatur (usually found on the copyright page at the beginning of the book). Vatican II approved no specific text.

BIBLICAL AGES • Why did people in biblical times live to be hundreds of years old? Noah and others lived to be almost a thousand years old. What has happened that we no longer live so long? — *John McMahon, Fort Wayne, Ind.*

No reputable scholar today accepts the patriarchal chronology of Genesis as literal but instead sees it as symbolic and theological. The writer of the Book of Genesis had no way of knowing what went on in the patriarchal period except by drawing on various oral traditions, legends, songs, etc., which existed among the people. Scholars assign four traditions that were used to write Genesis: Yahwist, which arose in the southern kingdom; Elohist, of the northern regions; Deuteronomic, generally restricted to the Book of Deuteronomy; and Priestly, the tradition taught by Hebrew priests. It was from the latter that the Genesis chronology was drawn. What I have said here in a few words would really take a book to properly explain. Many parts of the Bible do not lend themselves to literal and simple explanations. More understandable and accurate are some verses from Psalm 90 that relate time to God and human activity. About God the psalmist writes: "To your eyes a thousand years are like yesterday, come and gone, no more than a watch in the night." About life-span the psalmist says: "Our life is like a sigh. Our span is seventy years or eighty for those who are strong." This latter view is realistic and does not differ too much from how long we can expect to live in our own time.

OFFICIAL BIBLE • A friend told me that the *Douay-Rheims Bible* is the official Bible of the Catholic Church. If this is true, why do parishes use the *New American Bible*? If not true, is it permissible to read or own the *Douay-Rheims*? — *Sally Dytko, Marlborough, Conn.*

The *Douay-Rheims Bible* is a Catholic English translation of the Latin *Vulgate* of which the New Testament was published at Rheims in 1582 and the Old Testament at Douay in 1609. In England, Anglicans issued the *King James* translation, still in use by Protestants. A *Douay-Rheims* revision was made by Bishop Richard Challoner in 1750. This version of the Bible was the official Catholic English version until our own times, when scholars, using Greek and Aramaic texts (the *Vulgate* was a Latin translation of them), issued two new Bibles that have been accepted for English liturgical use — the *New American Bible* and the *Jerusalem Bible*. Protestant scholars have also brought out new translations that are accepted by the Church but not for official use. Recently completed by Catholic and Protestant scholars is a revision of the New Testament of the *New American Bible*. It is permissible to read the old *Douay-Rheims* translation, but it should be remembered that the modern translations are more accurate. You are also permitted to read other English (Catholic) versions, such as the *Good News Bible*, the *Living Bible*, and the *New English Bible*.

BELIEFS NECESSARY • I have never seen anything that explains what Catholics believe concerning the Bible.

Many Catholic theologians do not believe God dictated every verse and word in the Bible. I would appreciate any information on what we can believe as Catholics. — *Anton Hintz, Chippewa Falls, Wis.*

Catholics must believe that the Sacred Scriptures are inspired writings, that is, that they were written under the inspiration of the Holy Spirit in such a way as to show that God is the principal author. This does not mean that God dictated every word, as one would dictate to a secretary. Nor is it a vague inspiration, such as a poet gets when he sees something and is inspired to write a poem. The sacred writers were so inspired that they knew what God intended, although they may not have always been aware of that fact. At the same time, the sacred writer brought his own personality and knowledge to the work. Finally, it is the task of the Church, under the guidance of the same Holy Spirit, to interpret and explain the sacred writings.

BIBLE AND SCIENCE • I was thrilled that archeologists in recent years have uncovered overwhelming evidence that the Bible is true and accurate. Nevertheless, the age of the creation of Adam and Eve does not compare to the age of the anthropologists' Neanderthal and Cro-Magnon man. I am not taking the Bible literally, but the gap of thousands of years cannot be ignored. I feel there must be plausible solutions to these questions. — *Herman Kruszewski, Adena, Ohio*

You are correct in stating that recent archeology has substantiated biblical fact. Not too many years ago biblical scholars considered the text (words) of the Bible so corrupted by centuries of translation that little was thought trustworthy. The stories of Abraham, Isaac, and Jacob were considered by some as tribal myths. Biblical history was questioned (for example, the empire of the Hittites because the Hittites were unknown to history). Daniel was doubted because Greek history had no evidence of Belshazzar, a Babylonian ruler central to Daniel. Modern archeology, particularly the Dead Sea Scrolls, has proven that present biblical texts have been carefully transmitted. The facts surrounding the story of the patriarchs have been proven. The Hittites' language, laws, and history have been discovered and one can even visit their capital city, which has been uncovered in Turkey. A series of clay tablets was unearthed that named Belshazzar the last ruler of Babylon, co-regent with his father, Nabonidus. Having said all this, one must be warned about accepting all biblical dating and chronology as accurate. One must examine each book and determine what the author was aiming to do. The first chapters of Genesis, for example, were not written as a chronology but as testimony of God's creative powers. One need not accept days of twenty-four hours as pertaining to creation but six periods of time. The Church teaches that the Holy Scriptures are the written word of God, the collection of those writings inspired by God and placed in the care of the Church to protect, interpret, and hand down. We must be careful of personal interpretation that has led to all kinds of conflicts between interpreters and has resulted in many heresies.

BIBLICAL MYTHS • Our oldest daughter went to college this year, to what we thought was a Catholic girls' college. We found, however, that the college has gone "modern." She will not return next year. One big problem is the manner in which the Bible is taught, as consisting of "myths" or a series of stories, which in themselves have no meaning other than to relate a certain point. Could you let us know exactly what the Church's teaching on the Bible is? — *Art and Rosalie Llewellyn, Hampton, Va.*

This is a big question that I can only touch on. The Bible is the inspired word of God, God's revelation to man. The word "myth" should not be used in connection with the Bible because it only confuses. The Bible gives a historical record of God's covenant with man and it also teaches us in various ways. Some of that teaching is through stories that may or may not be actual historical happenings (for example, the parables of Jesus). The English word "myth" denotes fantasy or unreality. Even "allegory" is a word that can lead to confusion. The word "story" is best, but even that must be approached with caution and some clarification. On the basis of modern geological and archeological studies, even scientists are becoming cautious about the prehistoric period of Genesis (that is, before Abraham's time), which is an account of the origin of man, man's elevation to grace and fall from grace, told in story form. That story has elements of reality and truths revealed by God. Unless a teacher knows what these elements are and is able to impart them correctly without ambiguity or equivocation, that teacher should not be teaching biblical studies.

CANONICAL FORMATION • Who collected all the books of the Old and New Testaments and made them into the

Bible as we know it today, since all have different authors? — *E. Minerich, Fairbault, Minn.*

For Catholics it was the Council of Trent (1546) that solemnly defined the canon of Old and New Testament Scriptures and gave us the Bible as we have it today. This does not mean that the canon was not known before, but it was Trent that made it binding on the whole Church. The earliest listings were made by local councils and synods. The Council of Hippo (393) and the Third Council of Carthage (397) each gave the same list as was ultimately authorized by Trent. There were other similar actions over the centuries by popes and other councils. The Council of Trent made this universal decision because of challenges made by the Protestant reformers. Most Protestants accepted the Jewish canon of thirty-nine books for the Old Testament. Trent defined a canon of forty-six books (including Tobit, Judith, Wisdom, Sirach, Baruch, and 1 and 2 Maccabees, not accepted by the Protestants). It is an interesting note that all the Old Testament books accepted by the Church have been found in the recently discovered Dead Sea Scrolls with the exception of Esther. The twenty-seven books of the New Testament were written roughly between the years 55 and 100. Polycarp, in 110, mentions eighteen of them. The seven letters from St. Ignatius that still exist quote or mention twenty-four books. From these examples we can see that a consensus was forming of what were the inspired New Testament books. As with the Jewish canon, various local councils approved the twenty-seven books that were given definitive and final form by the Council of Trent.

Birth Control

Why is it that only Catholics cannot use birth control? Everyone else in the world can and it's okay. In our case, we have followed the Church's ruling and my husband would have to use self-control to the point where he would become so frustrated that he would get verbally abusive and angry beyond reason. After so many years of this kind of birth control, we find ourselves very bitter toward each other. Now, at fifty years of age or so, we could have sex with no worry, but I have put up with so much strain and verbal abuse that I have absolutely no desire. We are "private" type people and cannot talk it over with anyone. — *Name withheld, Northhampton, Mass.*

First, before I answer on birth control, a personal word. Now that the child-bearing years are past, you need to heal your marriage. In what should be meaningful and satisfying years, there seems to be an estrangement and lack of partnership. Maybe the partnership was always lacking because if it had been there your husband might not have been frustrated and angry. The resentments you have carried over as a result are poisoning the relationship today. If you were physically ill, you would see a doctor. Your marriage is ill and I urge you to contact the Catholic Marriage Counseling Center in Springfield. You and your husband have too many years left not to enjoy them. Birth control is not a disciplinary law of the Catholic Church, like fasting on Good Friday. It is the Church's teaching that according to the natural law which binds everyone — Christian, Jew, Muslim — each and every marriage act must remain open to the transmission of life. The Church teaches that this is all part of God's plan for creation, in which he allows men and women to share. This divine law binds everyone. By God's law, the social purpose of marriage is the continuation of the human race. He deliberately chose to make human partners in this plan. Moreover, NFP (natural family planning), which has been shown to be as dependable as the pill and more dependable than other methods of contraception, can be used to space children without violating God's plan. However, NFP will not work without the full understanding of both spouses. The other purposes of marriage — mutual love and support, companionship for life — are all part of a total picture of what God wants for us. The Church insists that the unitive and procreative meanings of marriage must be taken together because this is God's plan. The Church was told by Christ to make God's will known to mankind. That others do not choose to follow God's will is their own responsibility. The marriage act is intended to bring a man and woman together, not separate them. When that happens, there is usually a failure of communication, and the marriage needs outside help.

FOLLOWING CONSCIENCE • I have always understood that contraception is against the teaching of the Church. My married daughter, who is now on the pill, justifies it by saying that her priest told her that in such personal matters she must follow her conscience. I really don't know what to say to her. — *Name withheld, Rochester, N.Y.*

The official teaching of the Church is contained in Pope Paul's encyclical *Humanae Vitae*, which states that "each and every marriage act must remain open to the transmission of life." This teaching is simple and unequivocal. However, some (including some priests) have stated simply that the pope was wrong and have since instructed people to ignore the teaching and "to follow their consciences." While it is true that there is a primacy of conscience and one should never violate one's conscience, there is also the danger of creating a subjective morality. For conscience to be followed, a person must do all possible to form a correct conscience, and to do this the person must consider the teaching of the pope and the various national hierarchies that have upheld *Humanae Vitae*. Such teaching cannot be lightly dismissed because it is unpopular or goes against one's wishes. Vatican II in its *Declaration on Religious Freedom* said: "In the formation of their conscience, the Christian faithful ought carefully to attend to the certain and sacred doctrine of the Church. The Church is, by the will of Christ, the teacher of the truth. It is her duty to give utterance to and authoritatively to teach the truth which is Christ himself and to declare and confirm by her authority those principles of the moral order which have their origin in human nature itself." Therefore, people like your daughter must do everything possible to arrive at a correct decision. Only then can one be said to be "following conscience."

FAMILY PLANNING • I am puzzled. The Church teaches against use of birth control, yet it is my understanding it condones the rhythm method of preventing pregnancy and the new natural family planning method. Are these not methods of controlling births and hence sinful? How are we to know these natural systems are not against God's intentions? — *Name withheld, Toronto, Kans.*

The Church is not opposed to birth control, only *artificial* birth control. You should obtain a copy of Pope Paul VI's encyclical *Humanae Vitae (Of Human Life)*, for it contains the Church's teaching on marriage and morality. The pope tells us "that each and every marriage act must remain open to the transmission of life" in accordance with God's design for the human race. By artificial means, the users close the marriage act to human life. Natural means do not do this but work in accordance with God's laws. Pope Paul taught: "If, then, there are serious reasons to space out births . . . it is licit to take into account natural rhythms immanent in the generative functions, for the use of marriage in infecund periods only, and in a way to regulate births without offending." The present system of natural family planning (NFP) is far more accurate than the old rhythm method. Pope John Paul has spoken many times on this subject, stating the right of husband and wife to plan their family according to the natural means. When a person uses artificial means, that person interferes with natural processes taking place and prevents the act from being open to the end ordained by God. When one uses NFP, one is working in accordance with God's law and the act does nothing to forestall or nullify that law.

Black Priests

Can you please tell me when the first nonwhite person was ordained to the priesthood? A non-Catholic friend told me blacks were not allowed to be ordained until late in the 1880s. Is this true? — *Robert Berriger, Altoona, Pa.*

No, it is not true. There was never any rule, regulation, or law that barred blacks from the priesthood. However, it must be remembered that until 1865 the majority of blacks in this country were slaves and poorly educated. Even after emancipation the lack of education prevented blacks from rising higher in life. Also, very few blacks were Catholics. The first black priest ordained for the United States was James A. Healy, whose mother was a slave and whose father was white. He was ordained in 1854 and his two brothers also became priests a few years after him. He rose to be bishop of Portland, Maine, where he once had been embarrassed by a priest because of "his indelicate color." His brother, Patrick, also a priest, became president of Georgetown University. The first black priest of full African parentage was Father Augustine Tolton (born 1854) who became a priest in Chicago. Father Charles Uncles, S.S.J. (born 1859), was the first black Josephite priest. There are no records of the number of black Catholics in the period following the Civil War; however, I think it would be fair to state that they were few, but that even among those few, white priests did not actively seek vocations. The same unfortunate fact would be true of the mainline Protestant groups.

Blessed Articles

Can you tell me where I can purchase a Miraculous Medal and other small religious articles that have been blessed by the pope and not by subordinates? — *W. Coddington, Rahway, N.J.*

I know of no place where you can buy blessed articles. To sell blessings is a form of simony, a serious sin, which takes its name from Simon Magus who offered St. Peter and St. John money for the power of bestowing the Holy Spirit (Acts 8:18ff). There are a multitude of shops in Rome that sell religious articles, but they are not blessed. People buy them in quantities and take them to a papal audience where the Holy Father blesses them. If such people are buying such articles for others, they can be reimbursed for what they actually paid but nothing more because they are blessed. The best suggestion I can make to you is that you try to find an acquaintance or someone in your parish going to Rome, and ask that person to buy what you want and take the articles to a papal audience where they will be blessed.

Blessings

I would like to know if any Catholic is authorized to extend the outward sign of the cross to friends and relatives. I am not familiar with the canon law on this. Also, how do you address an archbishop? — *Albert K. McKee, Midwest City, Okla.*

Canon 1168 says: "The minister of the sacramentals is a cleric who has been given the necessary power; in accord with the norm of liturgical books and according to the judgment of the local ordinary, some sacramentals can also be administered by lay persons who are endowed with appropriate qualities." This new canon is not as restrictive as was the old. Thus in interpreting the above, a lay person can distribute ashes on Ash Wednesday; a parent can bless his or her children; a eucharistic minister can bless a communicant. What the Church wishes to avoid is a confusion of roles that are proper to authorized ministers and those of the laity. However, I would not see a difficulty in offering a blessing to one's relatives and close friends, since they would understand the sense in which it is given, but I do not think it should go farther than that. One addresses an archbishop the same as a bishop: "Your Excellency," or simply "Archbishop."

Blind

Is there any organization that supplies religious tapes or records for the blind? — *Elizabeth Parks, St. Albans, W. Va.*

Yes. Xavier Society for the Blind, 154 E. 23rd St., New York, NY 10010, provides publications for the blind in Braille, large type and on tape. The society has a circulation library of seven thousand items. It puts out a monthly review of articles selected from Catholic publications. All services are free.

Blue Army

I know that the Blue Army is involved in praying the Rosary for peace, but what other activities is it involved in? Where can I write for more information? — *Michael J. Neuverth, Colorado Springs, Colo.*

The Blue Army was formed to promote the appearance of Mary at Fátima and to urge people to carry out the requests she made. The group publishes the magazine *Soul*, which makes known its activities. Information can be had by writing to its headquarters: Blue Army (World Apostolate of Fátima), Washington, NJ 07882.

Born Again

We hear so much about "born again." Jesus spoke of it in John 3:1-12. What does the Church teach by this? As Catholics are we born again when we are baptized, when we are confirmed, or when as adults we affirm our living faith in Jesus Christ and turn our lives over to his care? — *Margaret M. Regnier, Phoenix, Ariz.*

The term has different meanings, particularly among Protestants. For some it means accepting baptism, for others it means an independent decision to accept Jesus as one's Savior and thus commit one's life to him. The Catholic interpretation of the term would be in the sense used by Jesus to Nicodemus where he was stressing the necessity of spiritual birth through the reception of baptism. Some charismatics use the term loosely in connection with "baptism of the Spirit." I have always been of the opinion that at some point every Catholic should make a free and positive commitment to Christ apart from infant baptism. The logical place to do this is at confirmation if the sacrament doesn't come too early. There should be some formalized point of decision rather than just being a Catholic by osmosis. Critics of this opinion say that we would lose many Catholics. My reply is that it is better to lose them than to have people calling themselves Catholics who refuse to live as Catholics and thus give scandal.

FUNDAMENTALIST MEANING • You were asked a question about being "born again." Being a Protestant, I looked in my concordance of the *King James Bible* and found "born again" twice, in John 3:3 and 3:7. I'm not going to say anything more about "born again" — because the Bible explains it well in these verses. — *Lester V. Tinnin, San Francisco, Calif.*

Mr. Tinnin and others who wrote me about these verses missed the point of the question and answer. Jesus, in speaking to Nicodemus, was talking about the necessity of baptism. Nicodemus had not been baptized and Jesus was telling him that if he wanted to enter into God's kingdom, he must be begotten of water and the Spirit. The question I answered concerned people who had already been baptized, namely Catholics, and whether they could be "born again." The term as it is generally used today by many fundamentalist groups goes beyond baptism to a new conversion of even those who have been baptized. Catholics can have such a new conversion to commitment, but they are not "born again" in the sense of Christ's discourse, since baptism is given but once for all time. Loosely speaking, they can be called "born again" in their new dedication to the teachings of Christ.

Capital Punishment

What is the teaching of the Church on capital punishment? — *Carl Shamburger, Levelland, Tex.*

It is the traditional teaching of the Church that the political community has the right to defend itself from unjust aggression, to remove from society those who do not keep its laws, and in extreme cases punish with the death penalty those found guilty of serious crime against the individual or social order. However, even in the light of this teaching, there is a growing consensus among Catholic theologians for the abolition of the death penalty. The Catholic bishops of the United States have declared their opposition to the death penalty, stating: "Past history shows that the death penalty in its present application has been discriminatory with respect to the disadvantaged, the indigent and the socially impoverished. Furthermore, recent data from correction sources definitely question the effectiveness of the death penalty as a deterrent." Most European and Latin American countries have ended the death penalty, and rulings of the U.S. Supreme Court have limited its use here.

WHY OBJECT TO DEATH PENALTY? • I am puzzled about capital punishment. I suppose all murderers, rapists, and thieves are against capital punishment; and I can't blame them. But I can't understand why so many decent people are against it. What do they have in common with bad people to make them both work against capital punishment? — *William J. Shea, Jr., Belleville, Ill.*

While it is Catholic teaching that under certain grave conditions the state has the right to protect itself even by the taking of life, many people in recent years have come to question the usefulness of capital punishment. Some feel that life is so sacred that no one but God has the right to take it. Others believe that capital punishment is not really a deterrent to crime and therefore not justified. Still others hold that under the present system of long legal delays, the raising and defeating of expectant hopes constitute "cruel and unusual punishment," which is forbidden by Article VIII of the Bill of Rights. Still others believe that as long as there is a chance for the reformation and rehabilitation of the criminal, his or her life should not be taken. Some also argue that the present laws are discriminatory because a rich person who can afford good lawyers can always escape death by plea bargaining or some other legal means and that therefore the poor who do not have proper legal counsel are victims of the system.

Catholic Church

I am a catechist and find we have differences of opinion in this statement: "I believe in the holy Catholic Church." The word "catholic" means "universal." Is the Catholic Church universal? What about the Eastern Rite, Western Rite, the Orthodox Church? Are they under the pope? — *Julie Handel, Wautoma, Wis.*

The words you quote are from the Apostles' Creed, amplified in the Nicene Creed. You are correct in saying that the word "catholic" means "universal"; it comes from the Greek word *katholikos.* It was applied to the Church because Christ opened his Church to all peoples of all places and of all times. It is also universal today because it exists in every part of the world. The Church is defined in many ways, but a legal definition might be: "the congregation of all baptized persons united in the same true faith, the same sacrifice, the same sacraments, under the authority of the Vicar of Christ and the bishops in communion with him." The Church is made up of Western and Eastern Rites (the latter being composed of the Antiochene, Alexandrian, Armenian, Byzantine, and Chaldean Rites). Since the Orthodox Church does not recognize the authority of the pope, it is not considered a member of the Catholic Church. One of the goals of ecumenism is to reunite the Catholic and Orthodox Churches, which gradually drifted apart between 1054 and 1472. The Catholic Church recognizes the orders and sacraments of the Orthodox Church as valid, and in recent years there have been meetings between the two churches, including the pope and the patriarch of Constantinople, who is first in precedence in the Orthodox Church.

"GOOD CATHOLIC" • Would you give me your explanation of a good Catholic? I hear many definitions of a good Christian, but I would like to hear your definition of a "good Catholic." A lot of Catholics have their own ideas. — *Mrs. F. Lapointe, Peekskill, N.Y.*

I suppose a whole book could be written to answer your question, but to give a simple reply I would say a good Catholic is any baptized person who belongs to the Catholic Church and who is united with other Catholics in the same true faith, the same sacrifice, and the same sacraments, under the authority of the Holy Father and the bishops in communion with him, and living to the best of his or her ability according to the laws of God and the Church.

CHURCH ORIGIN • When and in what year did the Catholic Church start? Did the Roman Catholic Church start when Christ asked Peter to build his Church? A Protestant told me that the Roman Catholic Church did not get into power until after the year 350. The same person said that Peter was never in Rome. How, when, and where did the Protestant Church start? — *Bob Powell, Wampum, Pa.*

When Christ appointed Peter the head of his Church, he spoke in the future tense (Matthew 16:18), as he did not intend the Church to begin until it received the Holy Spirit who would vivify it. After his resurrection (John 21:15-17), Jesus confirmed Peter in his role and instructed him to nurture the Church. The Holy Spirit descended upon the apostles on Pentecost Sunday, in the year 33, and the apostles left their hiding places and went forth to preach the new religion. This is considered the birthday of the Church. Jesus had predicted that Peter would die a martyr (John 21:18-19) and tradition tells us that Peter went to Rome and died there by crucifixion. Because of the Roman persecution of the Church, it existed as an underground religion, holding its services in the catacombs. These conditions continued until the year 313 when Constantine the Great in the Edict of Milan recognized the new religion and allowed it to emerge from the catacombs. At the urging of his mother, St. Helen, a Christian, Constantine built a church over the tomb of the apostle Peter. This tomb, identified by the inscriptions of pilgrims, was discovered not too long ago directly under the main altar of the present St. Peter's Basilica. The Protestant Church is generally considered to have begun in 1517 with the revolt of the Augustinian friar Martin Luther, although Luther borrowed some of his ideas from John Wycliffe and John Hus, who had lived earlier. Luther triggered the revolt against the papacy and was followed by John Calvin in Switzerland and Henry VIII in England.

CHRIST IN THE CHURCH • How do we know that Christ's promise to remain with his believers did not go with the Protestants who were also obviously believers, rather

44

than remaining in the Catholic Church, or that it does not extend to both? After all, Christ never specified that his promise extended to an institution of any particular form. — *Name withheld, Antioch, Calif.*

Your presumptions are not correct. Christ did found a specific Church (Matthew 16:17-19), based on the primacy of Peter and his successors. He would be in that Church and its bishops always (Matthew 28:20). He gave that Church certain teachings and placed within it certain powers. This Church continued through an unbroken series of popes for fifteen hundred years, before the Protestant founders broke away and rejected selected teachings of Christ (the Eucharist, penance, marriage, primacy of Peter, etc.). The Protestant justification was that the Catholic Church no longer represented the teachings of Christ and they, the Protestants, were restoring them. To do this they had to reject the power of the keys and also indirectly make Christ a liar, since he had promised to be *always* in his Church, the Catholic Church, until the end of time.

Celibacy

Will you please explain "celibacy"? I have a hard time making a non-Catholic friend understand. She wants to know why priests and nuns want to remain unmarried. — *Mrs. J.H. Brunton, Decatur, Ind.*

Celibacy is the unmarried state of life required for priests of the Western Church, chosen in the light of Christian faith and one of the duties of Western priests who freely give themselves to a life of continence. Permanent deacons are allowed to be married, but transitional deacons are not. Celibacy is also a requirement for Western religious sisters and brothers, although some exceptions have been made. The first local legislation for celibacy came into being at the Council of Elvira (Spain) in 306, and this was followed by other local enactments. By the twelfth century it was a universal practice, and the first universal law was made by the Second Lateran Council in 1139. The present legislation was ruled by the Council of Trent in 1563. In the Eastern Church, candidates for holy orders may be married before becoming deacons, but marriage after ordination is forbidden. Eastern Rite bishops must be unmarried. Celibacy was adopted so that the clergy might better imitate Christ and devote themselves wholeheartedly to their vocation. Celibacy has its roots in the sayings of the Lord about not marrying (Matthew 19:10ff); also the saying about leaving one's family for the sake of Jesus and the Gospel (Mark 10:29) or for the reign of God (Luke 18:29) and that in the resurrection there will be no marriage (Matthew 22:30). Paul wished all to be unmarried as himself (1 Corinthians 7:7) because the attention of the married is divided (1 Corinthians 7:32ff). These sayings were not considered mandates but counsels for those seeking higher perfection. The Church regards celibacy as a gift of grace.

CELIBACY AGAINST NATURE • I am the only Catholic in my office. Every time the subject of Catholic priests is mentioned, the subject of priestly celibacy invariably follows. They always say the same thing to me: "It's going against nature." Will you please give me a good answer? — *Mrs. R. Jones, Norfolk, Va.*

It is one of the fallacies of modern thinking that people cannot control their sexual drives. This is put forth as an argument against celibacy and for birth control methods. God has given each of us intellect and will that can be trained to do our bidding. Moreover, Jesus implied (Matthew 19:11) that special grace would be given to those who could accept the teaching of celibacy to which he gave the challenge, "Let anyone accept this who can." He would not ask something impossible. Celibacy is a gift of the Spirit, just as faithful married love is also such a gift. St. Paul (1 Corinthians 7) states that he is celibate and wishes others to do "even as I do myself." However, he adds: "If they cannot exercise self-control they should marry." A priest who commits himself to celibacy does so only after training that lasts a number a years at the end of which through reflection and prayer he has reached the firm conviction through practice that Christ is giving him this gift for the good of the Church and the service of others.

CELIBACY VOW VS. MARRIAGE VOW • Please tell me why a priest can leave the priesthood and marry, but in marriage it is till the death. In both sacraments there is an indelible mark imprinted on the soul. A priest takes a vow and marriage is also a vow. It is confusing when I try to explain it to my grandchildren and my children. — *Name withheld, Bellevue, Iowa*

You are correct in that both the priesthood and marriage are sacraments that leave a mark on the soul and that both the priest and the married person take a vow. Once married, the person is always married until death ends the marriage. Once a man becomes a priest he is always a priest. Those who leave the priesthood, are laicized, and get married are still priests and could absolve from sin in a real emergency. But they are no longer legally able to act like priests because the Church has changed their position to that of the lay state. Your question is how can the priest who takes a vow of celibacy get married while a married person who takes the vow cannot remarry. The answer is in the nature of giving the vow. Celibacy is a discipline the Western Church imposes on its priests. It is not a divine requirement. It does not exist in the Eastern Uniate churches where priests are allowed to be married. Because the Church imposes this discipline, it can also release from it. In granting laicization with the right to marry, the Church says in effect: "I release you from your vow of celibacy; however, you can no longer function as a priest but must live like a layman in the world." In marriage the matter is different. The indissolubility of marriage is not a law of the Church but God's law about which the Church can do nothing. This teaching comes from the New Testament. In Mark 10:2-12, Jesus gives his teaching on divorce. He says that no man can separate what God has joined and concludes: "Whoever divorces his wife and marries another commits adultery against her, and the woman who divorces her husband and marries another commits adultery." Do you see the difference? The Church makes the law of celibacy and can release from it. Christ makes the law of indissolubility and the Church cannot release from it.

Chain Letters

I received a letter in the mail that read: "This is not a chain letter. It is a novena to St. Theresa that began in 1955. It has never been broken. Within 24 hours, send a copy to four people. In the next four days say one Our Father and one Hail Mary. Notice what happens on the fourth day. Please do not break this novena." I sent a copy to four friends and the following day I received a telephone call from one. She informed me in no uncertain terms that sending such a letter was "heresy" and asked me to recall the letters I had sent out. I would like your opinion as to whether or not she is right. — *Name withheld, Lafayette, Ind.*

Your friend was not correct in calling it "heresy," but she was correct in chiding you because you were aiding and abetting superstition. Although the letter you received calls it a novena, it is not a novena but a chain letter. It puts pressure on you not to break the chain and strongly suggests that you will be rewarded on the fourth day. A novena is a devotional practice carried on for nine consecutive days and by extension has come to mean a devotion also practiced one day a week for nine weeks. Some spiritual writers do not like even novenas because too often superstition can be mixed in. Superstition is a violation of the virtue of religion by which God is worshiped in an unworthy manner or creatures are given honor that belongs to God alone. Chain letters are a form of superstition because they prey on people's fears and seemingly bind God to a course of action. Another example of superstition is allegedly unfailing prayers, which are often made part of chain letters.

Chalice

> Our church bulletin says: "Today the cup may be made of silver or gold, wood or glass and other less precious ingredients." This doesn't seem to say the same thing as your answers do. — *Lucian Szymanski, South Bend, Ind.*

This does not contradict anything I have said, except with wood one must be careful because some woods are absorbent. The rules on sacred vessels are simple. Vessels are to be made with solid materials that are considered suitable in each region. The conference of bishops is the judge in this matter. Chalices and other vessels that are intended to hold the blood of the Lord should have a cup of nonabsorbent material. The base may be of any other solid and worthy material. These rules allow wide options. The basic choice is that the material used should be considered worthy, valuable, and appropriate in the culture of the area.

Charismatics

> I have been bothered by some happenings in the Catholic Church in charismatic meetings. We worry that the actions listed could be either overactive imaginations or even works of the devil. These are: 1. Being slain in the

Spirit (touched by someone and losing consciousness). 2. Speaking in tongues. 3. Life in the Spirit classes, to obtain the gifts of the Spirit. What is the Church's feeling on these matters? — *Charles M. Brush, Jackson, Fla.*

The charismatic movement is a big umbrella that covers a diversity of activities and people. At one end is a solid worship of the Spirit in which people open their lives to the movements of grace, resulting in deeper prayer and faith. At the other end is a fanaticism that seeks the bizarre rather than a sincere and humble piety. Both the Holy See and the American bishops have approached the movement with caution. One cannot deny the working of the Spirit in his people. One cannot fault Catholics for trying to live deeper spiritual lives in the love of the Holy Spirit, opening their lives to the prompting of God's grace. However, where pride, elitism, ostentation, and a searching for the unusual enter, condemnation can only be given. 1. I have seen people "slain in the Spirit" and while the Holy Spirit could do such a thing, my own opinion is that it is almost exclusively the result of self-hypnosis and is purely psychosomatic. I have seen the same thing take place in voodoo and pagan practices. 2. Speaking in tongues was a valid charism in the apostolic Church, and St. Paul refers to it (1 Corinthians 12). He does stress, however, that it was given for the common, not the individual, good, and for the upbuilding of the Church. 3. The charisms are gifts of the Spirit and one cannot learn them.

CHARISMATIC MASS • What is a charismatic Mass? I am living in Cleveland and have never assisted at one. — *Maria L. Cady, Cleveland, Miss.*

There is no such thing as a charismatic Mass. The Mass itself is the same no matter who attends it. Some charismatic groups, while attending Mass, may be more vocal and emotional than ordinary Catholics, but this has nothing to do with the Mass itself. Charismatics are people who are trying to renew their spiritual life in the Holy Spirit. They place strong emphasis on prayer, openness to the Spirit, and a sharing of spiritual gifts. They attend prayer meetings, often weekly, which include spontaneous prayer, sharing of experience, fellowship, and study of the Scriptures. They place great emphasis on baptism of the Holy Spirit, which is not a new sacrament or rebaptism but the experiencing of grace, already sacramentally received.

Children

Years ago I married a non-Catholic in the Church but was forced to raise my two boys in a non-Catholic atmosphere. However, they were baptized, made their First Communions, were confirmed, and were married in the Church. Now, they are both fallen-away Catholics. I say the Rosary every day, pray to St. Jude, make novenas. What else can I do to rectify my *big* mistake? — *Name withheld, Salt Lake City, Utah*

I wouldn't say that you have done badly. You saw to it that they received the sacraments, and undoubtedly they were instructed at each of these steps. There is not much more any mother can do, particularly in a hostile religious environment. The faith has been presented to them and they are adults now, responsible for their own actions. Think of St. Monica who prayed thirty years for her son, Augustine. Continue to pray for your sons and let them know that you are praying for them, but do it in such a way that it doesn't sound like nagging. God's grace works its own wonders in time.

THE MASS AND CHILDREN • In our parish in recent years the priests have made it very clear that young children are not welcome at Mass. When we bring them for such occasions as the Feast of St. Blase and Ash Wednesday we get looks of disapproval. This year on Ash Wednesday we were refused ashes for our four-year-old. The priest who refused stated he was "theologically correct." When this was pursued with our pastor he flatly stated that the bishop refused distribution to children. At a later service, across town, our three- and five-year-old children were totally welcomed. Is the position of our priests right or wrong? — *Michael Veitch, Albany, N.Y.*

My first thought in answering was simply to refer to Matthew 19:14 and let it go at that. Having spent considerable time in mission countries where children run around the church and sanctuary I may be a little more immune to distractions than others. Very young children can be a nuisance to others during Mass, but a three- or four-year-old is at an age when he or she should be under control and I do not think that parents should be discouraged in bringing them to Mass. Children should experience going to church as a natural part of family life and growing up. Parents should bring their children to get their throats blessed on the Feast of St. Blase, but Ash Wednesday is something else. The Church uses ashes to signify mortality, sorrow, and penance and we receive them on Ash Wednesday as a reminder of values we should have in life as Christians. The distribution of ashes presupposes an intellectual act that small children cannot make. This is probably what the priest meant when he stated that he was "theologically correct." I myself give ashes to small children, not in the expectation that they will understand, but as a means of instructing them in the life of the Christian community; however, I can see how a priest might prefer to do otherwise. I have not heard of any bishop making a rule on this point, but I suppose it is possible. If such a regulation was made, I would not consider it wise or prudent.

Christ

If Christ did not descend into Lucifer's hell during the time between his death and resurrection, where did he wrestle with Lucifer over the keys to death, hell, and the grave? I've heard of this happening during those three days of death. Then Jesus rose from the dead and had victory over it all. Where did he wrestle with Lucifer over the keys (if in fact he did)? — *Jean C. Stoops, McLoud, Okla.*

There is nothing in the Gospels that tells of what Christ did between the time of his death on the cross and his resurrection. The Apostles' Creed, to which all Catholics must subscribe, states, "He descended into hell." The hell meant here is *sheol*, the Jewish word for "the place of the dead." The Catholic teaching is based on 1 Peter 3:18-19: "In the body he was put to death; in the spirit he was brought to life. And in the spirit he went and made his proclamation to the imprisoned spirits." The general teaching of the Church is that after his death, Jesus went to *sheol* to release those good souls who had died before him but could not enter heaven because it had been closed by Adam's sin. The sacrifice of Jesus reopened the gates of heaven. The incident you mention has no foundation in Scripture. It is based on a book, *City of God*, which purports to tell of a private revelation. Not only are we *not* required to believe such claimed revelations but in this case prudence would demand some skepticism.

Christmas

Most Catholics decorate trees at Christmas and celebrate Christ's birth. But the Bible speaks against those things. In Jeremiah 10:2-4 it says: "Thus saith the Lord, learn not the ways of the heathen. . . . For the customs of the people are vain: for one cutteth a tree out of the forest. . . . They deck it with silver and gold." So the practice appears to be paganism. Also, there is no New Testament record of Christians celebrating Christ's birth but only commemorating his death. — *Mark Browder, Huntingdon, Pa.*

Old Law practices do not apply in the New Law, which Christ established. The Old Testament tells us to stone a woman taken in adultery, proscribes all kinds of dietary practices, etc. We cannot interpret the Old Testament apart from the New Testament. Jeremiah in the passage you quote was not talking about Christmas trees. The newer and more accurate translations speak of "wood cut from the forest, wrought by craftsmen with the adze, adorned with silver and gold." Jeremiah here is referring to pagan idols that are carved from wood and dressed in precious metals. Likewise, nowhere in the Bible does it say we should not celebrate Christ's birth, but the Bible does show the shepherds hurrying to Bethlehem and the magi coming a long distance to commemorate the birth of Jesus. Christmas is in a sense an artificial feast, since we do not know exactly when Jesus was born. Even before Christmas there was the Feast of the Epiphany, but people wanted to celebrate Christ's coming into the world. So around the year 200 the feast was instituted on December 25, a date proximate to the Epiphany and coinciding with the winter solstice, a time of rejoicing among pagan people. It thus replaced a pagan feast for new Christians. Various countries contributed to our Christmas customs: the Christmas tree is from Germany, carols and holly from England, the Christmas crib from Italy, and so on.

Church and State

I would like to know the Church's position on the separation of church and state. Are there any countries where the church runs the affairs of government or would if voted into power? — *Bob Bartlett, Sioux Falls, S. Dak.*

Historically, this is a complex question and quite long. I will confine my answer to the present day and to Christianity, since there is a very close involvement of church and state in Muslim countries. Examples of church and state identification today would be England — where the monarch is head of the church, appoints all bishops (acting on the advice of the prime minister), and where even revisions of the Book of Common Prayer must be submitted to Parliament — and the Scandinavian countries where there is also a close identification between church (Lutheranism) and state. The present position of the Catholic Church (it was not always thus) can be found in two documents of Vatican II, *Declaration on Religious Freedom* and *Pastoral Constitution on the Church in the Modern World*. While recognizing the need of cooperation between church and state, the latter document declares, "The Church, by reason of her role and competence, is not identified with any political community nor bound by ties to any political system." The document insists that "the political community and the Church are autonomous and independent of each other in their own fields." This is very much in the spirit of Vatican II's *Pastoral Constitution* and its adoption was largely the work of the late Father John Courtney Murray. One should also read Vatican II's statements on the rights of the individual conscience to be respected by all governments.

Church of Christ

I have a problem dealing with my sister's new belief. After being raised a Catholic for thirty-eight years, she has left the Church for the Church of Christ. She has been baptized in this church and is taking private Bible lessons. I am angry, hurt, and confused. She is godmother to all three of my sons and I'm afraid that she might try to influence them to her way of belief. My parish priest tells me not to discuss religion with her. Please give me some background on the Church of Christ so I will know what to say to some of her religious claims. — *Name withheld, Charleston, W. Va.*

Your priest's advice is good because unless you are firmly founded in the teachings of your faith and in Scripture, debating with your sister can only confuse you more. Some years ago a church in the town where I lived put up a new sign: "Church of Christ. Founded AD 33." This is of course nonsense. The Churches of Christ are an offshoot from the Disciples of Christ, which in turn broke away from the Baptist Church. These churches evolved from Campbellism, after Alexander Campbell, a Calvinist Baptist who in 1830 severed ties with the Baptists. He began his own evangelical and fundamental church, which resulted in numerous congregations today. The Churches of Christ are now loosely organized and differ among themselves on doctrine, forms of worship, Bible translations, etc. They call themselves a restoration of New Testament Christianity and do not consider themselves a part of the Protestant Reformation. Their main strength is in Tennessee, West Virginia, the Ozark area of Missouri, Arkansas, and the plains area of Texas. As each church is autonomous, beliefs and liturgies vary, and theology goes from fundamentalist to rationalist; thus unless one is familiar with the particular congregation to which your sister belongs, it is difficult to comment on her new beliefs. The best way for your sons and yourself to protect yourselves is to study your own faith through adult-education courses and Bible studies. There are answers to any arguments your sister might make, but you have to know your own religion well to give adequate response. Since she probably has the zeal most new converts possess, she may not be open to reason or willing to listen to objective argument, particularly if she was a lonely person before and has now found new friends to fill her time. You can find out more about the Churches of Christ and Campbellism in the book *Separated Brethren* by William J. Whalen (Our Sunday Visitor).

Cloning

If it ever became possible for a person to have himself cloned, would the person's "copy" and his descendants have immortal souls? Persons who were the result of cloning would not be created the way God intends. — *Name withheld, Oradell, N.J.*

Cloning has been unprofessionally described as a scientific method for remaking exact copies of an individual. Cloning has already been accomplished by scientists in several lower forms of life, including frogs, and it is very possible that it will soon be done with human life. God is the principal and source of life, and once human life begins, God infuses an immortal soul into it, even if that life is artificially aided in its conception. The morality of cloning is another question entirely, with moralists being strong in their condemnation of the procedure. The legal and scientific communities are divided on the ethics of the question, which is fraught with the most frightening implications, particularly because of the abuses to which it could be subjected.

Commandments

Is not this a commandment of God also: "Love your neighbor as yourself"? In reading the prayer book this is how the commandments were: 1. I am the Lord your God, you shall not have strange gods before me. 2. You shall not take the name of the Lord your God in vain, etc. No mention of love your neighbor. I always thought that was a commandment of God also. — *Stella Kibartas, Chicago, Ill.*

The commandments in your prayer book are the Ten Commandments of the Old Law God gave to Moses, which bind us even today. Jesus summarized these commandments into his two great commandments (Matthew 22:36-40). These are the commandments of the New Law. The first is to love God with one's whole being and the second is to love your neighbor as yourself. In his parable of the Good Samaritan, Jesus showed us that our neighbor is everyone on earth, even an enemy. These two great commandments are summary commandments because they include the Ten Commandments. If we love our neighbor we will not lie to him, or steal from him, or harm him, or covet his possessions. Since Jesus is God the two great commandments are commandments of God also.

OLD LAW COMMANDMENTS • Since there are over six hundred commandments (laws) of the Old Testament, why do we Catholics uphold some and not others? Who decides? — *Richard S. Thomas, St. Paul, Minn.*

The Church decides, since it is the authentic interpreter of the Bible. Those commandments in Deuteronomy (the Ten Commandments), which come from God, are meant for all people of all times, since they are the law of God. The other regulations in Deuteronomy came from the Jewish priestly class. While some of them are ritual, others were a reaction to the pagan cultic environment that surrounded the Jews of the time. The priests of Israel had a horror of the possibility of pagan practices diluting Judaism and hence made rules that would keep their religion centered on the one God, untainted by these practices. The early Church had to face the very question you ask. The Council of Jerusalem (Acts 15) ruled on some of these laws. Peter had been prepared for this meeting by a vision (Acts 10:9-16). It takes a study of anthropology, sociology, and theology to understand the Jewish regulations and why most of them do not apply to us.

Communion, Holy

I would like the following questions answered, and also a direct statement on them from the new Code of Canon Law. What is the Church law on giving the bread and wine to the people? Should it be given at all the Masses? Should the blood of our Lord be kept overnight? Just how long? Should the consecrated host be dipped in the blood by lay people? — *John Whitte, Richmond, Ind.*

These rules are not contained in the new code but in the general regulations of the Church, which have been promulgated by the Holy See through the Congregation for Divine Worship. The instruction *Sacramentali Communione* gives episcopal conferences the right "to decide to what extent . . . ordinaries may concede Communion under both kinds." The bishops of the United States used this regulation to permit general Communion under both species. This regulation was issued on June 29, 1970. The *Norms on Eucharistic Practices* (April 17, 1980) ruled: "The consecrated wine is to be consumed immediately after Communion and may not be kept. Care must be taken to consecrate only the amount of wine needed for Communion." The people are forbidden to self-communicate. The same decree states that Communion is a gift of the Lord and that this is to be shown by its being given through the minister appointed for this purpose. The decree adds: "It is not permitted that the faithful should themselves pick up the consecrated bread and the sacred chalice; still less that they should hand them to one another." The regulation on self-communicating would prohibit the communicant from dipping the sacred host into the sacred blood. This must be done by the Communion minister, regular or extraordinary.

UNDER BOTH SPECIES • I am a Lutheran reader of your column and I find it not only enjoyable but also informative and interesting. I would like to know if receiving both species at Communion is still optional in the Catholic Church. If so, could you please explain the rationale behind this position? — *David L. Burklund, Lawrence, Kans.*

It is not optional for the priest celebrating the Eucharist. To complete the sacrifice Christ established at the Last Supper, the celebrant must consume both the body and blood. As for Communion, the Vatican II documents teach: "The meaning of Communion is signified as clearly as possible when it is given under both kinds. In this form the meal aspect of the Eucharist is more fully manifested, and Christ's intention that the new and eternal Covenant should be ratified in the Blood is better expressed." However, the Church does not mandate Communion under both species for varied reasons: danger of irreverence; very large congregations; personal reasons of communicants, such as abstention by alcoholics, sanitary fears, etc. While Communion under both species is ideal, they are not necessary in order for us to actually receive Christ. He is totally present in every crumb of bread and drop of wine. The Council of Trent taught that Christ whole and entire is received under one species alone. Nevertheless, more and more parishes are offering the faithful the opportunity to receive under both species.

COMMUNION AND CONFESSION • I notice in recent years that a larger and larger percentage of people at Mass are receiving Communion. Lately, about ninety-five percent receive. I was taught that a person could not receive without confession if the individual had a sin unconfessed. Surely some of the ninety-five percent must lack the necessary confession. — *Name withheld, Appleton, Wis.*

It is true that years ago many people had the idea that they could not go to Communion without going to confession first. However, this was not a theological teaching of the Church, which holds that the only time one must go to confession is when a person is in the state of mortal sin (which is a very serious state whereby we have removed ourselves from God's life). As you know, for a sin to be mortal there must be serious matter, full deliberation, and full consent to the sin. Less serious sins (venial) are forgiven by our own sorrow and in the penitential rite of the Mass. I do think that pastors must caution their people from time to time so that Communion doesn't become simply routine or something subject to social custom or pressure. To go to Communion when separated from God by mortal sin would be sacrilegious and sinful in itself. But at the same time we cannot presume that some of those going to Communion (or those who don't) are in a state of serious sin.

PROTESTANTS RECEIVING • A Catholic girl is dating a Lutheran boy. At times he goes to Mass with her, and on special occasions when he would take communion in his own church, he goes up to receive Holy Communion at ours. Apparently he is doing this in good faith. The question is, should he be told not to go to Holy Communion or should he be free to go? This is of great concern to the girl's parents. — *Name withheld, Cincinnati, Ohio*

The admission of non-Catholics to Holy Communion is governed by stringent and limited rules, and then only by way of exception. The case you give would not be such an exception. If the girl's parents are concerned, they should speak to their daughter, who in turn should instruct her friend in Catholic practices. It should be done tactfully in order not to alienate him from the Church. If she needs advice on the Church rules, she should ask her pastor to inform her on the contents of the decree entitled *On Admitting Other Christians to Eucharistic Communion in the Catholic Church.*

Communion of Saints

Would you please explain the phrase "communion of saints" as used in the Apostles' Creed? I always thought it meant sharing in the merits of the saints, since they by their holy lives stored up merits in heaven. — *Mary Losey, Bellevue, Ky.*

You are correct in your understanding except that you do not go far enough. It is the sharing of spiritual goods between the Church Militant (we on earth), the Church Suffering (those in purgatory), and the Church Triumphant (the angels and saints in heaven). It is more than just our sharing in the merits of the saints. Each of the three divisions can pray for the other two and we can share our own merits with those in purgatory (indulgences, etc.), thus helping to shorten their period in purgatory.

A CONVERT'S DIFFICULTY • One thing I cannot accept as a convert is that prayers of others for me will help me to enter the kingdom of God. Where in the Bible does it say prayers of the people left behind will help the dead enter into God's kingdom? Reference to the Bible is most important, instead of always referring to the Church. Instead of "the Church says" it should be "the Bible says." — *Angelina Adamo, Orange Park, Fla.*

It's too bad that in your instruction the doctrines of the communion of saints and infallibility of the Church were not given to you in greater detail. The communion of saints is the sharing of spiritual good between the Church Militant, the Church Suffering, and the Church Triumphant. Each of these divisions can pray for the others. We are all affected by the acts of others. Jesus suffered for us, even though he himself was sinless. A mother instinctively prays for her children. If I can pray for you when you are alive, why can I not pray for you after you are dead? If you have a Catholic Bible, read 2 Maccabees 12:43-46, wherein Judas Maccabeus makes atonement for the dead that their sins might be forgiven them. The Bible frequently tells us that only those who are totally free from sin and the attachments to sin can enter heaven. When most people die, they still have some attachments to sin, and sins which may have been forgiven by Christ will have to be atoned for. These are the people we can help through the authority of the Church. For Catholics, what "the Church says" is as important as what "the Bible says." This again is on the authority of Jesus. Catholics look upon Jesus as the founder of their Church. Jesus promised that the Holy Spirit would guide his Church "to all truth" (John 16:13). Moreover, he promised that he would remain in his Church until the end of the world (Matthew 28:20). He gave that Church great powers to bind and loose on earth, promising that what that Church did would be approved by God (John 20:23, Matthew 16:17-19). Thus what the Church does as Church takes on great importance. We refer to this as tradition, Christ acting through his Church. Some non-Catholics ridicule tradition and declare only their belief in Scripture. Yet the Old Testament is nothing but the traditions of the Jewish people, and the New Testament was not written until many years after the death of Christ, and it was composed from the traditions kept alive in the Church. Although you have been received into the Church, I hope your study of Catholicism is not over. The Catholic Church has two thousand years of richness and much accumulated wisdom, all guided by the Holy Spirit, the soul of the Church.

Confession (Reconciliation)

Why is confession so important in the Catholic Church, since the Church itself says Catholics do not need to confess venial sins and only go to confession once a year? What does mortal sin and confession have to do with each other with regard to perfect and imperfect contrition? Is it true that a Protestant can be forgiven mortal sin with only imperfect contrition but a Catholic cannot outside confession? — *Hulin Benoit, Lake Charles, La.*

Christ willed the sacrament of confession to be the ordinary means for sins to be forgiven. He established the sacrament on the night of his resurrection when he appeared to the apostles and gave them the power to forgive or retain sins, promising what they did would bind heaven. The apostles passed this power on to their successors, the bishops, who in turn delegated priests to assist them. Sin is an offense against God. Sin can be a grave (serious or mortal) offense, which demands serious punishment, or it can be light (venial), which is punished less severely than condemnation to hell. Mortal sin is a deliberate and free rejection of God and his teaching. Venial sin is a rejection of some teaching of God but is not a rejection of God himself. Since mortal sin is a rejection of God, if one dies in mortal sin, one dies rejecting God and hence will be separated from him for all eternity. If one dies in venial sin, one is not separated from God but must be purified of attachment to sin to be admitted into God's presence. Confession frees one of all sin and joins that person again to God. Contrition (sorrow for sin) is of two types: perfect contrition (sorrow for having offended the good God) or imperfect (sorrow because one will be punished). Either sorrow suffices to receive absolution in confession. However, outside confession, sin is only forgiven by God through perfect contrition; this applies not only to Catholics but anyone else. Also, the difficulty in confessing directly to God is that we do not know whether our contrition is truly perfect and hence there can be uncertainty whether the sin has been forgiven. In confession we have certainty in knowing because of the power given by Jesus to his apostles and their successors. Thus mortal sin is forgiven in confession or by perfect contrition. (Although mortal sins can be forgiven through perfect contrition, the person is supposed to go to individual confession as soon as possible.) Venial sin can be forgiven in confession or outside confession by an Act of Contrition to God (telling God you are sorry for your offense and promising to avoid such acts in the future) or through a penance service such as the one at the start of the eucharistic liturgy. The Church law on annual confession applies only to persons who are in a state of serious (mortal) sin. However, confession is not just for mortal sins. Canon 988.2 says, "It is to be recommended to the Christian faithful that venial sins also be confessed."

STRANGE ADVICE • Recently in the confessional I was advised that sins of thought against the Ninth Commandment shouldn't deter me from receiving the Eucharist weekly, provided I confess every three months. This confused me, since I always regarded these sins as serious matter; but the priest stated that was "a long time ago." Later I thought he might have considered me scrupulous. I would appreciate your comments. — Name withheld, Philadelphia, Pa.

I do not wish to comment on your confessor's advice, since he had more to judge on than a short letter. He may have thought you scrupulous or perhaps confusing temptation with actual sin. However, I am puzzled by the "long time ago" remark. Internal sins have the same gravity as external sins. Indeed, fidelity to God is always first broken internally, even before the external act. If I read the New Testament correctly, Jesus seems to be more condemning of internal sins than external sins (Mark 7:20-21, Matthew 5:28, Matthew 15:19, etc.). Every sin begins in the mind. The sinful act is thought about and then presented to the will. When the will gives consent, the sin has been committed, even though the act may not have taken place. St. Thomas Aquinas tells us that sin is formally in the will and this is an internal act. St. Augustine classically defines sin as any thought, word, or deed against the law of God. Existentialism has had a great effect on modern theologians with the result that some seem to be more anthropologists than theologians. Sin is sin because of God's point of view, not man's. There is a sentimentalism in some modern theologies that stresses our way of looking at things. But we do not lead God — he leads us. God is love and wants good for us. But he has also given us parameters inside which that love operates. Internal sins are as much a violation of that love as are external ones.

WORRIED ABOUT PAST SINS • Besides having three abortions I have committed acts of unnatural sex, but I made two lifetime confessions at two missions when we had missions and both priests forgave me my sins. But my mind still bothers me. Are my sins forgiven? — *Name withheld, Wichita, Kans.*

I receive many letters similar to yours from people who, having committed serious sin, confessed it and are still troubled by guilt. When a sin is forgiven by the Church through a priest, it is forgiven and we must try to forget it. We must have confidence in Christ and his Church to whom he gave the power to forgive sin: "Whose sins you shall forgive, they are forgiven them." You did all that was necessary for the forgiveness of sin: you repented what you had done, you went to confession, and you resolved not to commit those sins in the future. In confession, Isaiah tells us, things are set right and as the Lord says, "Though they [our sins] be scarlet, they will be made white as snow." Very often the devil uses the past to trouble our present by filling us with doubts. We must not allow this to happen. Our confidence is in the love of Jesus who died that our sins might be forgiven. We should never doubt the efficacy of that sacrifice.

CONFESSING CIRCUMSTANCES • When going to confession to admit consenting to impure thoughts, must you specify if they are heterosexual or homosexual impure thoughts? — *Name withheld, Ossining, N.Y.*

If this question was asked because it was troubling a person's conscience, my reply would be: "In conscience matters, always follow the safer course." Confession to be effective should be made humbly, frankly, and entirely. After all, we are telling our sins primarily to God who already knows them. So that the priest can make a proper judgment, we are obliged to confess circumstances that alter the character of the sin. The two sins you mention would require different advice from the confessor and hence the distinction should be confessed. We not only receive absolution in confession but also spiritual direction to aid us in the future.

Confirmation

In the Baptist religion they speak of a born-again Christian. Is there something comparable in the Catholic religion? — Mrs. A. Cooper, Darby, Pa.

A born-again Christian is a person who freely commits his or her life to Jesus Christ. This is done through a positive act of the will. Every Christian should be "born again" in this sense. Baptists baptize later than we do and therefore the person being baptized is old enough to make this commitment personally to Christ (instead of by proxy, as in infant baptism). Catholics have an ideal place to do so at confirmation, and catechesis in preparation for this sacrament should aim to have the recipient make such a commitment.

UNFRUITFUL SACRAMENT • If a person knowingly received the sacrament of confirmation in the state of mortal sin, would the confirmation be valid? Or would the person have to be confirmed again after a good confession? — Name withheld, Glencoe, N. Mex.

The confirmation would be valid and would not have to be received again, but it would be ineffective until the mortal sin was removed. The validity of the sacrament depends upon the matter and form and the intention of the recipient. Theologians divide the sacraments into two types: sacraments of the living (Eucharist, confirmation, holy orders, matrimony, and anointing of the sick) and sacraments of the dead (baptism and penance). To receive a sacrament of the living, one must be spiritually alive (in the state of sanctifying grace); otherwise, while the administration is valid, the sacrament is unfruitful. To make the sacrament become fruitful, the obstacle would have to be removed, in this case the mortal sin. Once the sin has been confessed and forgiven, the grace of the sacrament then takes effect.

Conscience

Many Catholics today maintain that the primacy of the individual conscience entitles one to believe or act in accordance with that conscience regardless of the teaching of the Church. Many also maintain that only that which is dogmatically defined must be believed. As a consequence, papal encyclicals, declarations, and the like may be safely ignored if they contradict one's honest belief. The accumulation of dissent clearly causes confusion. Can you comment? — *Alan T. Harvey, Santa Monica, Calif.*

There are several complex questions here. Conscience is the practical judgment of the rightness or wrongness of an act. Everyone must obey conscience (*Declaration on Religious Freedom*); however, conscience can err from invincible ignorance (*Pastoral Constitution on the Church in the Modern World*). Ignorance is not excusable when it results from negligence, complacency, self-centeredness, or prejudice. So while one is obliged to follow one's conscience, one is also obliged to form one's conscience in the mind of the Church. This is necessary because Christ rules in the Church ("He who hears you, hears me" — Luke 10:16). Therefore, the Christian must conform his or her conscience to the teaching of Christ of which the Church (the magisterium) is the authentic teacher (*Declaration on Religious Freedom*). This authentic teaching is far more than a few defined doctrines. As Vatican Council II states: "When their bishop speaks in the name of Christ on matters of faith and morals, the faithful are to accept this teaching and adhere to it with religious assent. This religious submission . . . must be shown in a special way to the authentic magisterium of the Roman Pontiff even when he is not speaking *ex cathedra.*"

FOLLOW CONSCIENCE • My conscience bothers me regarding killing, whether it's war or self-defense. Our Lord says, "If you get slapped, turn the other cheek." Why don't the bishops of the country take a public position regarding killing? — *Bob Beeson, San Diego, Calif.*

It is Catholic teaching that one must follow his or her conscience and that is why the Catholic bishops have always spoken out (and did so again recently) in behalf of the rights of conscientious objectors to war or military service. They have also spoken out against the arms race and for peace. Theologians divide the teaching of Christ into two types: counsels and commandments. Observance of the Ten Commandments is necessary for salvation. The counsels, while not necessary to salvation, are a means of perfection. Christ's admonition to "turn the other cheek" (Matthew 5:39, Luke 6:29) or his approval of celibacy (Matthew 19:12) are counsels. Theologians teach that one has the right to self-defense and to use the minimum amount of force necessary to repel an unjust aggression. All Christians should work to outlaw war and in behalf of peace. The higher Christian way is one of nonviolence and the bearing of injuries. One seeking higher Christian perfection would not engage in killing for any reason.

Cooperation in Evil

Could OSV run a clear-cut article on cooperation with evil (for example, mailman delivering anti-Catholic literature)? Since divorce, remarriage, and contraception are woven tightly into life here, it is helpful to know what the bare miminums are — even if the ideals are known and strived for. — *Name withheld, New Ulm, Minn.*

In speaking of cooperation with evil, one must distinguish what the theologians call formal and material cooperation. Formal cooperation in the sin of another is always sinful in itself. Formal cooperation is when a person aids another to commit the sin as a sin. Material cooperation is sometimes permitted. Material cooperation is in itself a good act that is used by another to commit sin. Thus delivery of mail in itself is a good act, even though it might be abused by bigots or pornographers or con men. The mailman would be allowed to deliver the mail, although in some instances a bad result might ensue. I don't see how the rest of the question applies to cooperation. The teaching of the Church is clear and not subject to dimunition. Concerning divorce, remarriage, and contraception, here is the Church's stand: Once validly married, one cannot divorce and remarry. Based on the teaching of the Second Vatican Council, Pope Paul VI issued an encyclical concerned with marriage doctrine and morality in which he said that each and every marriage act "must remain open to the transmission of life." Therefore, on the authority of Church teaching, direct contraception is never allowed. While some priests contested this teaching, the succeeding popes and the body of U.S. bishops have consistently affirmed it.

NO COOPERATION HERE • I am a court reporter in New York. I am only starting. My problem comes when it comes to reporting on states like New Jersey that recently instituted capital punishment. I as a Catholic do not agree with capital punishment. My concern comes when I may be sent to report an "examination before trial" or things that involve the legal justice system of such a state. Should I tell my superior that I do not want to go to a state like that because of the incompatibility of principles? Or is it for the benefit of justice that I become involved? — *Name withheld, Long Island City, N.Y.*

I do not think you should be troubled about what you are called upon to report or where you are sent. You are not directly involved in finding guilt or innocence (which is the jury's job) or in passing sentence (the judge's responsibility). Your work is simply to report what has taken place and you have no responsibility for what results from that reporting. Making a record of legal proceedings is in itself a good thing and necessary for the rendering of true justice. Your record is useful in appeals and even reversals of judgment. I am sure that as you record, you will record many things you disagree with or find offensive; however, your responsibility is simply to record, not to pass judgment. We are never allowed to cooperate by taking part and consenting to the sin of another (formal cooperation). I do not wish here to go into the subject of capital punishment, which is a complicated theological issue, only to say that your reporting is in no way formal cooperation in the result and is in itself an indifferent act. You may feel upset, outraged, sorry, etc., regarding the outcome, but you are in no way responsible for it and your part has no determination of the end result.

Cosmetic Surgery

Is it a sin to have cosmetic surgery such as a face-lift, dermabrasion for acne scars, or having your nose straigthened? Is this vanity? — *Name withheld, Nashville, Tenn.*

There is nothing morally wrong in having cosmetic surgery, provided the risks are not excessive. In the type of surgery you mention, the risks are minimal. Vanity is an inordinate love for the esteem of others, and this could be involved but not necessarily. True, good looks are not the most important things in life, but certain improvements can bring peace of mind and greater self-assurance. God expects us to take care of what we have and if we can improve it, so much the better. God is not opposed to beauty. In opting for such surgery, one must consider the risks involved, the skill of the surgeon, and the costs, which often run high. It should also be noted that while improvements can be made, one should not expect a miracle. To answer your question directly, it is not a sin, nor need it be vanity. In fact, in many cases it would be a recommended procedure.

Creation

Recently someone asked me, "How do you know God created the world?" She wanted to know who witnessed this, and the fact that he created it in six days. How would you have answered? — *Name withheld, Elkhart, Ind.*

The world was created long before there was anyone to witness it. Philosophers have long pondered the problem of exnihilation — something coming from nothing. If anything comes into being from nothing, it needs a cause. That cause is God. Scientists today incline toward the so-called big bang theory to explain the universe. But that theory only explains the present state of the universe. There had to be something there to create the big bang, something before it. So we go back as far as we can until we get to a first cause, which is another name for God. Philosophers also argue from the order in nature, the laws by which the universe operates. This presupposes a Creator who made the laws and put order into the universe. There are other arguments, particularly a powerful ontological argument from St. Anselm, but these require some philosophical training to understand. I know of no Catholic theologian who holds to a literal six days of twenty-four hours each as the period of creation. The inspired writer of Genesis was writing to a simple people who had little knowledge of the universe. He explained creation in a way that they could understand. A day of creation could just as easily have been millions of years. Time means nothing to God, who is timeless.

Creed

At Sunday Mass the congregation recites the Nicene Creed, which was defined at the First Council of Nicaea in 325. What is the origin of the creed we call the Apostles' Creed? — *Homer W. Ashley, Prescott, Ariz.*

The Apostles' Creed is not of apostolic origin but seems to have originated in the second century as a summary of what the apostles taught. It was used as a formula of faith by catechumens preparing for baptism. By the fourth century it was in wide use throughout the West. As the Church aged and grew, doctrinal difficulties arose, particularly with Arianism, which the original creed did not answer. Hence the development of the more complex Nicene Creed.

Cremation

Can a Catholic be cremated? I want to be cremated, but I have been told the Church will not allow it. Since I started my quest for information, I have heard of a man who died in Florida, was cremated, and his ashes sent to New York where there was a Christian Mass and burial. I do firmly believe in the soul. I do not hold with wakes. All I want are Masses and prayers. — *Mrs. Goldie Czyzewski, Derby, N.Y.*

Cremation is not against any article of faith. It was legislated against because in Europe it was the equivalent of the denial of Catholic doctrine (the resurrection) and a repudiation of the Church by secularism. In 1963 the Congregation for the Doctrine of the Faith issued a decree permitting cremation for a serious private or public reason as long as it does not involve contempt of the Church or religion. In Japan the Church has long permitted the cremation of Catholics, even going so far as to enshrine ashes within the church building. This is a matter to talk over with your pastor. Any arrangements about death and after should be settled well in advance.

Crucifix

What is the reason the Catholic Church has the image of Christ hanging from the cross while other religions simply show the empty cross? — *Arthur Hilgert, Oakdale, Pa.*

I presume you are referring to a crucifix, which is the image of Christ superimposed on a cross, usually represented at the time of his passion but sometimes depicted as Christ the King. When the Protestant rebellion took place, the reformers sought to do away with as much Catholic symbolism as possible, so crucifixes and statues disappeared from their churches. Up until very recent years (and still largely true), one could even tell the Catholic Church as the building with the cross on top of it. The symbolism of the crucifix is that one does not separate the person of Christ from the sacrifice on the cross. The cross is the means of our salvation through the sacrifice of Jesus as well as a reminder of what our sins cost the Son of God.

Crucifixion

The apostle John, in his Gospel, says that the soldiers broke the legs of the men crucified with Jesus, but that when they came to Jesus and saw that he was dead they did not break his legs. Why did the soldiers break the legs of people crucified? Was it further punishment or so they could not escape? — *Robert L. Bauer, New Orleans, La.*

The soldiers broke the legs to hasten death. Most people do not understand the crucifixion. They think that the pain and the death came from being nailed to the cross or from loss of blood. Death on the cross came from suffocation, preceded by the terrible agony of strained muscles aching for oxygen, the lungs struggling to breathe. In order for the crucified to breathe, he had to lift his torso by pushing with his feet so that his lungs could expand to enable breathing. As the crucifixion wore on and strength ebbed, this was harder and harder to do. Death could be hastened by breaking the legs. No longer could the crucified lift his body to breathe and so he suffocated, strangling as he struggled for breath. This was the death Jesus suffered, about as terrible as the human mind could concoct.

Deaconesses

When women were appointed deaconesses in the early Church, did they receive the "laying on of hands" as did the deacons in the same era? — *Charles J. Sippel, Hardy, Ark.*

We do not know. There is argument today whether the role of deaconess was part of holy orders or was only a ministry. There is evidence that the early Church had deaconesses who fulfilled a role of serving women that would be embarrassing or possibly cause scandal if done by a man (for example, baptism by immersion). There is evidence also that some of these roles were also fulfilled by widows. Did deaconesses come from the ranks of widows or unmarried young women or both? We do not know. If they did exist, we do not know why they declined and ceased to exist. Some think their need may have declined with the increase of infant baptism, others that they came into competition with the increase in nuns. In short, we know very little about deaconesses in the early Church and not very much more about deacons.

Dead

My brother died a few months back. The chaplain and the parish priest were present when he died. Both consoled my sister-in-law, telling her she had nothing to be sad about, that my brother is now in heaven with the saints. There are a number of Masses to be offered for him. If he is already in heaven, will he be helped by these Masses? — *Name withheld, Palmertown, Pa.*

Neither you nor I can presume salvation for ourselves or another. Even the Church, which has the power of binding and loosing, only proclaims salvation in a limited number of cases (canonized saints) and then only after long examination, testing, and proven miracles. Salvation is a matter we must leave to the mercy and justice of God, and even when one is saved there can still be a period in purgatory when Christ's merits in the Mass can help. Hence the Bible tells us that it is a good and worthy thing to pray for the dead. What then happens to the merits of Masses offered for a person who is already in heaven? They are joined to the merits gained by martyrs and saints and applied according to the wisdom and mercy of God.

RESUSCITATION • What is the Church's teaching regarding cardiopulmonary resuscitation efforts and is this or is this not a threat to dying with dignity? This has been on our minds since we faced a life-saving situation that turned out to be fruitless, since the person died. Also, what do moral theologians teach about the length of time the soul remains in the body after death? Is it true that in sudden death the soul may remain longer than death from a long illness? — *Mrs. Lorna Case, Cincinnati, Ohio*

I don't like to use the term "dying with dignity," since in too many areas this has become synonymous with euthanasia. As cardiopulmonary resuscitation, or CPR, is a relatively new technique, there is no body of moral teaching on it. Formerly, death was presumed when there was no evidence of breath or heartbeat. Today, guidelines for death are more complex, involving a lack of response to stimuli, no excitable reflexes, and the absence of brain waves on the brain-wave machine (the electroencephalograph). Nevertheless, doctors are still debating the definition of death. Theologians hold that we are obliged to use ordinary means to preserve life. Ordinary means include normal food, drink, rest, medicines, treatments, and operations that offer reasonable hope for the preservation of life. I would include CPR among normal means, since it is a standard technique to restore breathing and heartbeat that may have been temporarily interrupted. CPR has had almost miraculous success among victims from apparent drowning or heart attacks. CPR in many cases may be fruitless in the end, but we are bound to try it when available. Because of the uncertainty of the moment of death, most theologians allow the administration of the sacrament of anointing up to half an hour after apparent death and some even allow longer. However, in the case of apparent death, the sacrament can only be given conditionally. There is no distinction made between deaths caused by sudden or long illnesses.

NEAR-DEATH EXPERIENCE • I would appreciate your comments on the so-called testimony on life after death by patients clinically dead but later revived. — *Mrs. Lucia Beaudoin, New Ipswich, N.H.*

It is my opinion that once a person is truly dead there can be no revival. However, clinical death and actual death may be two different things. Modern medicine is wrestling with the problem of true death now. The best opinion seems to be that death occurs when there is a total lack of brain activity, and heartbeat and respiration have ceased for fifteen minutes. Even so, the Church allows conditional absolution to be given to a person declared dead after a long illness for up to a half hour after apparent death and up to three hours in the case of a person who had been well and strong and has died suddenly, violently, and accidentally. Even if the medical profession agrees on the moment of death, the Church will still make the distinction between apparent death and real death, the latter being the point where the soul is fully separated from the body. There is a growing body of testimony from people who have been thought dead and later revived who tell of experiences they seem to encounter outside the body. They were obviously not dead if these impressions were recorded in the brain for later recall. It may be that they are on the threshold of eternal life and subject to influences that are not of this world. I have heard some of these people talk of what is to them a very real experience. Was it reality or a dream that left a strong impression? At the moment, we do not know the answer.

> **FEAR OF DEATH** • My ninety-year-old mother has said the Rosary every day, went to Mass every day she could, but is afraid to die because of the flames of hell for past sins. Can you tell me anything to reassure her? — *Rosemary Crocker, La Mesa, Calif.*

I think one of the more successful ruses of the devil is to prompt people to despair because of past sins. Your mother should not allow herself to fall into this trap. Anyone who has said the Rosary daily — and been faithful with the sacraments as your mother has — has no reason to despair of salvation. Such a person has not turned her life away from God, even though there may have been temporary failures. St. James (3:2) reminds us that "we all make mistakes" and Jesus taught his own disciples to pray, "Forgive us our trespasses." These sins have long since been forgiven and atoned for and to let them trouble us is vanity and a loss in trust in the mercy of God who sent his Son so that sins could be forgiven and we can be joined with him. The whole life of Jesus was spent reconciling us to God and this work is carried on today through his Church. We must have confidence in God's work and refuse to allow the devil to trouble us about the past.

Death Penalty

> What is the Church's stand concerning the death penalty? I have read articles that the Church was not against capital punishment when administered by duly constituted civil authorities. — *Name withheld, Midwest City, Okla.*

The Church as such has never made a definitive ruling on capital punishment, although the theologians of the Church have taught that the political community has the right to defend itself against unjust aggression and may in extreme cases put to death people found guilty of serious crimes against the social order. However, in recent years modern theologians have been tempering this position by declaring that the death penalty is essentially vindictive and question its value as a deterrent to serious crime. This view has been adopted in Europe and Latin America where, except for communist countries, the death penalty is no longer used. Pope John Paul II has spoken against the death penalty. In 1974 the U.S. bishops issued a statement in opposition to the death penalty. This was repeated in 1978 when the bishops reaffirmed the 1974 statement, declaring that "a return to the use of the death penalty can only lead to the further erosion of respect for life in our society. . . . We do not challenge society's right to punish the serious and violent offender, nor do we wish to debate the merits of the arguments concerning this right. Past history, however, shows the death penalty in its present application has been discriminatory with respect to the disadvantaged, the indigent and the socially impoverished. Furthermore, recent data from correction sources definitely question the effectiveness of the death penalty as a deterrent to crime." There are those who argue that the death penalty is a deterrent, at least for those who suffer its effects. On the reverse side, others argue that life sentence without possibility of parole is sufficient protection for society. From my own experience of serving in a state prison with a death house at a time when executions were common, I would agree with the bishops' position. Murderers and those who seriously endanger public safety should be removed from society, but ultimately punishment should be left to God's justice.

Depression

Pertaining to going to heaven, God doesn't judge a person by his or her illness, does he? My sister lost her son in a tragic accident. Since then she has become very emotionally ill. She is grieving all the time, is insecure, can't sleep, and has a troubled mind. She is a good Christian, loves God, but finds it hard to find trust and find faith and peace. She worries about this. Can you give her some answers? — *Name withheld, Redford, Mich.*

Our God is a God of love and mercy who delivered his own Son to death. His judgments are not made on a disordered and distorted mind but on a person's real worth of being. Tragedy touches the lives of all of us, and countless parents have suffered the tragic loss of a child. Most are able to pick up the shattered pieces of their lives and go on with the daily task of living. Some few, however, find difficulty and need help. Your sister may be one of these. She needs a period of counseling by a good priest-psychologist or someone qualified in mental health counseling.

Deuterocanonical Books

1. What is the historical basis for those Old Testament books that are found in the Catholic Bible but not in the original Hebrew Torah nor subsequent Protestant translations? What evidence do we have that these books are canonical? 2. What is the scriptural basis for the existence of a hierarchy in the Church? How do we justify it in view of Jesus' instruction to the apostles that they are to be servants and not concern themselves with the ambition of exercising authority over others? 3. How and when did Latin become the universal language of the Church, since Greek was used by many of the Church Fathers? — *William E. Pollock, Cheltenham, Pa.*

1. The Catholic canon of the Old Testament was stated by the Council of Hippo (393), the Council of Carthage (397), Pope Innocent I (405), and was dogmatically defined by the Council of Trent in 1546. The Catholic canon follows the Alexandrian collection of sacred writings and is known as the Septuagint version of the Old Testament. The Jewish canon, which gradually evolved through the consensus of the rabbinical schools, does not have all these books, omitting 1 and 2 Maccabees, Tobit, Judith, Sirach, Wisdom, Baruch, and small portions of Daniel and Esther. There has never been any binding Jewish legal decision (similar to the decision of Trent) but only common acceptance. Some rabbis pay heed to the Deuterocanonical books mentioned above and quote from them. When the Protestant revolt came, the leaders rejected the Catholic Bible and chose to follow the Jewish listing. Since the definition of Trent the Catholic canon is a matter for Catholic belief. 2. The term "hierarchy," while originally used to denote bishops, is broader in actuality. It refers to the orderly arrangement of the clergy in

providing the spiritual care of the faithful and the government of the Church. Jesus himself established Peter as head of the Church and appointed Judas as treasurer of the apostolic band. In establishing a Church (Matthew 16:18) Jesus willed that it would have the necessary means of functioning and governing. Acts and the Epistles show how this hierarchy developed. Apostolic tradition is also important here. You are correct in assuming that Jesus did not wish those in charge to be lords and masters (his washing of the feet at the Last Supper gave the example) but to be servants of the people. This is why one of the pope's titles is Servant of the Servants of God. 3. At the time the Church began its spread, Greek was the *lingua franca* of the then known world. It was used even in Rome. Thus the Catholic Scriptures were mainly written in this language. With the domination of the Roman empire, however, Latin grew in importance and in the second and third centuries a Christian literary Latin began to develop. St. Jerome (circa 343-420) made the first authorized translation of the Scriptures into the common language (the Latin *Vulgate*). With the headquarters of the Church in Rome, Latin thus became the official language of the Church.

Devil

Are we obliged to love the devil? This is not a facetious question. Our pastor brought this up at Sunday Mass. He spoke of the love God has for all things he created because everything he created was good. We were exhorted to love the devil because God does. Is this a new concept? We were always led to believe that the devil was the essence of all evil. It is hard to visualize a God, who is supremely good, loving that which is supremely evil. — *Walter J. Nachtwey, Fon du Lac, Wis.*

Your pastor may be a bit ontological for the average parishioner, but he is on solid ground. We must distinguish between a person and his act. As the late Bishop Sheen used to say: "Hate the sin, but love the sinner." A parent punishes an unruly child but doesn't stop loving that child. In an extreme case of "tough love" a parent may banish a child from the home because of an intransigent nature. This does not mean that the parent loves the child less. Thus with God. He created Lucifer in his own image, a brilliant spiritual being who somehow failed the test of free will and because of God's justice was banished for all eternity. The difference between God and Lucifer is that God still loves him while Lucifer is filled with hate. The true Christian feeling should be one of sorrow for Lucifer for what he has lost and what he has become. We can hate the evil he represents but have love for him as part of God's creation. Such love would be a greater agony for Lucifer than the pains of hell. So theologically your pastor is right, but he may be asking for more than many people are able to give. He is holding up to you a counsel and at least causing you to think, which is what a good homily should do.

PROBLEM OF EVIL • Why does the all-powerful God permit the devil to do his evil work in our souls and elsewhere on earth? — *John G. Bowen, Pleasanton, Tex.*

What your question raises is the problem of evil, one of the most complex questions in theology. Evil has no substance in itself but is the absence of good, or more simply the absence of God. God gave his rational creation the gift of free will, which has for its end the choice of himself. But because it is free, some angels chose (just as some humans choose) to reject God and to propagate evil in the world in opposition to God. Why doesn't God prevent them? To do so he would have to take away their freedom and they would be little more than automatons, which is not God's intention. Why doesn't God utterly destroy them? In creating angels and men, God gave them a soul, which is an eternal principle. Those who choose evil in preference to God suffer for it eternally. At the same time we must remember that the Father gave us Jesus Christ, who, being "obedient unto death," thus rejected evil and won for humanity the graces necessary also to reject evil. This is the good news of the Gospels. Jesus showed us how love overcomes evil, and in giving us the sacraments he gave us the means for our own victory. Jesus is our reconciler, willing for us what God wills and showing us the way to put God in our lives, which in itself is a rejection of evil. This is a simplified explanation for what has been the subject of many, many treatises.

Divine Office (Liturgy of the Hours)

Is a priest required, under the new Code of Canon Law, to pray the Divine Office daily? How do the new requirements differ from the old? Are there any provisions for cases such as illness or traveling, when a priest cannot say the Office? — *James Bartos, Auburn, Ind.*

Canon 276 states: "Priests as well as deacons aspiring to the priesthood are obliged to fulfill the Liturgy of the Hours in accordance with the proper and approved liturgical books; permanent deacons, however, are to do the same to the extent it is determined by the conference of bishops." (Permanent deacons in the United States, by decision of the hierarchy, are exempt from this requirement.) Canon 1174 repeats this requirement for clerics and adds that members of religious institutes are bound according to their constitutions. This same canon adds: "Other members of the Christian faithful according to circumstances are also earnestly invited to participate in the Liturgy of the Hours inasmuch as it is an action of the Church." This later exhortation is new to the revised code. A cleric may be dispensed from the obligation of the Divine Office for a proper motivating cause, for example, an eye ailment or missionary journey. The 1918 code was taken more strictly than the present law, for it considered even the omission of a single hour a grave sin. Recitation of the Breviary was looked upon more as an obligation than a sense of perfection. Also, the 1917 Breviary was in Latin while today's Liturgy of the Hours is in the vernacular. The present code must be interpreted in accordance with the official instruction given at the beginning of the Liturgy of the Hours, which while it calls upon clerics to faithfully recite the entire Divine Office as a means to perfection, also states that Lauds (morning prayer) and Vespers (evening prayer) are the two hinges of the Office and should not be omitted "unless for a serious reason," indicating a lesser reason can justify omitting one of the other hours while at the same time warning against "self-deception in this kind of a decision." In its guidelines for the permanent diaconate, the U.S. hierarchy notes that while permanent deacons are not bound to the universal Church law, they are encouraged "to pray the Liturgy of the Hours, since it is the official prayer of the Church, and gives firm liturgical direction to their prayer," adding, "permanent deacons should not hold themselves lightly excused from the obligation they have to recite morning and evening prayer."

Dogma and Doctrine

How do I respond to an Episcopalian friend as to the definition and differences of "dogma" and "doctrine"? — *Lucienne M. Dreyfus, Cambridge, Mass.*

While these words are sometimes interchangeable in general usage, they have a precise meaning within the Church. A doctrine is a teaching of the Church on faith and morals. A dogma is a doctrine or body of doctrine formally stated by the Church in an authoritative manner and necessary for belief. Someone once put it more simply: Doctrines are those teachings of the Church that are not yet dogmas. Vatican Council II was a doctrinal council, giving Church teachings but making no formal definitions. Vatican Council I was a dogmatic council, defining the dogma of papal infallibility. Other dogmas of recent times were the dogma of the Immaculate Conception and the dogma of the Assumption of the Blessed Virgin Mary, each of which was solemnly pronounced *ex cathedra* by the pope. Once a dogma has been declared, it is no longer open to question by theologians but is an accepted truth of the Church. Doctrine, on the other hand, is open to discussion, debate, and alteration. Limbo, for example, is a doctrine put forth by theologians, but it has never been defined by the Church. Doctrine on orders within the Church formerly included porter and exorcist in minor orders, and subdeacon in major orders, but as the result of the last council these orders were dropped and are no longer taught. Doctrine is subject to revision and expansion, but a dogma is a fixed teaching.

Dogmatism

I don't agree with the answer that it is an obligation under pain of sin to attend Sunday Mass. Also, in a recent article about the virginity of Mary, again the dogmatism is evident. While we stress tradition and good reason we should not impose as an intimidating dogma what is commonly accepted, though in a very highly disputed situation. — *Father Flavio, O.F.M., Provo, Utah*

In making answers here I try to rely on Church documents, rather than solely on my own opinion. Regarding the obligation of attending the Sunday and holy day Eucharist, this is laid down in precept by Canon 1247, which obliges the faithful to participate in Mass on Sundays and holy days. This canon must be interpreted in the light of the foundational canons (897-899), which state what the Eucharist is, and the highest honor the faithful are to give this august sacrament. Because of the nature of this sacrament and the august Person who is its center, the obligation for the faithful to participate is a grave one and those failing to do so through their own choice incur a grave fault (sin). As for the perpetual virginity of the Blessed Virgin, this doctrine was taught and held in the early Church. The Lateran Council (649) in its Fourth Canon stated, "If anyone does not properly and truly confess in accord with the holy Fathers, that the Holy Mother of God and ever Virgin and Immaculate Mary (did not have) her virginity remaining indestructible even after His birth, let him be condemned." This teaching was confirmed by the Council of Toledo XI, by Popes Leo III and Sixtus IV, and was accepted by all Christians until the Protestant Reformation when the Council of Trent in its ordinance against the Unitarians and promulgated by Pope Pius IV reaffirmed that Mary was ever a virgin, repeating this teaching in its profession of faith required of all Catholics. Vatican Council II in its teaching on Mary refers to her as "ever virgin," using words previously given by Popes Pius XI and XII.

Easter

Please explain how the system of arriving at the date of Easter originated. I know it is always the first Sunday after the first full moon after the first day of spring, but why?
— Mark E. Kolb, Crown Point, Ind.

In the early Church there was controversy over the day on which Easter should be celebrated. Some wanted to celebrate it on the fourteenth day of Nisan of the Hebrew calendar, no matter what day it fell on; others wanted to celebrate it on the nearest Sunday in memory of the day of the week on which Christ rose. In the year 190 Pope Victor I ordered a Sunday celebration of the feast. In 325 the Council of Nicaea ordered that Easter should be observed on the first Sunday following the first full moon of spring. There is still a difference between Catholic and Orthodox practice and some studies are going on in an attempt to arrive at a uniform date.

EASTER DUTY • Contradictory counsel from various clergy causes confusion. One of your columns said "Easter duty" was still a rule. Our parish newspaper says the "Easter duty" has been dropped. Can this contradiction be resolved? — *Mary Conces, Battle Creek, Mich.*

Canon 920 of the new Code of Canon Law states: "Once admitted to the blessed Eucharist, each of the faithful is obliged to receive holy communion at least once a year. This precept must be fulfilled during paschal time, unless for a good reason it is fulfilled at another time during the year." This law corresponds to Canon 859 of the old code. The Church makes this rule so that its members will fulfill the warning command of Christ: "If you do not eat the flesh of the Son of Man and drink his blood, you have no life in you" (John 6:54). Thus by the above canon all Catholics are bound to receive Communion during Easter time unless for a serious reason it must be received outside the Easter season (for example, if you were going to be in a part of the world where a priest was unavailable during paschal time). The item in your newspaper is misleading.

Ecumenical Councils

Many of us senior citizens recently were discussing the Second Vatican Council. What year was the first one? None of us could recall the reasons that made it necessary. What success resulted from the ecumenical councils? Any information as to the availability of reading material would be appreciated. — *Mrs. Alice Cores, Chicago, Ill.*

Would that more people discussed the councils of the Church! Even more important than the history of these gatherings is the doctrinal import of what they decided because each gave direction to the Church for all time. The first council held by the Church was the Council of Jerusalem, attended by SS. Peter and Paul, at which it was decided not to oblige Gentile converts to Jewish practices. However, historians do not count this meeting as one of the twenty-one ecumenical councils. The first such council was the First Council of Nicaea (325), which condemned Arianism for denying the divinity of Christ, and which fixed the date of Easter. In more modern times there have been three important councils. The Council of Trent

(1545-1563) responded to the Protestant rebellion and issued many decrees that covered such things as the sacraments, purgatory, indulgences, the nature of the Mass, and the jurisdiction of the pope over the whole world. The catechism produced by this council was the basis for Catholic teaching up to our own time. Vatican Council I (1869-1870) met in response to Modernism, which was affecting the Church. It defined the infallibility and primacy of the pope and issued decrees on natural religion, faith, and revelation in its dogmatic constitutions on faith and the Church. Vatican Council II was convoked by Pope John XXIII to update the Church. It opened on October 11, 1962, and ended on December 8, 1965. It issued two dogmatic and two pastoral constitutions, nine decrees, and three declarations, which covered such things as the nature of the Church, divine revelation, sacred liturgy, the Church in the modern world, ecumenism, missions, the life of priests, renewal of religious life, laity, Christian education, and the use of mass media. It would be well for your group to study these documents. They can all be found in at least two paperback editions: *Vatican Council II — The Conciliar and Post-Conciliar Documents* (including its companion volume), and *The Documents of Vatican II.*

Ecumenism

With the renewed interest in ecumenism between the Catholic Church and various Protestant churches (Episcopal, Lutheran, etc.), have there been any recent changes in Church policy regarding such activities as attendance at one another's church, receiving Communion, etc.? There seems to be much confusion and no clear guidelines to follow. Are there any reading sources that you would recommend? — Michael W. Beard, Kansas City, Mo.

I agree that there is much confusion as to what ecumenism means. It does not mean that one religion is as good as another or that religions are interchangeable. It does mean that we respect the honest beliefs of others and cooperate with them as far as possible without compromising their beliefs or ours. Catholics may not receive Holy Communion in a Protestant service and Protestants may receive Communion in a Catholic church only under limited conditions. The rules for all this are set down in various decrees and instructions, but unfortunately these important documents never seem to get down to the people. I recommend that every Catholic family have in their libraries one of the paperback books on the Second Vatican Council documents mentioned in the question-and-answer item immediately preceding this. My personal preference is the two-volume work *Vatican Council II — The Conciliar and Post-Conciliar Documents* and *Vatican Council II — More Post-Conciliar Documents*. They can be purchased at any Catholic religious goods or book dealer. They will answer all your questions on ecumenism and they contain the official teaching of the Church on current questions.

SENSITIVITY TO OTHERS • Why is it that when we Catholics pray among ourselves we make the Sign of the Cross before and after, but when we are among our Protestant brothers and sisters we don't? Why do we hold back and don't say the Our Father and Hail Mary when we share a prayer with a non-Catholic group? Are we Catholics afraid to pray what we are taught to pray? — *Ray Lerma, Stockdale, Tex.*

It is not a question of watering down our own beliefs but a sensitivity to the beliefs of others. Catholics and Protestants frequently pray the Our Father together, since both religions have respect for this prayer. However, Protestants vary in their beliefs about Mary, so in order not to offend their beliefs, we use this prayer only among ourselves. I am always embarrassed when at a mixed religious gathering some minister insists on saying a prayer "in Christ's name." While this is good Christian practice, it can be offensive to good Jews, and Christian charity should compel us to respect their beliefs. It is just as easy to pray from the Psalms or offer a prayer to the God of Abraham in whom we both believe. We must be careful always not to force our own beliefs on others; great tragedies have happened in the world because of this. We can be firm in our beliefs if asked about them; however, we must always respect the honest beliefs of others. God himself is a respecter of free will — it is his great gift to us. If he will not violate this freedom, we must be prepared to allow others who differ from us the right to their beliefs.

Episcopal Orders

Do the Episcopalians have the true body and blood of Christ in their Holy Communion as we do? Would a Catholic be permitted to receive Holy Communion in their church? — *Margaret Curley, Salem, Mass.*

Your first question may sound easy, but an answer is quite complicated. To change bread and wine into the body and blood of Christ, a priest must be validly ordained. Thus the question must be asked, "Are Anglican orders valid?" Pope Leo XIII in 1896, after lengthy investigation, declared Anglican orders invalid because they were conferred in a rite that was defective in form and talent, brought about by Michael Parker when he became head of the Anglican Church in 1559. He said that they were probably invalid then, citing declarations by Pope Julius III in 1553 and 1554, and Pope Paul IV in 1555. He ordered that convert Anglican priests had to be reordained. However, since that time Old Catholic bishops (although schismatic clergy have valid orders) have been used at times in ordinations and those ordained by them have valid powers. The situation is further complicated by the fact that females are now being ordained to the priesthood of the Episcopal Church, which the Holy See states is invalid and which has severely complicated and handicapped discussion going on between Catholic and Anglican scholars. Until the situation is definitively clarified by the Holy See, I believe a Catholic would have to presume that Episcopal consecration of bread and wine is invalid. Apart from this question, the Church has declared that intercommunion between Catholics and Protestants is not permitted because the unity of the sacrament reflects the unity of the Church, which is not now present between Catholic and Protestant churches. As the Church teaches, "Of its very nature, celebration of the Eucharist signifies the fullness of profession of faith and the fullness of ecclesial communion." This reason alone would forbid the reception of Holy Communion in an Episcopal church.

Equality of Religions

I have some close friends who left the Catholic Church for a non-Catholic religion. They insist all churches are the same and they can join any church. They also claim they can be buried from the Catholic Church even if they are not members, and that one can confess sins at home, make an act of contrition, and the sins are forgiven. — *Name withheld, Stevens Point, Wis.*

It is not true that one religion is as good as another. Jesus Christ founded one Church that he wanted everyone to join. One has an obligation to determine which is that true Church. The various churches teach different things, often contradictory. All cannot be true. The Catholic Church claims direct descent from Christ and the apostles. If your friends have apostatized from the Catholic Church, they are excommunicated and cannot be buried from a Catholic church. People who commit apostasy, heresy, or schism are excommunicated automatically (Canon 1354). It is true that out of charity the Church will bury a non-Catholic, but only if the bishop gives permission and the non-Catholic's own minister is unavailable. I don't think a bishop would give permission to a public apostate. It is also true that sins can be forgiven outside confession by an act of perfect contrition — total sorrow for and renunciation of attachment to sin arising from pure love of God. Perfect contrition is not easy to come by, and one is never sure if one has it. Confession is the ordinary means for forgiveness of sin willed by Jesus when he established the sacrament of penance after his resurrection (see John 20:22-23).

Eucharist

Why don't they take a poll of Catholics and see how many actually believe they are eating the flesh and drinking the blood of Christ at Communion? The Bible clearly states in John 6:63 that the flesh is useless and that God is spirit and certainly spirit isn't flesh. It even states in the Bible that "flesh and blood cannot inherit the kingdom of God." Something's cuckoo someplace. No wonder kids leave the Church. — *Andy Dwongi, San Francisco, Calif.*

I think your poll would be a good idea. I sometimes wonder, too. In John 6:64 Jesus tells us of the necessity of grace. He is speaking in terms Paul repeats in 1 Corinthians 15:45. Jesus is not speaking of himself. He is not speaking of "my flesh" as he does in the eucharistic passages; for example, "Unless you eat the flesh of the Son of man and drink his blood, you shall not have life in you'' (John 6:54ff). Jesus is using "the flesh" in the passage you cite in the sense of John 1:14 and 3:6. He is speaking of us. We are composed of body and soul. After death our body will disintegrate in the grave, but our soul continues living. St. Paul in 1 Corinthians 15:50 teaches that the corruptible body of man must be transformed to share the joys of the kingdom. So, in the passage you cite, Jesus is not talking about the Eucharist but about your flesh and mine.

NO FAST FOR THE SICK • When one is hospitalized and a eucharistic minister arrives to give Communion, may one receive, even though the one-hour fast is not observed? It seems so strange and ungrateful to refuse. — *Judy Bailey, Charlottesville, Va.*

The one-hour fast does not apply to the ill. Pope Pius XII granted the privilege whereby "the sick, even if not confined to bed, can take non-alcoholic drinks and medicines in either liquid or solid form before the reception of the Eucharist without any restriction of time." This has been made legal in the new Code of Canon Law (919), which exempts from any fast the aged, the infirm, and those who care for them.

Eucharistic Ministers

My problem is about men and women giving Communion. When I went to Catholic school I was taught that no one except the priest was to touch the Holy Eucharist and I still feel that way. But it seems to me that either I accept the way things are now or don't go to Communion when it is being distributed by a lay person. What would you advise? — *Name withheld, Owensboro, Ky.*

Under the eucharistic rules resulting from Vatican II, the Church allows properly constituted lay persons to act as extraordinary ministers of Holy Communion who assist the celebrant in distributing the Eucharist. This follows the practice of the early Church when Christians were given the Eucharist to take home to the sick. Perhaps there were abuses, but the custom arose of only the priest (or deacon) touching the Eucharist. There was never a divine law in this regard. However, there are some people who feel as you do and we must respect their consciences and preferences. My advice is that since the priest is also distributing Holy Communion, you get in the line going to him. It would be sad to miss receiving at Mass, since reception of Communion is your full sharing in the eucharistic supper.

OPPOSED TO WOMEN MINISTERS • Where in Christ's teaching, in the Bible, or in canon law, does it say that women can give Communion? Many of us find it impossible to accept, and we all talk about it. Are we sinning? If the Church is us and we support it, why is this forced on us? We hear the pope does not allow it — yes or no? Why educate and ordain men when any woman can do the same? — *Mrs. Clarence Stenzel, Ness City, Kans.*

We have two kinds of law in the Church: divine law (Ten Commandments, law on remarriage as adultery, etc.) and ecclesiastical law. Neither the pope nor the bishops can change divine law. Ecclesiastical law can change with circumstances and times. The rules governing women in the Church are ecclesiastical laws and can be changed. Thus the instruction *Liturgiae Instaurationes*, approved and authorized by our Holy Father, ruled that women, girls, married women, and religious are prohibited from serving the priest at the altar. However, the same decree allows women to proclaim the Scripture readings, offer the prayers of the faithful, and act as ushers. The instruction *Immensae Caritatis*, issued three years later and also approved by the Holy Father, allows women to act as extraordinary ministers of the Eucharist. To reject wholly or stand in contempt of these rules of the Church would be sinful. It is my experience from traveling about the country that the majority of Catholics approve of these changes. For some, like yourself, these changes are hard to accept. My advice is: "Receive Communion from the priest." We train and ordain priests to lead our sacramental life — to consecrate the body and blood of Christ, to forgive sins, and to do those things only a priest can do.

Evolution

I hold a fundamentalist and literal interpretation of Genesis. I heard the whole story for evolution from high school, college, and graduate faculties. All I got were vague statements such as "It is thought. . ." and "Most scientists believe. . . ." My question to you, Father, is what scientific evidence are you talking about? I've seen nothing to change the arguments against evolution I obtained from G. K. Chesterton and David Goldstein. — *Gerald T. Griffin, Falmouth, Maine*

The whole question of evolution is complex and it is difficult to treat it here in the short space allowed for an answer. There is a distinction between the evolution of man and the development of man. The former is an unproven theory, the latter a provable fact. To someone who does not believe in God, evolution would seem to be the only logical explanation for man and the universe; yet even logic fails here when the evolutionist is pinned down to explain first cause or the origin of primal matter or gas or what-have-you. If one believes in God, creation is then a reasonable explanation. This does not mean that Genesis must be taken as a historical document right down to the last detail. The inspired writers were primarily concerned with theological statement. My difficulty with many Creationists is that they deny provable fact. The carbon-14 method developed after World War II and the newer potassium-argon method do give relative dates. Biology, anthropology, and archeology also contribute. I know there are those who deny provable facts, but that doesn't make them less true.

Excommunication

How can our Church excommunicate someone? On what grounds? Is there an age limit? What procedures are followed? Whose approval is necessary? Who can remove the excommunication? — *Adolfo Jiménez, Pomona, Calif.*

An excommunication is a penalty or censure by which a baptized person is cut off from the life of the Church. The Church has this right because Jesus gave it the power of the keys (Matthew 16:17-19, John 20:22-23). An excommunication is given for sins (crimes) specified in canon law, which also says no one is liable to canonical penalty who has not completed the sixteenth year. Some excommunications are automatic, arising from the act itself, and go into effect as soon as the act is committed; others must be imposed by ecclesiastical authority. Certain excommunications can only be removed by the pope, others by a bishop or delegated priest. Automatic excommunications reserved to the pope are: violation of the Sacred Species; physical atttack on the pope; absolution by a priest of his accomplice; unauthorized episcopal consecration; direct violation of the seal of confession. Other automatic excommunications are: apostasy, heresy, or schism; procuring of an abortion. Excommunications imposed by judgment are: violation of the confessional seal by an interpreter or others; pretended celebration of the Eucharist or conferral of sacramental absolution by one not a priest. Other crimes are punished by interdict, suspension, or censure, in that order of gravity. All of these rules are spelled out in canon law.

NO PREJUDICE AGAINST AMERICA • In reference to the lifting of the ban of excommunication of divorced and remarried Catholics, please explain the difference between excommunication and the denial of confession and Communion. Are they one and the same? Tell us why this punishment was meted out solely to American Catholics. Why the glaring prejudice? — *Elizabeth Kerin, Orlando, Fla.*

At the time of the great immigration influx at the end of the nineteenth century, many Catholics were being married outside the Church and hence being lost to the Church. As a means to deter this situation, the American bishops petitioned Rome for permission to impose excommunication on those Catholics who married outside the Church. Rome granted the American request, so this was not a case of prejudice against the United States but a response to something sought by American bishops. Recently the American bishops asked Rome to remove this automatic excommunication; this was granted and received headlines and much misunderstanding. Excommunication is a censure whereby one is excluded from the communion of the faithful and which involves certain penalties in canon law. An excommunicated person cannot share in the sacraments, indulgences, Catholic burial, suffrages, and other public prayers. An excommunicated person is forbidden certain ecclesiastical acts; is limited in participation in ecclesiastical trials; is forbidden participation in Church election procedures; is incapable of acquiring any position in the Church; cannot be raised to holy orders; is deprived of all ecclesiastical income, benefices, pensions, or office in the Church. Now all these effects have been removed and the person in an irregular marriage is no longer cut off from communion of the faithful. Confession and Holy Communion are another matter, and these are still to be denied but not from any canonical reason. The sacrament of reconciliation presupposes a purpose of amendment, which a person in an irregular marriage probably cannot make. Holy Communion presupposes freedom from serious sin, and the Church holds that the marriage act within an irregular marriage is either a form of fornication or adultery. The problem of an irregular marriage is now not one of canon law but of pastoral practice.

Exorcism

Jesus conferred upon his disciples the authority to forgive sins and also overcome demons. I have seen very little use of priests' authority over demons and diseases. Why can't I go to a priest when the devil plagues me with a cold and be rid of it? — *Jan Leitheiser, Emery, S. Dak.*

The power to forgive sins and to overcome demons was not given to Christ's disciples but to his apostles and through them passed down to the bishops and through them to priests. All priests exercise the power of forgiveness of sin in the sacrament of penance and in the rite of penance at Mass. As for exorcisms, part of the baptismal rite is exorcism, and therefore all priests exercise exorcism every time they baptize. However, in cases of adult possession (which are rare), the Church limits this power to certain priests who by their knowledge and sanctity of life can oppose Satan. Such priests must have great discretion and knowledge, able to discern true possession from hysteria or mental disease. They can only act on the authority of the local bishop. As for healing, Jesus cured only certain people and then only when certain conditions were met. There were many thousands of infirm and ill that he did not cure because this was not the will of the Father. Every priest in the sacrament of anointing of the sick exercises a healing ministry, and many people are restored to health; but again, this depends on God's will. Also, it is wrong to presume that every bad thing that happens to us is the work of the devil, such as being "plagued with a cold." Most of our problems come from our imperfect human nature, which because it is imperfect must suffer sickness and pains. Unfortunately, we look upon these trials as something evil, rather than opportunities offered by God to perfect ourselves and offer our suffering for the salvation of others. In the time of our Lord, people did not have much knowledge of disease, particularly mental disease, hence they were prone to attribute what they did not understand to the work of the devil. The New Testament writers reflect this attitude. We must understand the Bible in light of the times in which it was written and not make facile applications despite our greater knowledge.

Faith and Morals

What precisely is the infallible "faith and morals"? What precisely isn't? — *Mary Longo, North Palm Beach, Fla.*

Faith is the religious belief of the Catholic Church in those truths revealed by God through the Bible and tradition as interpreted and proposed by the infallible teaching authority of the Church. Morals concern the standards of right conduct as found in the commandments of God and the Church, in conscience, and in law. Thus when the pope speaks of these matters of faith and morals *ex cathedra* (in his role as supreme teacher) to the whole Church, with the intention of making an infallible statement, only then is the pope infallible. Infallibility does not extend to anything beyond faith or morals, such as scientific fact and future predictions.

Fátima

As a recent convert to the Catholic faith, I am disturbed by your answer to the woman who wrote about Our Lady of Fátima. You seem to favor the ramblings regarding a so-called vision over the words of Scripture. Nowhere in the Bible is Fátima mentioned. I feel much of the Fátima and other appearances of a visionary nature are manifestations of the devil. — *Name withheld, Magnolia, Ohio*

First, the Bible is not our sole rule of faith. We also have apostolic tradition and the teaching of the Church. Second, the Church moves very slowly regarding visions because they can be a case of self-delusion or, as you point out, the work of the devil. One need only read the difficulties the Fátima children went through or the trials given by church and state to St.

Bernadette at Lourdes to understand the skepticism that first exists. It is only after time and deep scrutiny that the Church makes a ruling that a certain incident is worthy of belief. The Church has given approval to Fátima, Lourdes, and Guadalupe in Mexico. In each of these places miracles, carefully attested to and examined, give further reason for credence. From details in your letter not printed above you seem to have a misunderstanding of what happened at Fátima. For example, our Lady never called upon Russia to repent or perish. She did ask Catholics to pray for Russia that it might be converted because otherwise its errors would harm the world, a fact we see happening. I suggest you get one of the excellent books that exist on Fátima and study it. It may add to the dimension of your faith. For a succinct account of Fátima, you might be interested in Catherine M. Odell's *Those Who Saw Her: The Apparitions of Mary*, covering the best-known visions (from Guadalupe to Medjugorje), available from Our Sunday Visitor.

Father

I was reading the Bible, and in Matthew 23:9 Jesus tells us not to call anyone on earth our father. He says that only one is and he is in heaven! Why do people in the Church address the priest as "Father"? When did it start? — *John Landrey, Dallas, Tex.*

In reading the Bible we have to understand what is behind the words; otherwise what we read is subject to misinterpretation. The verse you cite is part of a passage in which Jesus is rebuking the Jewish religious establishment, accusing it of idle formalism and vain display, constantly seeking honors and titles. He condemns their use of three titles: *rabbi* (master), *abba* (father), and *moreh* (teacher), implying that they are not worthy of these titles. He also means that there is one Father, God, and one teacher, the Messiah. He did not mean that you shouldn't call your dad your father, or not refer to a teacher in school as your teacher. Christian tradition from the first days has interpreted this verse in its restricted sense, that Christians should not crave worldly honors and that they should be servants of one another. St. Paul was probably the first to use the word "father" in the sense of referring to a priest. In 1 Corinthians 4:15 he writes: "Granted that you have ten thousand guardians in Christ, you have only one father. It was I who begot you in Christ Jesus through my preaching of the Gospel." St. Paul looked upon himself as the father of the Church in Corinth because through his preaching and baptisms the Corinthians were brought to new life. Thus today, through the priest's hands, Christians come to new life. Just as a natural father serves the material needs of his family, the priest serves their spiritual needs. The use of the term in this sense takes nothing away from God the Father and, in the restricted sense mentioned above, does not contradict Matthew.

Fear

> Nowhere in the Bible have I ever seen that fear is a sin. It is not something that we can help. I mean the kind of fear that comes from insecurity or the loss of a loved one. Still, my lady friend says that fear is a sin. — *Name withheld, Detroit, Mich.*

Fear is an agitation of the mind, often with physical effects, produced by a present or threatened evil to oneself or another. Grave fear can lessen responsibility for one's acts, thus a marriage contracted under grave fear would be invalid. Fear is a natural reaction and a means of self-defense, since it alerts us to a threatening danger. Fear in itself is not sinful. Unreasoned fear, or groundless fear, could be sinful, as it indicates a lack of trust in God and could be the result of superstition (for example, fear of a black cat crossing one's path). However, ordinary fear is a protective device instilled in our nature. The bloody sweat of Jesus in the Garden of Gethsemani was the result of fear of what lay ahead, but Jesus overcame this natural fear and surrendered himself to his Father's will. The Bible does speak of fear in the sense I have described it. Other times it uses the word in place of "awe," as in Proverbs 1:7, "The fear of the Lord is the beginning of wisdom." So your friend is not correct if she says categorically that fear is a sin.

Final Repentance

> When Rita Hayworth died she was buried from a Catholic church. She had been married five times. Then Jackie Gleason, married three times, was buried from the Church with a Mass of Resurrection, celebrated by no

less than a bishop. Are these cases of fame and/or fortune overriding the rules of the Church, or have I missed some changes in these rules? — *James H. Ackerman, Greensburg, Pa.*

I do not know the details surrounding the death and burial of Rita Hayworth, but in the Gleason case the archbishop of Miami issued a statement which said that Mr. Gleason had been reconciled to the Church and had received the sacrament of anointing of the sick before death. There should not be criticism but rejoicing that these and others returned to the Church before they died, for as our Lord said, there is more joy in heaven over the return of one sinner than for ninety-nine just. He illustrated this teaching with parables (for example, the Lost Sheep and Prodigal Son). Jesus also warned us about judging others, promising that the same measure with which we judge will be used in judgment of ourselves. Jesus did not turn sinners away but instead reached out to them, and the Church must do the same. Many years ago a notorious Jewish gangster was gunned down on his way to lunch. He was rushed to a hospital where he asked for a priest and baptism. He died on the operating table. When he was buried from a Catholic church, many people wrote letters to papers protesting this fact, and some were upset that so notorious a man could gain heaven at the last minute, while they had to lead good lives for years and years. But Jesus even covered this matter with his parable about the vineyard payments where each worker received the same pay no matter how many hours each worked (see Matthew 20). Jesus proved his words by promising the criminal on Calvary instant salvation. So be happy that Gleason and Hayworth returned to the Church and repented past failures, and rejoice that "one who has been lost has been found."

First Fridays

How does one receive the indulgences for the nine First Fridays when your church doesn't have them, the priest resides at another parish thirty-six miles away, and you only see him for the eleven o'clock Mass on Sunday? I would like to take part in this but am at a loss how to go about it. — *Mrs. Jerre Chapman, Carlton, Tex.*

You are speaking of a devotion in which the first Friday of each month is set aside in honor of the Sacred Heart and in reparation for sin. Among the promises said to have been made to St. Margaret Mary Alacoque, who promoted this devotion, was that the reception of Holy Communion on nine consecutive First Fridays would gain the grace of final repentance. You will note the requirement is not for attendance at Mass, although this is laudatory, but solely the reception of Holy Communion. I do not know of conditions in your mission church, but if there are extraordinary ministers of the Eucharist, one of them could give Communion on this day. Otherwise, the only solution is to drive to the nearest place Communion can be received on the first Friday of the month. I realize that this sounds hard, but the nine consecutive First Fridays were meant to present some difficulty. Why don't you discuss this with your priest when he comes for Sunday Mass? He may have a better solution to serve your needs.

First Saturdays

Can you tell me when or how the First Saturdays began and what indulgences are gained if you make them? — *Mrs. S. C. Pinto, Angola, N.Y.*

At Fátima our Lady told the three children that she wished Russia to be consecrated to her Immaculate Heart and that on the first Saturday of every month Communions of reparation be made for the atonement of sin. She promised if this was done, Russia would be converted. According to Sister Lucia (the only surviving Fátima visionary at this writing) the Virgin appeared to her again on December 10, 1925, and said: "I promise to assist at the hour of death, with the graces necessary for salvation, all who on the First Saturdays of five consecutive months confess, receive Holy Communion, recite five decades of the Rosary, and keep me company for fifteen minutes meditating on the mysteries of the Rosary, with the purpose of making reparation to me."

Flags in Church

What is the Church position with regard to the U.S. and papal flags in the church? My priest more or less stated that it is not "in" anymore. I have always been taught to love God and country and wonder if this is the result of Vatican II. — *Name withheld, St. James, Mo.*

There is no regulation from the Holy See concerning the removal of national or papal flags from Catholic churches. In the mid-1970s the Committee on the Liturgy, made up mostly of diocesan liturgists and some bishops, drew up a document called "Environment and Art in Catholic Worship." This document stated: "Identifying symbols of particular cultures, groups or nations are not appropriate as permanent parts of liturgical environment. While such symbols might be used for a particular occasion or holiday, they should not regularly constitute a part of the environment of common prayer." A number of bishops disassociated themselves from this conclusion. The document was prepared in the heady days following Vatican II and it was a time of Vietnam protests when draft cards were being incinerated on altars in Catholic colleges, and American flags were being burned on campuses. One archbishop told the writer that he thought the opinion was the result of "Vietnam syndrome." However, the document was never rescinded and is still quoted today. Nevertheless, Catholic theology has always taught that patriotism (not nationalism) is a virtue. Vatican II's *Pastoral Constitution on the Church in the Modern World* tells us: "Citizens should cultivate a generous and loyal spirit of patriotism." The flag, which is the symbol of one's country, is a reminder of that patriotism. Many parishioners have served their nation, and others have lost sons and daughters in the service of their country. There are deep-felt feelings for the flag of that country. As the Holy See's liturgical instruction reminds us, "In the adornment and appointments of a church it is the piety of the entire community which should be the first consideration." Hence pastors in their quest for "liturgical purity" should be mindful of the patriotic feelings of their Christian faithful and not offend those feelings, even though they are within their rights of being ultimately responsible for the conduct of the churches put in their charge. While the altar of sacrifice should be the visual focus of the people, church adornment can be done in such a way that it does not distract the people's attention from the ceremonies. There are other places in the church where flags can be placed apart from the sanctuary. The document of the committee quoted above was an advisory document, not a legislative one.

Flying Saucers

What is the Church's stand on flying saucers? Many people, including a member of my family, swear that they have seen them. Is it against the Catholic religion to believe that there may be beings on other planets? — *George Vetari, Daly City, Calif.*

The Church has no stand on flying saucers. This is a scientific question and not a theological one. It is not against Catholic teaching to hold that there may be other life in the universe. One does not limit God's creative ability or the universality of his love. The possibility of other life raises interesting theological questions. If it exists, would it be human life? If so, would it share in redemption? Did it have its own revelation? And on and on. The universe is a vast and diverse place and it is reasonable to suppose that there must be other regions capable of sustaining life, but whether it is there or not can only be a matter of speculation.

Forgiveness of Sin

Recently a visiting liturgist informed us that "it is the activity of the assembly (People of God) that absolves sin, ordains priests with the leadership of the bishop, and that is the source of all graces." Is this the teaching of the magisterium? — *Jerome W. Schneider, Jasper, Ind.*

No, it is nonsense and is a waste of time for those who listen to such claptrap. Christ gave the power to forgive sins to his apostles, not the assembly. The bishop ordains in his own right whether or not the assembly agrees with him. Christ is the source of all grace, not the People of God.

Forty Hours

Years ago we had an annual devotion called Forty Hours, during which the Blessed Sacrament was exposed and venerated. It was arranged among the different parishes so that somewhere in the diocese this devotion was taking place. We don't hear about Forty Hours anymore. Is it now forbidden? — *Herbert Brown, Studio City, Calif.*

Canon 1275 of the old Code of Canon Law ordered that the Blessed Sacrament be exposed for veneration once a year in every parish. Canon 943 of the new code does not make this mandatory but does recommend it "during a suitable period of time, even if not continuous, so that the local community may meditate and may adore the Eucharistic Mystery more profoundly; but this kind of exposition is to be held only if a suitable gathering of the faithful is foreseen." Thus exposition is not only allowed but encouraged, as long as a suitable number of people will be present. This particular devotion should be an expression of popular piety. There is also another difference from past practice. Formerly, Mass was celebrated during Forty Hours before the exposed Sacrament. Canon 941 now forbids this. The Sacrament would have to be reposed while Mass was celebrated. The present legislation envisages three types of exposition: (1) lengthy exposition described above; (2) short exposition, which also includes Scripture reading, hymns, both vocal and silent prayer, and can conclude with a blessing by the Sacrament; and (3) perpetual adoration by religious communities. The ordinary minister can be either a priest or deacon; however, an acolyte or extraordinary minister may, for good reason, expose and repose the Sacrament.

Free Will

Johann Wolfgang von Goethe stated in *Conversations with Eckermann*: "If we grant freedom to man, there is an end to the omniscience of God; for if the divinity knows how I shall act, I must act so perforce." How am I to know that man has free will? Please answer. — *Name withheld, Ellinwood, Kans.*

Over the centuries there have been long arguments resulting in shelves of books and treatises on such subjects as causality, determinism, and predestination, both philosophical and theological. The subject has involved such thinkers as Aristotle, Plato, Augustine, Bellarmine, Luther, Molina, Leibniz, Kant, Hegel, and Marx. While accepting free will, Kant said it could not be demonstrated even theoretically. Alexander Willwoll wrote: "Final agreement on this thorny problem has not yet been reached; and perhaps such agreement is not psychologically possible because of the impossibility of man's being able to grasp with his limited intelligence the nature of God's activity both in itself and in relation to creatures." As regards Goethe's statement, I think he is confusing apples and oranges. He is mixing up omniscience with omnipotence. Because God knows what answer I will make to a proposition the intellect presents to the will does not mean that God has foreordained this result over which I am powerless. I am free to choose A or B, and while God knows which I will choose, he does not force me into the choice, which may be, as in the case of sin, against his own choice and will. This is the greatness of free will, namely that we can will against the choice of the Almighty.

Freedom of Religion

In the enclosed article the pope says we should have freedom of religion. I was taught the Catholic religion is the religion approved by God. Please explain. — *Name withheld, Fort Atkinson, Kans.*

The article you refer to concerns the Holy See's new family rights charter. When the pope speaks, he is speaking to the world, not just to Americans or even only to Catholics. In communist countries the Church and even priests are not allowed to give religious education to youths. In Lithuania lay people have been imprisoned for giving Catholic education. With this in mind the charter declares: "Parents have the right to educate their children in accordance with their moral and religious convictions." And again: "Parents have the right to freely choose schools or other means necessary to educate their children in keeping with their convictions." Also: "Every family has the right to live freely its own domestic religious life under the guidance of the parents, as well as the right to profess publicly and to propagate the faith, to take part in public worship and in freely chosen programmes of religious instruction, without suffering discrimination." The difficulty with a short article in the press is that it can distort the full meaning. The pope in this charter is speaking in behalf of the religious freedom of all peoples and for their right to follow their consciences in the raising of their children.

Funerals

I have some questions about the Funeral Mass: 1. Why doesn't the priest recite the *Dies Irae*? 2. Why aren't there six lighted candles placed around the coffin anymore? 3. At what times during the funeral Mass are the bells of the church to be tolled? 4. Is there a dogma known as the Assumption of Masses? — *Ronnie McCarty, Hodge, La.*

In the liturgical revision of Vatican II, a whole new thrust was given to the liturgy for the dead. Where formerly the emphasis was on judgment and punishment, which we begged God to spare the deceased, and sorrow for the loss, the new revision is one of hope and joy in the resurrection. The black vestments of sorrow have been replaced by the white vestments of joy. 1. The *Dies Irae* is a good example. This long hymn began: "That day of wrath, that dreadful day." It reminded us of "What terror then to us shall fall, when, lo, the Judge's steps appall." It goes on: "The book is opened that the dead may hear their doom from what is read." These dire threats are not what the Church wishes to teach but life in Jesus through the individual resurrection. 2. The present rule on candles is: "Lighted candles may be placed about the coffin or the paschal candle alone may be placed at the head of the deceased." Most pastors opt for the latter, since the paschal candle is a symbol of Christ's resurrection, which is a promise of our own. 3. There is no requirement to toll the bell, except for local custom. In some parishes it is the custom to toll the bell as the body is brought into the church and when it leaves. This is a matter for pastoral choice. 4. There is no dogma or Church teaching called the Assumption of Masses.

Fundamentalism

I have a problem answering two questions of my Christian fundamentalist co-workers. First, where in the Bible does it state that Catholics may pray to Mary and other saints to intercede for us to God? They refer to John 14:6, I Timothy 2:5, and others, inferring that it is proper to pray only to God or Jesus Christ. Second, they say that Roman Catholicism is not Christianity or a religion by definition, for Christianity relies only upon the interpretation of the Bible and a religion relies upon rules and precepts made by man. Please answer these questions with biblical source, disregarding the "traditions" that are used to answer many controversial questions. — *Emil J. Sereda, Jr., Fresno, Calif.*

Just as it is very difficult to argue with fundamentalists who make up their own definition of things and set the limits for debate, so it is difficult to respond to you if you are ruling out tradition. There is a total of almost two thousand years of Church practice since the Church defined what is in the Bible that your friends are using. One of the failures of Catholic education today from the seminary down to elementary catechisms is that too little attention is paid to ecclesiology or the theology of the Church itself. Jesus Christ founded a Church (Matthew 16:18) and appointed a head of that Church to whom he gave power to bind and loose and promised that this binding and loosing would be recognized by God (Matthew 16:19). He commanded this Church to go out to the world, baptizing and teaching, and that this Church would endure to the end of time and that he himself would be present in it (Matthew 28:19-20). He also promised that the Holy Spirit would be in this Church to keep it from error (John 14:16). Hence in the Bible we find the preparation for and completion of the Church, the foundation of the Church by Jesus, and the early development and life of that Church. Hence what that Church does in matters of faith and morals is guided both by Jesus and the Holy Spirit and assumes equal importance with the Scriptures, which have gone before. Your friends in defining Christianity and religion are creating their own definitions to serve their own ends. Christianity is a religion (a form of worshiping God) as is Islam or Judaism or Buddhism. The problem for the seeker after truth is to determine which is the true religion. Your friends have decided what Christianity is. In each religion over the years, different modes developed for giving worship. Among Jews we find Orthodox, Reformed, etc., with shadings among these groups. Among Muslims we find Sunnites and Shiites and other forms. Among Christians we find various churches — Catholic, Methodist, Episcopalian, etc., and even people who think they are a church unto themselves. Again, the problem is in determining which is the true Church, the Church founded by Jesus Christ. Only the Catholic Church (Eastern and Western Rites) traces itself back in an unbroken line to Peter and Jesus Christ. A church which began fifteen hundred years after Jesus is a church that represents the dissent and teachings of its founder, not those of Jesus. Finally, those who insist on "Bible only" proof should be the first to recognize the Catholic Church if they only approached the Bible openly and not with a host of prejudgments and biases brought to its interpretation. If they truly followed the Bible, they would be seeking the Church Jesus Christ founded and which exists, according to his promise, in the world today. Once that Church is accepted, there is no problem in asking Mary to intercede for us with Jesus or asking saints to pray for us. That is why I say ecclesiology is so important and Catholics need more study of it and why Catholics have two rules of faith: the Bible and tradition. Because so many fundamentalists do not really believe the Bible (for example, that Jesus truly established a Church), they do not seek that Church and hence it is very difficult to argue with them, since there is no real basis (meeting of minds) on which to argue.

HOW TO REPLY • I work in a large factory with many Protestants who really try to teach me their ways of belief. They tell me I'm not saved because I am Catholic. I love my faith and do my best. I read the Bible and other Catholic materials. But I am not wise like you. They say that Christ died for our sins once and for all and we don't need Mass or Communion. Also, they say they are certain they are saved and going to heaven. How can they be so certain? — *Name withheld, Pinconning, Mich.*

This column on a number of occasions has advised the average Catholic not to argue religion with fundamentalist Protestants because they have been raised in bigotry, have closed minds, and selectively misinterpret texts of the Bible. It is not that they have ill will, for they believe that they are acting in your best interests in trying to convert you. Unless a Catholic is trained in the science of apologetics (answering objections), he or she can suffer in faith because the skill to point out the falsity of the argument is lacking. For example, on the Eucharist texts, the fundamentalist holds the Last Supper institution as symbolic. But this flies in the face of the eucharistic discourse in John 6:25-58, which the Jews and disciples took literally and caused many to leave Jesus because of it (John 6:60-66). The early Church took the words literally also, as Paul shows (1 Corinthians 10:16 and 11:23-27). So did the early Fathers, as any reading of their sermons will show. So did people for the next fifteen hundred years until the Protestant reformers came and threw out the central doctrines of the Church. Protestants make the Bible their sole rule of faith, yet most Protestants today accept divorce. How does this square with Mark 10:2-12 wherein Christ forbids divorce? I know of a man who was bothered as you are bothered. A neighbor, acting out of good faith, was continually trying to "save" him. Finally, after another attempt, the man asked his neighbor: "How do you know you are saved?" The neighbor replied, "I have been baptized and have accepted Christ as my Savior." The man said: "I, too, have been baptized and I accept Christ as my Savior. So I, too, am saved. Let us now pray together for the salvation of the rest of mankind." They prayed together for a moment. "Thank you," said my friend, as he turned away. He was never bothered again.

Gambling

We are residents of Pennsylvania, where *all* forms of gambling are against the law, except for state-operated lotteries. How then do Catholic bishops and priests justify the many forms of illegal gambling permitted on church grounds, from cash bingos to various lotteries and ticket sales? Is it not a matter for the confessional by participants? — *Name withheld, Plumville, Pa.*

It is the traditional teaching of the Church that gambling is not wrong in itself and is permissible if it does not lead to a waste of money needed to pay one's just debts or support one's family, and provided that cheating and fraud are absent. The state seems to recognize this as it does permit a lottery. Hence, the regulations against bingo and parish raffles are somewhat hypocritical. However, where laws do exist it can be a source of scandal to ignore these laws. Catholic groups should obey the laws and work to change those that seem unjust or unrepresentative of the people. Since there is no sin involved in gambling, as noted above, there is no matter for the confessional. Contempt for law, however, can become matter for the confessional.

General Absolution

A friend of mine from another diocese has taken part in a communal penance service several times, and is now doubting its validity. The service is announced in the church bulletin and takes place a couple of times a year. There are some prayers in common, then all participants are told to think of their sins and be sorry for them. After that, everyone is given general absolution. There is no opportunity for private confession and no mention of the obligation to confess all serious sins. From what I have heard, this is not valid except in the case of unforeseen inability to hear confessions of a large number of people and then all serious sins must be confessed at the penitent's next confession. Does such an obligation exist? If so, how soon must it be fulfilled? Are any such penance services allowed in some dioceses on an experimental basis? — *Teresa Groebner, Clements, Mich.*

Ordinarily, such a penance service includes a Liturgy of the Word, penitential prayers, *individual* confession and absolution, and prayers of thanksgiving. General absolution can only be given in special circumstances in which it is morally or physically impossible for persons to confess and be absolved individually, and who have a need for reconciliation and reception of the Eucharist, with judgment on the circumstances warranting such a ceremony being the right of the bishop. In such a general ceremony, penitents who have had grave sins absolved are required to confess them at their next individual confession. Such a ceremony as you describe would be illicit. Several years ago a southern bishop who celebrated a similar ceremony was sternly reprimanded by the Holy See. Such a ceremony is not allowed anywhere on an experimental basis, and theologians are divided on the validity of the absolution given in the manner you describe.

Gifts of the Holy Spirit

I have a question about the gifts and fruits of the Holy Spirit. Relative to Galatians 5 we seem to have added the fruits of faith, modesty, and chastity, and our seven gifts are quite different from the nine of 1 Corinthians 12. Would you explain the basis? — *R. E. Reeder, Chatham, N.J.*

Sometimes the terms are used loosely and there are varying lists of gifts, fruits, virtues, and charisms of the Holy Spirit. However, in a more precise catechetical sense the gifts of the Holy Spirit are traditionally enumerated as wisdom, understanding, counsel, fortitude, knowledge, piety, and fear of the Lord. These gifts come from Isaiah 11:2-3. The fruits of the Holy Spirit are enumerated as found in Galatians 5:22-23: Love, joy, peace, patience, kindness, goodness, faithfulness, gentleness, and self-control. There are the principal virtues of faith, hope, and love, plus the cardinal virtues of justice, fortitude, temperance, and prudence. St. Paul, in 1 Corinthians 12, lists the charisms as prophecy, teaching, wisdom in discourse, utterance of knowledge, faith, healing, miracles, tongues, and interpretation of tongues.

Gideons

What religion is the one called Gideon? I've heard that its members are the ones who put Bibles in hotels. And I read something about a great man by that name who was connected with Moses. What can you tell me about this? — *Mrs. Dorothy E. Schuder, Long Beach, Calif.*

Gideon was one of the great judges of Israel who opposed the cult of Baal. He defeated the Midianite oppressors and refused the kingship of Israel saying that only God was the King of Israel. You can read about him in the Book of Judges, Chapters 6 through 8. The Gideons are a group of Protestant laymen, of varying denominations, founded in Wisconsin in 1898 as the Christian Commercial Men's Association of America. It undertook the apostolate of placing Bibles in hotel rooms where they could be read by commercial travelers and others. It is now internationally known. It is said that there is not a room in a decent hotel in America that has not had a Bible placed there by the Gideons.

Girl Altar Servers

The laity of both sexes are allowed to receive Communion in the hand. The laity of both sexes are allowed to be eucharistic ministers. Why then are females barred from being altar servers? What is the thinking behind that rule? Aren't we females good enough? — *Anne Black, San Francisco, Calif.*

It is not a question of being "good enough." Certainly if women are allowed to touch the Eucharist, the most sacred element of

Catholicism, they must be considered "good enough" to bring the priest wine and water or wash his hands. I admit it seems illogical to bar women from service at the altar while opening more important ministries to them, such as reader or eucharistic minister. Neither is there any scriptural reason that would prohibit women servers. However, the Bible is not the sole rule of faith for Catholics. Tradition is a very strong motivating force in defining Catholic positions. While uninterrupted custom can be altered because of changing insights and cultural patterns, as we have seen done as a result of Vatican II, Rome is very cautious and hesitant in departing from tradition. This is not a bad thing, since it gives continuity to the faith as a whole. I would not be opposed to women servers, if they were permitted by Church authority. However, as I have written here before, it is wrong for a pastor to allow women or girls to serve at Mass as long as the present regulation stands. We have a hierarchical Church, founded that way by Christ. To decide which laws will be obeyed and which will not is anarchistic, disruptive of the authority on which the Church is built, and it weakens the faith of the laity who are aware of the disobedience. We are free to work to change laws, but while they exist they must be obeyed (Luke 10:16).

God

An argument came up. Who is God? No one here can give a definite answer. Also, who was the founder of the Jewish religion? — *Margaret Hughes, Osceola Mills, Pa.*

Because God is infinite and limitless, he cannot properly be defined. Even the word "he" is misleading. The best we can do is describe God as the one and only Supreme Being, uncaused and the First Cause, eternal, completely self-sufficient, all-intelligent, all-knowing, all-powerful, completely free, the beginning and the end of everything created. You can take every superlative and good word and apply them to God and the description would still be inadequate. As for the founder of the Jewish religion, you could say God is, since he revealed it; or you could say Abraham was, since he made the original covenant with God; or you could say Moses was, since he received the commandments, codified the law, and established the Jewish priesthood under his brother Aaron.

Good Friday

I have a question a young friend asked me that I couldn't answer. Why is it called "Good Friday" when it is the day that Christ died on the cross? — *Lillian Kenny, Sarasota, Fla.*

The Church sometimes uses unusual forms to bring home a deeper truth. Thus in one of its hymns it refers to original sin as, "Oh, happy fault!" This does not mean that original sin was not a tragedy; rather, through this sin Christ came into the world and that is our happiness. Thus while on Good Friday we mourn the suffering and death of Jesus, in God's view this is a most propitious day, since through it Christ won the salvation of mankind and reopened the doors of heaven. Hence while there is a historical sadness to the day, in the long view there is happiness because of what that sacrifice means for us. Theologically, it is "Good" Friday because of the many good things Christ's sacrifice earned for all humankind.

Good Works

Is there any difference between "good works" and serving Christ? Or are they one and the same? — *Marianne Vernile, Belle Vernon, Pa.*

They are not exactly the same. Serving Christ is a good work, and doing good works is the way we serve Christ. Generally, good works are moral actions of kindness and generosity toward others that are performed from a spiritual motive and earn merit for the doer. More specifically, good works are those actions resulting from following the precepts and counsels and those which fall under the heading of prayer, fasting, and almsgiving. Good works in themselves are not the cause of justification, which also requires faith. However, they are necessary for salvation. There is greater merit when we do them for Christ.

Gospels

What is the Catholic Church's teaching concerning the time and origin of the four Gospels? I like to believe that the Gospels were written less than twenty-five years after Christ's death. According to the writings of Sister Mary of Agreda, the Blessed Virgin told her: St. Matthew wrote the first Gospel in Hebrew in the year 42; St. Mark wrote in Hebrew in 46; St. Luke wrote in Greek in 48; and St. John wrote in Greek in 58. Can you offer a more reliable and authentic source? — *Lloyd Ostendorf, Dayton, Ohio*

There is no definitive teaching on this subject and Scripture scholars are far from certain themselves. However, there is general agreement that Mark's Gospel was the first written possibly in Rome, for a Gentile audience, in nonliterary Greek, sometime between A.D. 50 and 65, although a few place a later limit. The second Gospel, which like Luke depended on Mark, is Matthew, which was written in the last third of the first century. This is based on the known date of the destruction of Jerusalem. Predicated on a reference of Papias it has been assumed that it was written in Aramaic for a Jewish audience. Some modern scholars hold Papias suspect and say that the copy St. Paul used was in Greek. Luke wrote in Greek for a Gentile audience. The dates given for Luke extend from 65 to 80, with a date around 70 as probable. It is generally agreed that St. John's Gospel was not written after 100; it was probably closer to the year 90. It was not written for pagans but more likely a Jewish-Christian audience. There is no scholarship that would agree with Sister Mary of Agreda. While many hold that Mark was based largely on the testimony of Peter (who died around A.D. 67), there is no evidence Peter influenced the other Gospels.

AUTHORSHIP • While I was listening to a Sunday morning religious program, a Mr. Robinson from a theological school in California said that the Gospels of John, Matthew, Luke, etc., were not truly written by these holy men. He claims that the Gospels were only assigned their names. Would appreciate your opinion. — *E. Hesse, Rhinebeck, N.Y.*

The authorship of the books of the Bible is a complex question and each book must be taken separately. The Church has never defined authorship, only canonicity (that is, which books are inspired). It is true that in the ancient world a book would sometimes be attributed to a famous person, or a disciple who wrote the teachings of the master. It is also true that after two thousand years it is difficult to prove conclusively that authors wrote the books assigned to them, but it is even more difficult to prove that they did not. There are books of the Old Testament in which scholarly opinion holds the author to be other than the name assigned, and this is generally true on the Epistle to the Hebrews, on which the consensus is that it could not have been written by Paul. There have been debates about authorship of the Gospels. In such an examination three things must be considered: external evidence as to authorship, internal evidence, and tradition. Using each of these three, the weight of evidence seems to be in favor of the authorships as we know them. There are those who make a career of trying to debunk things, but the burden of proof has to be on them. As regards the Gospels, on the evidence available a jury would have to find in favor of the assigned authors.

Grace

How does a person receive the grace of God? In what manner does it come to you and what do you have to do to receive it? When I was a small boy my father was a great teacher and he spoke often about the saints and grace. Please let me know how to receive it and does it take good works and lots of prayers? — *Paul Dembiczak, Moses Lake, Wash.*

Grace (or "favor") is the means by which God gives us new life. It is a gift of God and gives us a share in his life. It is necessary for salvation and is given to us through the merits of Jesus Christ. The principal means of grace are the sacraments (particularly the Eucharist), prayer, and good works. Grace is of two kinds: sanctifying (habitual) and actual. Sanctifying grace, which is given to us in baptism and renewed through the other sacraments, makes us children of God, brothers of Jesus, and heirs of heaven. Actual grace is that immediate help God gives us to do good and avoid evil. It is not a permanent grace like sanctifying grace, which is only lost by committing serious sin and restored through the sacrament of penance, but is necessary for the performance of supernatural acts. If you would increase the grace within you, you do it by growing in holiness — and you grow in holiness by prayer, reception of the sacraments, and by good works.

Heaven

I hear so much about heaven and how beautiful it is. Is heaven more beautiful and better than life here on earth? Does the Bible say much about it? — *Name withheld, Redford, Mich.*

The word "heaven" appears often in the Bible. It is used to mean the place of the redeemed after death. It is sometimes used for God. It is also used to mean the sky, wherein the sun, moon, and stars are placed. In the sense used here it means the place where we will be with God after death and salvation. Heaven is beyond any adequate human description. St. Paul, paraphrasing the prophet Isaiah, writes in 1 Corinthians 2:9: "Eye has not seen, ear has not heard, nor has it so much as dawned on man what God has prepared for those who love him." The peace, happiness, and beauty of heaven are beyond anything the human mind can imagine. In 1 Corinthians 13:12 Paul says, "Now we see indistinctly, as in a mirror; then we shall see face to face. My knowledge is imperfect now; then I shall know even as I am known." In heaven we will have perfect happiness. Jesus told us that our treasure will be in heaven and promised that our reward will be great there. Some saints have claimed to have had visions of heaven and said afterward that the vision was beyond any words to describe. The greatest gift is that we will see and know God.

VISIONS OF HEAVEN • Has anyone in the history of Christianity ever been allowed to "see" heaven while still alive? Also, have individuals who have had the stigmata, such as St. Francis of Assisi and Padre Pio, had the marks in their hands or wrists? — *Name withheld, Philadelphia, Pa.*

In the Book of Revelation, John describes his visions of heaven. Other mystics have claimed similar visions. Both St. Francis and Padre Pio had the stigmata in their hands. Medical scientists have shown that nails through the hands would tear out from the weight of the body. However, a nail through the bones of the wrist would hold the weight. While the Church does rule on the sanctity of a stigmatist's life, the Church does not rule on the stigmata as a miracle. The stigmata could be psychosomatically induced, particularly by one who meditates deeply on and identifies with the passion of our Lord. The stigmatist is usually an ecstatic, and ninety percent of some three hundred reputed stigmatists have been women. I don't mean to suggest that the stigmatist deliberately wills the stigmata, but medical science is only now learning of the powerful effects of the mind on the body.

Hell

> Is there really a hell? I feel our hell is on earth and that a merciful and loving God could not be so cruel as to punish anyone for an eternity. — *Y. Ross, Highland, Ind.*

If we are to believe Christ, then there is a hell and it is for eternity. Christ spoke often of hell, warning his followers of this possible ultimate tragedy in its permanent separation from God's presence and love. The New Testament speaks frequently of hell being unending (Matthew 25:46, Mark 9:43-48, 2 Thessalonians 1:9, Revelation 14:9-11). The teaching of Origen that all sinners will eventually be brought to salvation was rejected by the Second Council of Constantinople and the eternity of hell was taught by the Fourth Lateran Council. It is not God who sentences the sinner to hell but the sinner himself by his free choice. God wishes the salvation of all but does not force it. He gave us free will to choose himself and by this same free will we can reject him. God gives us power to reform our lives up to the moment of death, but as we die so we remain. We make the choice, not God. So, in effect, God does not send us to hell — we send ourselves by choosing a way that is apart from God.

> **HARD TO UNDERSTAND** • In a recent question on predestination, you spoke of the concept that in God's knowledge certain individuals would be lost, not by God's choice but by their own. Can you explain this concept further, as I cannot conceive of the idea of anyone being "lost" for eternity? — *Ruth Gunderson, Madison, Wis.*

Many people have difficulty reconciling the mercy of God with his justice, yet Scripture and Christ himself speak of hell as being everlasting (see, for example, Matthew 25:41). Man only goes to hell because he has rejected God and thus in this sense says that he prefers hell to God. God merely affirms this action. I realize that it is disturbing to think that men and women make this irrevocable choice, but God's justice makes hell necessary. The death of Jesus on the cross made such punishment unnecessary for all who willingly choose eternal life. Christ spoke often of hell and warned men to avoid this terrible tragedy (Mark 9:43-48).

AVOID PRESUMPTION • In recent years I have been picking up a trend of thought that seems to me heresy. Even my own pastor expressed the opinion that there probably isn't such a thing as hell for mortal sinners because God is too loving, too forgiving, to allow most sinners to be lost forever. Is this what they call Modernism? — *Name withheld, Seattle, Wash.*

Based on many different utterances of Jesus, it is the teaching of the Church that hell exists, that it is a place of punishment for those who die self-alienated from God (mortal sin), that the punishment of hell begins immediately after death, and that it lasts for all eternity. The Church does not define the nature of hell, other than it is separation from God; neither does it indicate the number of people in hell. It is true that some people have difficulty reconciling God's mercy and justice, but this is their problem, not God's. Common sense should tell them that a person who spends his or her life trying to do the will of God would not be treated the same as one who rejects God and his law. It is good for us to meditate on the two men who were crucified with Jesus — one who was saved and the other presumably lost. This incident teaches us that we should never despair and, at the same time, never to presume. The opinion you state could be a facet of Modernism.

Holy Spirit

What has been the basis, doctrinal or theological, for the Church's changing the name of the Holy Ghost to Holy Spirit? — *D. A. Miele, Norfolk, Va.*

There is no doctrinal or theological reason, only one of semantics and the changing usages of language. Latin, which is the official language of the Church, uses the term *Sanctus Spiritus*, and this is how it is found in the *Vulgate*, which is the official scriptural text. When in the late 1500s the English translations were made, the common word for *Spiritus* was Ghost, and thus the English rendition of *Sanctus Spiritus* was Holy

Ghost. The word ghost was in turn derived from the middle English *gost* which came from Old High German *geist*, meaning spirit. Over the centuries the meaning of the word changed until its present usage means the soul of a dead person that can appear to the living in bodily likeness. When the new translations of Scripture were made, the translators chose the term Holy Spirit to more accurately render *Sanctus Spiritus* in today's usage. Protestants who accept only the *King James* translation as authentic still cling to Holy Ghost. In making the modern translations of Scripture, one aim was to use the vernacular and drop archaic expressions and words such as "thy," "thine," "shouldest," "say unto him," "ye," "hath," and similar anachronisms.

WHY A DOVE? • Why are we made in the image and likeness of God, yet the Holy Spirit is not an image of God but a dove, a bird? It is so hard to feel close to a bird. Also, would you please explain how Jesus can be both God and Son? — *Name withheld, Utica, N.Y.*

God is pure spirit and we are made in the image of God, not in our bodies but in our souls, which are pure spirit. The Holy Spirit is not a dove any more than the Holy Spirit is the tongues of flame that appeared above the heads of the apostles on Pentecost. The dove that appeared at the baptism of Jesus was representative of the Holy Spirit, just as the tongues of flame were representative at Pentecost, each reflecting the unseen presence of the Holy Spirit at these incidents. The Holy Spirit is also described as the unseen bond of love that exists between the Father and Jesus. We must also understand that Jesus had a twofold nature: divine (God), existing from all eternity, one with the Father; and human (Jesus Christ), born in time and capable of suffering life's vicissitudes. It was this human nature that cried out to the Father at his crucifixion. Furthermore, we must remember that the Holy Trinity is a mystery that our limited human minds cannot comprehend.

Home Best Teacher

What influences children the most in growing up to be good practical Catholics? Is it the blood of good Catholic parents, their good example, the environment in which they grow up, the Catholic school, or what? — *Bertha Lorenzo, Buffalo, N.Y.*

There is no question in my mind about the home being the major influence. Bishop Fulton J. Sheen once said that Christianity is not taught but caught, meaning that it is example that is the best teacher. The home is the natural school. The great churchman and educator Edwin V. O'Hara once said, "The Christian home is the school of Christ." Pope John XXIII in his encyclical *Pacem in Terris* wrote that the family "must be considered the first and essential cell of human society." Too many parents delegate the religious training of their children to priests and nuns, but these have nowhere near the influence of a Christian home. The family should be a little church for the child where he or she sees Christianity lived daily.

Homosexuality

Could you give the Church's view on being a gay Catholic? — *Name withheld, Forest Park, Ill.*

The story of our sexuality is briefly told in the Bible. "Male and female he created them," says Genesis 1:27. Why did God so create them? Again Genesis (1:28) has God commanding the first man and woman: "Be fertile and multiply, fill the earth and subdue it." On these texts the Church develops its theology of sexuality. God created man and woman to complement each other and share with him in the continuation of the human race. This sexuality is an intimate and basic part of our lives that can only be totally fulfilled in another complementary person. It is the Chinese principle of *yang* and *yin*. That is the way that things are ideally to work. However, this is an imperfect world, as a result of which things often go wrong; people are born sterile, or blind, or deaf, or with a sexual drive that is directed to its own sex rather than to the complementary sex. Most homosexuals can no more help what they are than can a heterosexual. The Church teaches that Christ died for every human being and that each one of us can share in our Lord's redemptive sacrifice. At the same time the Church condemns all acts, both homosexual and heterosexual, that are opposed to Genesis 1:28. The Church's attitude is that of Christ to the woman taken in adultery: he condemned her sin but showed his love to the person. While heroic virtue is the ideal, both Christ and the Church know that people will not always attain it — hence the sacrament of reconciliation where the past is forgiven and we start out anew. The important thing for everyone is to stay close to Christ and serve him to the best of one's ability. Neither Christ nor the Church asks more than that.

FAILURE TO DISTINGUISH • Enclosed is a letter of mine that was printed in the daily paper. I found your answer on homosexuality after I had sent my article in. I was stunned by your statement: "Homosexuality in itself is not sinful." This sounded to me like, "Adultery in itself is not sinful." Is there a contradiction between your statement and my assertions? — *Name withheld, Wheeling, W. Va.*

Yes, there is. Your statement was a blanket condemnation and did not distinguish between a homosexual condition and homosexual acts. The latter are always sinful. There are many homosexuals who lead virtuous and chaste lives. I'm sure you do not mean to imply that they live in a state of sin because they have homosexual orientation? I refer you to the "Statement on Moral Life" issued by the National Conference of Catholic Bishops on November 11, 1976: "Some persons find themselves through no fault of their own to have a homosexual orientation. . . . They should have an active role in the Christian community. Homosexual activity, however, as distinguished from homosexual orientation, is morally wrong. Like heterosexual persons, homosexuals are called to give witness to chastity, avoiding, with God's grace, behavior which is wrong for them just as non-marital relations are wrong for heterosexuals." Homosexuality is a psychic disease, usually inborn but sometimes acquired. It is a complex problem. Few homosexuals prefer to be homosexuals. One is not to be blamed for an innate condition but only for deliberate acts that flow from that condition. Adultery is another matter, since this does not refer to a psychic condition but a deliberate violation of God's law.

HOMOSEXUAL VOCATIONS • What difference does it make if a man or woman, priest or sister, who *lives* a celibate life, is heterosexual or homosexual? Might it be possible for a person with homosexual tendencies, but living a truly celibate life, to give better understanding and counsel to those persons who are not celibate but would like to control their sexuality? I have a grandson who is a practicing homosexual, and I can remember so well his early years and the atmosphere of his childhood home life. — *Name withheld, Tampa, Fla.*

I don't think it makes any difference under the condition you place, but the Church must be cautious because of the possibility for future scandal if the person stops living a celibate life. For a person vowed to celibacy, any deviation (whether heterosexual or homosexual) is wrong. As for the homosexual, as we have said here before, the sin is not in the psychological or sexual orientation of the person but in the practice of homosexuality. Living a celibate life is not easy, but God has promised sufficient grace to the person who tries.

Hypnosis

I have heard of a class that helps one lose weight through hypnosis. The person who conducts this class is reputable and holds a professional degree. I would like to attend these classes, but I am concerned about one thing. I am afraid that by allowing myself to be put into a suggestible state, I might leave my mind open to evil spiritual influences. Can you reassure me on this point? — *Name withheld, Bremen, Ind.*

In itself, hypnotism is not wrong. It has become a valuable tool in medicine and psychiatry in treating certain illnesses and conditions. There are two types of hypnotism: slight hypnotism, in which the subject remains conscious and aware of what has happened, and deep hypnotism, in which the sensory system and muscles are greatly affected. Susceptibility to hypnotism varies greatly with individuals. While the hypnotic state heightens suggestibility, most psychologists assert that the subject would not do in a hypnotic state what he or she would not do in an awakened state. Hypnotism is not a toy to be played with, but in the hands of a competent psychotherapist it can be a useful tool. The Church approves of legitimate uses of hypnotism but condemns its abuses. One should not expect miracles from hypnotism. To lose weight or give up smoking still requires willpower, although hypnotism might make it somewhat easier.

Icons

Some time ago I came into possession of a very old icon of St. Nicholas of Myra. Although I am a Latin Rite Catholic, I have a fair understanding of the origin, use, and veneration of such holy images. Such attitudes toward holy images are no longer a mark of the Western Church, and in some churches of the Latin Rite an almost Protestant iconoclasm exists. What is the proper place of icons in the Roman rite? Is veneration appropriate? Does the Western Church possess any prayers or liturgical rites that include devotion to icons? — *Mike Perigo, Lafayette, Ind.*

Icons, or paintings of our Lord, the Blessed Virgin, and other saints, are venerated in the place of statues in the Eastern churches. These paintings are done on wood and metal, and some of them, like some statues in the West, are held in high regard. In the eighth century a group arose that condemned the use of images (which is iconoclasm, from the Greek for image destroyer), but this heresy was condemned in 787 by the Second Council of Nicaea, the Church's seventh ecumenical council. I know of no antipathy to icons in the Western Church, and in fact some of the West's most honored images are icons. The celebrated image of Our Lady of Czestochowa is an icon, and the pope has gone to Poland to venerate it. There are copies of the famed icon of Our Lady of Perpetual Help in many Latin Rite churches in the United States, and devotion to this icon is promoted by the Redemptorist Fathers. A special chapel has been built at Fátima to enshrine an ancient icon of the Virgin with funds largely raised by American Catholics. I have seen icons in many Catholic churches and in many rectories. There are prayers and ceremonies attached to the icons I mentioned just as there are to venerable statues.

Impotency

According to a story in the newspaper, impotency is no longer an impediment to valid marriage because there is some hope of reversal. If hope of rehabilitation could be used as an excuse to validly marry, please give me some cases where there are no loopholes. I personally feel that the pastor was correct in refusing to marry this couple. Since impotence is reversible, when is it an impediment? If these two people are now validly married, what would the Church do in the future if the woman requests an annulment? — *Bernard T. Fabry, Youngstown, Ohio*

I don't want to comment on a specific story, since newspapers are not always accurate and I do not know all the details of the case you mention. I will, however, answer generally. Impotency is the impossibility of sexual intercourse because of some defect of mind or body, or both, which prevents a person from exercising the marriage act with another in a normal way. It is not the same as sterility, and the latter neither prohibits nor annuls marriage. According to Canon 1084: "Antecedent and permanent impotency to have intercourse, whether on the part of the man or the woman, whether absolute or relative, annuls marriage by the very law of nature. If the impediment is doubtful, either as to fact or as to law, marriage is not to be impeded nor is it to be declared null as long as the doubt exists." There are two words here to be noted: permanent and doubtful. Not all impotency is permanent. That caused by mental defect can be reversed by treatment. Even some physical impotency can be reversed by surgery or treatment. We are now in the age of microsurgery when things deemed impossible a few years ago are being done — vasectomies, for example, are being reversed. Some cases of paralysis yield to operation and physical therapy. When the permanence is doubtful, the marriage may be permitted. Cases on the part of a male that would be considered permanent would be castration (lacking both testicles) or the lack of a male organ. The lack of a vagina would be a permanent case in a woman, but even here reconstructive surgery might be possible. According to most moral theologians, the pastor is held to try and resolve any doubt before marriage. However, if after such an attempt the doubt persists, marriage is not to be forbidden. Again, here we must distinguish between doubt and moral certitude. It was on the basis of this doubt that the marriage you mentioned was permitted. It was a judgment made by the bishops, and I suppose that one could agree or disagree with it. However, he had all the facts and the responsibility, and his judgment is recognized as official. It is my opinion that if the parties concerned sought an annulment after a few years, it would be disallowed because of the investigation that went into the case beforehand and because the same reasons that allowed the marriage in the first place were still pertinent.

Indulgences

Would you explain what is meant by indulgences? Although I went to Catholic schools this was never explained to us. — *Emily Wojdula, East Chicago, Ind.*

An indulgence is the remission before God of the temporal punishment due to already forgiven sins, which the Christian can gain with the proper disposition and by the performance of an indulgenced act. The Church grants these indulgences from its spiritual treasury — the superabundant merits of Christ and the saints, through the power given it by Christ (see Matthew 16:19), and the sharing of spiritual goods through the doctrine of the communion of saints. An indulgence is partial or full, according to whether it does away with part or all the temporal punishment due to sins. Many outside the Church misinterpret this doctrine, thinking that an indulgence is freedom to commit sin. Just the opposite is true. To gain an indulgence one must be free of serious sin and have sorrow for one's own sin. A full (or plenary) indulgence requires confession, Holy Communion, and prayers for the pope's intention. A book from Our Sunday Visitor — *Life after Death* by Father Albert J. Nevins — has a chapter on the nature and history of indulgences, together with many indulgenced practices and prayers.

PARTIAL INDULGENCE • I have a prayer book that has many indulgenced prayers included in it. Under each is a notation that tells the time of the indulgence (three hundred thirty days, five years, etc.) and then if there is a plenary indulgence it will state with the further comment "on the usual conditions." I am unaware what the phrase "on the usual conditions" means. — *Name withheld, Brazil, Ind.*

Your prayer book is out of date, since partial indulgences are no longer given in a time frame and many former indulgenced prayers and acts have now been voided. In 1967 Pope Paul VI issued a new constitution on indulgences that explains what they are, why the Church grants them and how, and then lays down new rules for them. It was one of the first changes to come from Vatican Council II. A partial indulgence removes part of the temporal punishment due to sin. Like plenary indulgences, they can be applied to souls in purgatory. A partial indulgence can be granted more than once a day (for example, each time the indulgenced prayer is said), unless there is a provision to the contrary. According to the constitution partial indulgences shall no longer show any determination of the days or years, but the amount of remission is left to the mercy and justice of God, adding, "in addition to the remission of temporal punishment merited by the action itself, an equal remission of punishment through the Church's intervention." The only conditions for partial indulgences are the act itself and "a contrite heart."

Infallibility

Much has been said over the years concerning papal primacy and infallibility. It is especially important in light of the current Anglican-Catholic unity discourses. My question is: How many times has a pope chosen to invoke papal infallibility and proclaim a dogma? Not many I suspect. — *John R. McGoldrick, San Antonio, Tex.*

The doctrine of infallibility was defined at Vatican Council I in 1870. The pope is only infallible when he speaks *ex cathedra* ("from the chair," that is, deliberately and formally) on a matter of faith or morals. In the last one hundred twenty-five years, the pope has only spoken twice *ex cathedra*, in defining new doctrines: On December 8, 1854, Pope Pius IX defined the doctrine of the Immaculate Conception; on November 1, 1950, Pope Pius XII solemnly proclaimed the dogma of the Assumption.

Infant Death

My daughter, who lives in another state, recently gave birth to a stillborn child. I am deeply disturbed that my grandson was buried without any funeral service. My daughter told me nothing could be done because the child had not been baptized. Is this correct? — *Name withheld, Hammond, Ind.*

No, it is not correct. Among the funeral Masses in the *Sacramentary* is one "For a Child Who Died Before Baptism." Also, in the funeral rites (Chapter VIII) there are various texts for funerals of children who die before baptism. Your daughter must have the mistaken idea that because the child was unbaptized it was of no interest to the Church. Nothing can be further from the truth. We do not know what happens to an unbaptized child, but we do know that God's mercy and love are limitless. God's covenant with Noah embraced all of creation and God's love for a child who dies before birth is no less than that for a child born alive.

Inheritance

How responsible is a grown son for the promise he made by signing a legal document agreeing to share equally in the care and support of his widowed mother (now dead)? His argument for failing to do so is this: "Legally the promise of a dead man (his father) isn't worth the paper it is written on." Perhaps Dad was unwise in willing his property and business to his sons rather than leaving enough to provide for his wife. — *Name withheld, Toledo, Ohio*

While not knowing the other side of this case, I can only state some general rules. In accepting an inheritance one is morally bound to the conditions of that inheritance. One is also bound to the intention of the donor. Legality and morality are not always the same thing. One has moral obligations, such as the support of a parent, which may not be legal obligations. Where there are a number of children, this support fails proportionately on each child according to ability. However, all this is moot, since your mother has died — although it evidently still rankles in the family. I am sure that your father's intention was to do what he thought right, certainly not to split the family. It is unfortunate that many families fall apart because of inheritances. What you should do is forget the past and try to put the family together again. Reconciliation is a work of God.

Inquisition

I have a friend, and whenever I want to talk to her about my Church, she brings up the Inquisition and says that a church that could do such terrible things cannot be a church of God. How can I answer her? — *Name withheld, Mobile, Ala.*

The first thing to ask her is which Inquisition she is talking about. There were two of them, and they were quite different, as I'll explain in a moment. But before I do, this should be made clear: we must judge past events in the light of their own times, not with a twentieth-century mentality. Things back in the fifteenth and sixteenth centuries were much rougher than they are today. For example, King Henry VIII and his daughter, Queen Elizabeth, imprisoned or killed hundreds and hundreds of Catholics, several score of whom have either been canonized or beatified. This happened in other Protestant countries as well. There are cases of Protestants putting Protestants to death because of a difference of beliefs. Some Catholic leaders reacted in the same way. All of these events must be judged against national rivalries and enmities and political aspirations. To get back to the Inquisition, there were two Inquisitions, and the one most people talk about is the Spanish Inquisition, which began in Spain and was organized in the Spanish colonies of the New World. This was an instrument of the Spanish crown, originally set up by King Ferdinand and Queen Isabella, who had united Spain and driven out the Moors. It was established to inquire into the faith of Muslims and Jews who had converted to Catholicism and who were suspected of only a faked conversion. However, this Inquisition soon became a political instrument of the Spanish crown, used to punish the opposition by creating false charges and gaining "confessions" by harsh tortures. As such, it was opposed by Rome, and any historian of the period should be familiar with censures and reprimands given the Spanish Inquisition by a succession of popes. This Inquisition did not disappear until Spain lost its North and South American possessions. The other Inquisition was the Roman and Universal Inquisition, which was begun by Pope Paul III as part of the Catholic Reform in answer to the Protestant Reformation. Pope Paul was concerned with the heresies being propagated from Germany and Switzerland. He was greatly occupied with the teaching of Jesus: fear not those who kill the body, but fear those who kill the soul. He worried about souls being lost through heresy, so he set up a commission of a half-dozen cardinals entrusted with keeping the Catholic faith free of error. Later, this commission became a congregation of the Church, known as the Holy Office. It was kept independent of secular powers and had as its aim showing people in error their mistakes and leading them back to the Church. It had detailed legal procedures that had to be followed. Some abuses did creep in, as can happen with any human institution, but these were never sanctioned by the Church and were ended whenever they became known. The Holy Office existed up to modern times, when in 1965, as a result of Vatican II, it was redefined and given a new title: Congregation for the Doctrine of the Faith.

Insurance

What is the Church's stand on life insurance policies, fire and theft policies, signing your name to charitable checks, and accepting welfare from the state? — *E. Carey, Buffalo, N.Y.*

The Church has no specific teaching on these matters but expects us to use the common sense God gives us. Jesus has given us an ideal of detachment from all worldly goods; however, knowing that few can do this, he also gave us examples of people who planned ahead — the man guarding his possessions against thieves, the king who calculated the forces coming against him and made peace. In today's world we need protection against thieves and natural perils, so there is nothing wrong in having insurance against loss that could be ruinous. We do not accept welfare from some impersonal state. It comes from the taxes of our fellow citizens who thus care for their brothers and sisters in need. This is good Christian teaching and is the reason why welfare should not be abused.

Intercommunion

I attended a mixed marriage recently, which was celebrated at a Mass. Everybody in the wedding party, Catholics and Protestants, received Communion, including the groom's non-Catholic parents. Can a priest give Communion to non-Catholics indiscriminately? — *Name withheld, Toledo, Ohio*

No, he cannot. The *Directory Concerning Ecumenical Matters* lays down very strict and rigorous conditions for giving Holy Communion to non-Catholic Christians. Moreover, in a subsequent explanation authorized by the pope, it is made clear that permission for each particular case is reserved to the local bishop. A priest cannot on his own authority admit a non-Catholic to Holy Communion.

FORBIDDEN ACTION • Some good friends of mine are of the Presbyterian faith. On many occasions I have attended church with them and received Communion. Many family members have denounced this action because I am Catholic. I see no wrong in this. In my heart I am receiving my Lord. In your own opinion is it wrong? — *Name withheld, Chicago, Ill.*

Yes, it is wrong. Presbyterians and Catholics look at the reception of Communion in two very different ways. The Presbyterian service is symbolic. Presbyterians do not believe in transubstantiation, nor do they believe that they receive the actual body and blood of Christ. For a Catholic who understands his religion, the very foundation and unity of the Catholic Church is in the actual body of Christ, offered in sacrifice and given to the faithful as the Bread of Eternal Life. This is done by the ministerial powers given by Jesus to the apostles and passed down to their successors, who alone are empowered to make effective this sacramental act. The Eucharist is the sacrament of unity within the Catholic Church and for this reason non-Catholics are forbidden the sacrament, except under very special circumstances. The manner of your attendance at the Presbyterian service gives the impression to your friends that one religion is as good as another, that you subscribe to their beliefs and do not find them in any conflict with your own. I suggest you read Vatican II's *Decree on Ecumenism* and the regulations on admitting other Christians to Holy Communion.

DANGER OF SCANDAL • A religious order sister insists it is perfectly in accord with the Catholic faith to attend services in the interdenominational Union Church. She goes twice a month to these services. I say she is wrong. Who is right? — *Name withheld, Detroit, Mich.*

You are. The basis underlying an interdenominational church is that one religion is as good as another. No Catholic can give assent to this principle. Sister's regular attendance at such a church can be the cause of grave scandal and giving encouragement to the fallacy that one religion is as good as another. While the *Decree on Ecumenism* urges us to respect the beliefs of another, the decree limits joint worship to special occasions, "such as prayer services 'for unity.'" The decree also states that liturgical worship is not to be considered as a means to be used indiscriminately for the restoration of unity among Christians, adding, "The expression of unity very generally forbids common worship." Sister appears to be mixed up on priorities. I suggest that she study the *Decree on Ecumenism* and the *Directory Concerning Ecumenical Matters.*

Investments

Is it moral for a Catholic to invest in such things as stocks, bonds, options, commodities, and futures, or engage in short selling? Or are these things sinful or a form of gambling? — *Name withheld, Oakdale, Conn.*

I do not know enough about short selling to comment, but the other forms of investment you mention are licit and are not sinful. These investments are looked upon as loans made to another and come under the Church's teachings on justice and contracts. You are allowed to make loans and receive interest for that loan because of the use of your money and the risk involved. There are safer ways to invest money (for example, insured deposits, certificates of deposit, and U.S. Treasury bonds). Going into the market involves greater risks to your investment, and hence greater interest must be paid — dividend and increased value are forms of interest. Although there are risks in every investment, and some are riskier than others, I would not call such investments gambling. Gambling is a contest in which the outcome is largely due to chance, as in the case of the roll of dice or the fall of cards. While there could be elements of gambling in investments, their outcome is not so much due to happenstance as to good or poor business practices, which come from intelligence and experience.

Israel

This is my question: Why hasn't the state of Israel been diplomatically recognized by the Vatican? Is there any moral or political reason to deny such recognition? — *Clemente Medina Suarez, Brooklyn, N.Y.*

There is no moral reason why the Vatican cannot have diplomatic relations with Israel. The Church does recognize the existence of Israel as a state and has an apostolic delegate living in Israel. Moreover, Israel was visited by Pope Paul VI and the

Vatican has received in audience high Israeli officials, but political reasons have caused the Vatican to delay full diplomatic relations. The Palestinian situation is still not resolved and many of these Palestinians are Christians. Through war, Israel took possession of the West Bank (Jordan), all of Jerusalem (half of which, the Old City, is claimed by Jordan), and the Golan Heights (Syria), none of which acquisitions are recognized by the Arab world. There are many Arab Christians living in Muslim nations whose safety and protection the Church must consider, as well as their own feelings. It is a complex situation that can best be settled by a peace conference between Israel and its neighbors that would set permanent borders for Israel, and remove what amounts to a continuous state of war. Some of the same reasons affecting Vatican-Israeli relations also govern the Church's relations with Eastern-bloc nations where many Catholics live under communist domination. Just as the Church has to consider the welfare of Christians in Arab nations, so it must consider their welfare in communist nations. The Church has also argued for the internationalization of Jerusalem's Old City, which contains Christian, Muslim, and Jewish shrines.

Jehovah's Witnesses

Some years ago there was an article in *Our Sunday Visitor* about the beliefs of Jehovah's Witnesses. I gave this article away. I respect the rights of others, but their informers are too pushy. Can you please write about the do's and don'ts. — *Name withheld, Valparaiso, Ind.*

The Jehovah's Witnesses are a cult rooted in the novel biblical interpretations of its founder, Charles Taze Russell, and popularized by "Judge" Joseph Rutherford. The cult has gone under different names: Russellites, International Bible Students, Rutherfordites, Watchtower and Bible Tract Society. Its beliefs are a mishmash, and it is easier to tell what the group is against than what it is for. William J. Whalen, an authority on sects, writes: "The Witnesses oppose blood transfusions, business, Catholics, Christmas trees, communism, civic enterprises, the doctrines of hell and immortality, evolution, flag-saluting, higher education, liquor, lodges, Protestants, priests, the pope, public office, military service, movies, Mother's Day, religion, Sunday Schools, the Trinity, tobacco, the United Nations, voting, the YMCA, Wall Street and women's rights. This list does not pretend to be complete." Witnesses reject the divinity of Christ, original sin, and the Trinity. The cult appeals to people who lack discrimination, who are ill-educated and untrained in their own beliefs. Members undergo hours of training on key biblical texts and all are expected to proselytize. When these people call at your door, do not invite them in because they are difficult to get out; do not try to debate with them, as they are well-trained in what they have to say and they do not hear what you say. Do not accept literature from them and politely close the door.

TRINITY • My brother is thinking about becoming a Jehovah's Witness, and I think part of the reason is that the Catholic Church is misrepresented. They say, for instance, that the notion of the Trinity didn't even come into existence until the Nicene Council. I understood that the Trinity was defined at the Nicene Council in response to Arianism. Is there a book or something that I can read about how Catholics might respond to Jehovah's Witnesses? — *Name withheld, Howell, Mich.*

Our Sunday Visitor does publish a book, *Strangers at Your Door*, which methodically examines the Witnesses. The sect was founded by Charles Taze Russell about 1870. He taught a mishmash of Unitarianism, Arianism, Millennialism, Adventism, and some pet theories. When he died, his lawyer, "Judge" Joseph Rutherford, gained control of the group, which he named Jehovah's Witnesses, threw out some of Russell's teaching, and proclaimed his own prophecies and biblical interpretation. Witnesses are not Christians because they will not admit Christ is God. They will say he is "divine" and specially honored by God but will not admit he is coequal with God the Father and the Holy Spirit. They are carefully trained in selected texts and will confuse Catholics who have not been trained in the Bible. Witnesses draw their converts from nonintellectuals and people with little advanced education. They are completely subservient to their leaders and make great sacrifice of time and money for their beliefs. They are persistent, and one should not get into an argument with them or accept their literature unless one has been trained how to respond to their theological nonsense. The notion of the Trinity exists in the New Testament — God the Father, God the Son, God the Holy Spirit — and it was the denial that Christ was a coequal (Arianism) that led to the First Council of Nicaea and formal definition.

Jesus

I am a Jewish Christian who does not argue about gene-alogy, usually. But I am curious. Jesus' lineage in the Gos-pels of Matthew and Luke is traced to David through Jo-seph, not Mary. So Jesus is not biologically traceable to David because Joseph is Jesus' adopted father. Am I right in saying that Jesus is descended from David by adop-tion? — *Samuel Girard, Cavalier, N. Dak.*

The genealogies differ. Luke proceeds backward from Jesus to Adam while Matthew moves forward from Abraham to Jesus. The purpose of the genealogies is to show that Jesus is the Messiah King, son of David, son of Abraham. Luke by going back to Adam adds a universalist note that Jesus is the Savior of all mankind. In Jewish law of the time, ancestry was counted only through the father, even if the father was adoptive. The purpose of the passages is to show that Jesus was incorporated by divine command into the house of David. For the Jews gen-eration was not the only way of gaining a son. In Deuteronomy 25:5-10, a widow who has no son must be taken to wife by her brother-in-law and the first son born of the union is recognized as the son of the deceased husband. By Jewish law, at the time of Christ a man could adopt a boy by solemn declaration that he was his son, and legally and to all effects the boy was his son. The adoption by Joseph was not a casual act but was done in obedience to God's command (Matthew 1:20). So you are correct in your assessment that Jesus is descended from David by adoption. There are some who believe Mary was of David's line also, but there is no proof for such an assertion.

Jews

A friend asked me if "Jewish" referred to nationality or religion. I answered, "religion." Will you also explain "Jew," "Hebrew," "Yiddish," "Judaism"? — *Paul Licata, Raytown, Mo.*

A Jew is one who traces his or her descent to the people of Is-rael, specifically the tribe of Judah. Judaism is the religion of the Jewish people, but not every Jew is religious. Today many who call themselves Jews have been secularized and practice no religion, or even deny the existence of God. That is why the use of the word today is more cultural than religious. Hebrew is the ancient language of the northern Semitic people, including the Israelites. It was the language of the Bible, but it began to disappear as a tongue after the Jewish defeat by the Babylonians in the sixth century B.C. By the time of Christ, it had been replaced by Aramaic. The Zionist movement of the nineteenth century revived Hebrew and gave it modern form. It is the language used today in Israel. Yiddish is basically a High German language written in Hebrew letters used by Eastern European Jews; it also includes some words devolved from Polish and Russian. It was the language of the Jewish immigrants who came to the United States but is now dying out.

SALVATION • Recently my husband's friends and I had a discussion on the Jews. They said Jews cannot go to heaven. I had never heard this before, as I was raised to believe that anyone who believes in God and lived by his or her faith could go to heaven and that God was the final judge. They totally disagreed with this and said the Jews must believe in Jesus Christ as their Savior. Can Jews go to heaven? — *Maureen Anthony, Amarillo, Tex.*

Recently a Baptist minister said that God did not hear the prayers of Jews. He believed this because in his opinion every prayer to be heard must be offered in the name of Christ. This opinion is similar to that of your friends. The Church does not hold this opinion, and Jews, Muslims, and even pagans can be saved because Jesus Christ died for the redemption of all. In its *Dogmatic Constitution on the Church*, Vatican Council II taught: "Basing itself on Scripture and Tradition, it teaches that the Church, a pilgrim now on earth, is necessary for salvation: the one Christ is mediator and the way of salvation. . . . He himself explicitly asserted the necessity of faith and baptism (cf. Mk. 16:16, Jn. 3:5)." Having said this the council points out that there are various ways one can be joined to the Church, considering Protestants who accept the Gospel, Jews who are people of the covenant, and Muslims who profess the faith of Abraham and acknowledge the one true God. As for pagans, the council declared: "Those, who through no fault of their own, do not know the Gospel of Christ or His Church, but who nevertheless seek God with a sincere heart, try in their actions to do His will as they know it through the dictates of their conscience — those too may achieve eternal salvation." Your fundamentalist friends are limiting the mercy and justice of God.

Judgment

I understand God forgives sins when we are truly sorry and confess them. But does this mean that we will never have to suffer or atone for these forgiven sins? I know someone who does commit sin and she enjoys herself and is always happy. She will be forgiven when she is ready to confess these sins. Why should I be good? — *Name withheld, Pittsfield, Mass.*

While it is common today to stress the mercy of God, to be honest we must give equal importance to the justice of God wherein every person will get his or her due. So while your friend might seem to be getting away with sin, there will one day be a balancing of the books and fair judgment given. Some people believe they will always have time to reform and straighten out their lives, but as Jesus told us, not one of us knows the day or the hour he or she will be called to God. There is an old spiritual axiom, "As you live, so shall you die." One who lives in sin will probably die in sin. How foolish to deliberately take such a risk! But even if one does have time to have one's sins forgiven, the temporal punishment remaining must still be purged. St. Augustine says the "fire" of purgatory will be "more severe than anything a person can suffer in this life." There a person will come to understand how sin separates one from God and that this terrible loss, even though only for a time, is the result of one's own misspent life.

GENERAL JUDGMENT • In the general judgment how will souls be judged? According to their state at the time of death, or what? — *Anne Cialeo, Brooklyn, N.Y.*

It is Church teaching that there are two judgments — particular judgment and general judgment. The particular judgment is made at the moment of death and the general judgment at the end of time. How we fare at the particular judgment is something we have decided by our lives. St. Paul tells us, "It is appointed men to die once, and after that the judgment" (Hebrews 9:27). The moment of death is the fulfillment of all life and all that we have done is added up at that moment. If we are living in friendship with God at the moment of death, then we are assured of salvation. Since few of us are entirely free from attachment to sin, there is a period in purgatory to remove these attachments. The good things we have done in life can shorten this period. The general judgment is described in

Chapter 25 of Matthew's Gospel. In this judgment we are judged as members of society and we are judged on things that happen after we are dead. What we have done in this life does not necessarily cease with our death. Good actions and good seeds we have planted may not come to fruition until long after we are dead. The effects of sin on others may continue long after the sin was committed. On the last day everything will have reached its final result and a full and proper judgment made.

Justice and Peace

Should the Church espouse political and social issues, such as oppression and exploitation? We have the pattern of Christ. He told the rich that they would have difficulty entering the kingdom of heaven. Nevertheless, he never took part in protest movements or denounced the unjust distribution of wealth. He never joined subversive groups carrying posters that read, "Down with the Romans!" — *Terril D. Littrell, Evansville, Tenn.*

The position of the Church is best expressed in the *Pastoral Constitution on the Church in the Modern World*, issued by the Fathers of Vatican Council II. I suggest that you read this document, particularly numbers 77-82. Number 77, which sets the theme, states in part: "This council fervently desires to summon Christians to cooperate with all men in making secure among themselves a peace based on justice and love, and in setting up agencies of peace. This Christians should do with the help of Christ, the author of peace." On the basis of this document, peace and justice commissions were formed throughout the Church, including many dioceses. Their purpose is to make Catholics more aware of matters relating to peace and justice. The Church cannot be a political instrument, just as Christ was not a political instrument, but, by the nature of life, matters of peace and justice today sometimes touch politics. Christ frequently spoke out on injustice, one example you quote. He denounced the Jewish establishment and castigated the Judean King Herod. Christ did not concern himself with the political reality of his day, just as today the Church is not so much concerned with who Caesar is but with what Caesar does. I believe that some peace and justice groups oversimplify a terribly complex world. Some go to extremes not envisioned by the council, and some represent the "hot buttons" of their members more than theological reasoning. The Church, however, is committed to peace and justice and expects its members to be likewise concerned.

JUSTICE FOR WORKER • Could you please explain if the desire for efficiency can be more important than the performance of charity? For instance, I know of a man with a family of seven children who was fired from his job as a groundsman to make way for a young university graduate (a horticulturist) just out of college. — *Michael Connolly, Nelson, British Columbia*

The best we can do regarding your question is to lay down some general principles. There are two types of obligations, one in charity and one in justice, and both could apply here. Once a man is hired, the employer assumes these obligations. As Pope Leo XIII reminds us in *Rerum Novarum*, the great labor encyclical, "It is a most sacred law of nature that a father must provide food and all necessaries for those whom he has begotten." Therefore, once a person is employed, it requires an equally compensating reason to discharge that person. Moreover, as Pope Pius XI reminds us in *Quadragesimo Anno*, there are obligations in charity apart from justice, so that "if one member suffers anything, all the members suffer with it." Employment is not a one-way relationship, on the part of the employee who receives a salary for his labor. There is also an obligation on the part of the employer who removed the man from the labor force. As long as the man does satisfactorily that for which he was hired, he is entitled to employment unless there are sufficiently compensating reasons to end employment. Of course, a man who is incompetent or disloyal may be replaced for not fulfilling his obligation.

Killing

I am a deputy sheriff in southern California. Can you clear up a question I have? Is it permissible to kill another when necessarily committed in self-defense, or in defense of an innocent third party, or for the purposes of Catholic police officers in this country to kill when necessary to overcome resistance to or escape from a lawful arrest for a violent type of felony? — *Name withheld, Los Angeles, Calif.*

As a police officer you are sworn to protect the public against what theologians call the unjust aggressor. The moral theological principle that applies here is: One may defend oneself against an unjust aggressor even to the point of killing him, provided that one does not injure him more than is absolutely necessary to ensure self-protection. Thus a police officer may kill in self-defense or in defense of a third party, provided that there is a threat to your life or that of a third party. One may also use self-defense in the protection of one's property, but here the amount of force that may be used must be proportionate to the value of the property defended. Also, theologians teach that it is wrong to kill in defense of goods not yet possessed, for example, to kill in a stakeout before a crime is committed. They also teach that it is not permitted to kill an aggressor if his attack is not presently but only remotely imminent, for example, to kill a person who has made a threat against another but is not at the time carrying out the threat. As for killing to overcome resistance or prevent escape, the rule of proportionality would apply. Only enough force necessary to prevent the escape (and only proportionate to the crime involved) may be used. Thus it would be wrong to attempt to kill someone for speeding or fleeing a fender-bender simply to apprehend the person. In short, a policeman has the right to defend his life and property and the lives and property of others, and is allowed to use the minimum force necessary to accomplish this purpose. In some cases this minimum force may be lethal, as when a policeman is faced with an armed aggressor or to prevent the escape of one who has committed a serious violation of law. But when lesser force will be as effective, that should be used. This still means that a policeman must make judgments, but in cases of doubt he can always decide in behalf of his own safety and that of the public. By his acts an aggressor forfeits his rights — in serious cases his right to life, and in less serious cases his right to bodily safety.

Laicization

I cannot agree with your answer to a Benedictine sister. Holy orders says, "I am a priest forever." Matrimony says, "Till death do us part." Why should a priest get a dispensation, but married people can't? Just because a priest cannot obey his bishop's orders and the Church's laws is no excuse. These are two sacraments instituted by Christ. — *Name withheld, Daman, Kans.*

It is true that both holy orders and matrimony are sacraments that leave an indelible mark on the soul. A priest is a priest forever, even after laicization. This word simply means that the privileges of the priesthood are taken away from the laicized person, that is, he can no longer say Mass, hear confessions, celebrate weddings, etc. Also, in most cases, the obligation of celibacy is removed — but this really has nothing to do with the priesthood as such. For example, sisters and brothers take vows of celibacy, while in the Eastern Churches priests are allowed to marry. Celibacy is a discipline imposed by the Church on those who wish to be priests. When they choose to no longer act like priests, the Church can remove this discipline. A laicized priest can offer a valid Mass or forgive sins, although such actions would be illicit (illegal). He still has that power because he is a priest forever, but the Church now tells him he can no longer exercise this power legally. If he should be permitted back into the active priesthood, he is not ordained again because he already is a priest. When two people are married, they are married for life. But even here the Church permits a separation for sufficient reason. Christ instituted both sacraments, but he did not make celibacy a requisite for the priesthood. If he had, the Church could do nothing. Celibacy is a discipline of the Church and thus the Church, having instituted this discipline, can release from it. The difference is that when Christ instituted marriage, he said that no man or institution could do anything to dissolve a marriage; thus the Church has no power over divorce, any more than the Church can take a man's priesthood away from him. The only thing the Church can do is tell that man he can no longer exercise the powers of being a priest, even though he still retains those powers. The only thing the Church can tell a separated couple is that they cannot remarry.

Lazarus

Lazarus, we are told, returned from the dead after four days. Surely after this first-ever occurrence, Lazarus must have been questioned by many regarding the days during which he was dead and one wonders why some references to his experiences never did appear in the Bible.
— *Bill Gallachi, Ferndale, Mich.*

Lazarus was not the first-ever. Previously, Jesus had brought again to life the son of the widow of Naim and the daughter of a

Jewish official. But like yourself, I often wish that the evangelists had been better biographers, at least in the sense that we know biography today. However, the Gospel writers were not writing a biography. Their aim was to write a testimony that Jesus was the Son of God and that he came on earth to save mankind. They used events from the life of Jesus to prove their thesis. The Gospels leave many questions unanswered because the writers did not think these points added anything to what they were setting out to prove about Jesus. You are right in saying that there was interest in Lazarus. John 12:9 tells us that when Jesus returned to Bethany at the beginning of Holy Week a great multitude "came, not for Jesus' sake only, but that they might see Lazarus, whom he had raised from the dead."

Legion of Decency

What ever happened to the Legion of Decency? If it is defunct, now would be a good time to resurrect it. Until we got our VCR we just didn't realize how bad are some of the movies our children are seeing. — *Guido R. Schiavi, Wilmington, Del.*

The Legion of Decency unfortunately disappeared quite a few years ago. It has been replaced by a rating system that comes out of the U.S. bishops' office in Washington. Many Catholic papers carry these reviews of new movies with their morality rating that is not as easy to understand as the former Legion ratings. However, hardly any papers carry the complete current listings (Our Sunday Visitor prints recent ratings at least once a month); so unless the Catholic papers are saved, there is nothing for reference. Moreover, with VCR releases many noncurrent films are now available. Industry ratings are not much use, since they are based more on violence than on Christian morality. There are few motion pictures produced today that are not in some way offensive to Christian mores. Offensive language and immoral acts are purposely written into today's films. There is a greater need than ever for parental vigilance, not only for theatrical offerings but for VCR tapes that are rented and brought into the home.

Legion of Mary

As a new member of the Legion of Mary I am concerned with the wording of the "Promise" that will shortly be required of me, particularly the second paragraph: "But I know that Thou (Holy Spirit) who has come to regenerate the world in Jesus Christ, has not willed to do so except through Mary; that without her, we cannot know or love Thee; that it is by her and to whom she pleases, when she pleases, that all Thy gifts and virtues and graces are administered." I love our Blessed Mother deeply but wish to be assured that this statement is not in conflict with Christ's teachings. — *Name withheld, Nashville, Tenn.*

The Legion of Mary has long had Church approval, and the organization has done great work in spreading devotion to Mary, strengthening Catholic life, and bringing back fallen-away Catholics. The Holy Spirit came into the world according to the promise of Christ who said many times that after his death he would send the Holy Spirit. Jesus came into this world because of the consent of the Virgin Mary to the Incarnation. Thus it can be said that the Holy Spirit comes indirectly through Mary, since she was the direct cause in bringing Jesus to us through whom the Spirit came. Among the titles that Vatican Council II gave Mary in its *Dogmatic Constitution on the Church* is that of Mediatrix, adding, "This, however, is so understood that it neither takes away anything from nor adds anything to the dignity and efficacy of Christ the one Mediator." The promise you mention must be understood correctly in light of the theology of the Church and it could be misunderstood. I would suggest that you ask the chaplain of your presidium to elaborate on it at a future meeting.

Limbo

Please reply to your statement that the Church never did take an official position on limbo when the *Baltimore Catechism* stated that limbo was a place that unbaptized persons went to upon death. Limbo, states the catechism, is just like heaven except that a person will never see God. — *Jim Ostrom, Wahpeton, N. Dak.*

Limbo is the name given the place where the dead go who are not in heaven, hell, or purgatory. Neither revelation nor the earliest Christian tradition treats this subject. St. Augustine put forth the belief that children who die without baptism are condemned to the real (but mitigated) pains of hell. This teaching was tempered by St. Anselm of Canterbury and after him the Scholastics to the effect that although such children were deprived of eternal beatitude, they existed in a place or state of their own, namely limbo (the edge). The *Baltimore Catechism* follows this opinion. The Church has never defined this matter nor has a conclusion on it come from any council. The nearest to it came in a letter to the Armenians (1321) wherein it was stated: "It (the Roman Church) teaches . . . that the souls . . . of those who die in mortal sin, or with only original sin, descend immediately into hell; however, to be punished with different penalties and in different places." The matter is still discussed and argued today, but catechesis over the centuries and substantial theological tradition have posited a place called limbo, and weight has to be given to this history. While there is no definite doctrine of faith in this matter, parents who lose children before baptism should be encouraged to put their trust in a loving God who wishes salvation for all and whose grace knows no limits.

Living Will

Are Catholics permitted to make a "living will"? I feel rather strongly about not having life-sustaining machines and medicines when the brain is dead and it is only a matter of time. I've heard it is to make death easier and to allow death with dignity. Who says death should be easy or with dignity? Jesus Christ did not have such a death. — *Mrs. Rosemary Heckman, Cincinnati, Ohio*

You have to be careful using such terms as "living will" and "death with dignity." These are phrases coined by euthanasia adherents to promote their philosophy of death. Only the living can make a will and most people want to die with some sort of human dignity. Also, a will that is opened after death will have no bearing on what happens before death. If you have wishes regarding a final illness or a funeral, these should be communicated to the person or persons who will arrange the event and who will act in your name. While Catholic morality teaches that we must use ordinary means to prolong life, we are not obliged to use extraordinary means. These latter include those that involve extreme difficulty as regards pain, expense, or other factors, or those that do not offer reasonable hope for recovery. Ordinary means include proper care and nourishment of the body, usual remedies in case of sickness and illness, and ordinary medical attention when needed.

Lord's Prayer

In the Lord's Prayer the petition "lead us not into temptation" puzzles me. It is difficult for me to conceive how God would lead one into temptation. — *Theresa A. Surovek, Hammond, Ind.*

This petition does not refer to our daily encounter with evil or God leading us into this type of temptation. Many Scripture scholars prefer the translation "lead us not into the trial" as being more accurate, pointing out that the temptation meant is the great eschatological test (Matthew 24:22) that Jesus predicted, one that no one could bear unless it was shortened. The prayer is a plea to spare us from this trial that St. Paul calls "the wrath to come" (1 Thessalonians 1:10).

Lutherans

As a member of the Lutheran Church, I was most pleased to read that officials of the Catholic Church celebrated with Lutherans the birth of Martin Luther. These officials have agreed on numerous beliefs and traditions that to a point separated us. Do Catholics want Lutherans? How readily can they accept one another and on what terms? Is real unity possible? — *Jeff Schlieman, Yakima, Wash.*

Unity is always possible where there is good will and understanding. Vatican Council II echoed Christ's prayer that all his followers might be one. The council committed the Church to ecumenical efforts. As a result dialogue has been established between competent experts from different churches, common Christian projects have been undertaken, and there has been a coming together for common prayer where this is allowed. The Catholic-Lutheran dialogue has been going on for many years, and substantial points of agreement have been reached. Most important, bitterness has been removed and in its place has come respect. However, there is a long and difficult way to go before total unity comes. We can imagine this difficulty when we realize that even among Lutherans themselves not all divisions have been healed. However, both Catholics and Lutherans can commit themselves to prayer for unity, good will, and mutual respect.

Magnificat

Is there an official Church position on the source of the Magnificat in Luke 1:46-55? — *Joseph A. Jordan, Black Canyon City, Ariz.*

I don't know what you mean by an official Church position on the source. As you indicate, the Magnificat source is Luke. This is an official prayer of the Church, said daily by every Latin Rite priest as part of evening prayer (Vespers). If you are actually wondering what source Mary used, it was the Old Testament and shows her familiarity with Scripture. The Magnificat is made up of phrases borrowed from Isaiah, Malachi, Jeremiah, Exodus, etc. There are some Scripture scholars who believe that the Magnificat really belongs to Elizabeth. They cite several manuscripts which state (verse 46) "And Elizabeth said," in place of "And Mary said." They also cite the similarity of the Magnificat to the Canticle of Hannah (1 Samuel 2:1-10), suggesting Elizabeth, as both Hannah and Elizabeth were aged and barren. However, the manuscripts approved by the Church attribute the prayer to Mary, and both Western and Eastern Christendom have traditionally affirmed her authorship. Moreover, it has a completely different character than Elizabeth's immediate prior speech greeting Mary.

March of Dimes

The March of Dimes gives money to develop and support programs of amniocentesis, which leads to abortion. Shouldn't Catholics be told not to support the March of Dimes? — *Name withheld, Chicago, Ill.*

Amniocentesis is a diagnostic procedure in which some fluid is drawn from the sac containing the unborn child and analyzed for diseases such as sickle-cell anemia, Cooley's anemia, and Rh factor, as well as other defects. In itself it is a neutral procedure that enables the doctor to offer prenatal control if disease is found, enables medical treatment to begin before birth or at birth, and enables a family to adjust to an adverse situation. It is true that this knowledge can be abused and parents can make a decision to abort a defective fetus, but this is not the purpose of amniocentesis. The March of Dimes has stated over the years that its purpose is solely to sponsor medical research on birth defects. Some pro-lifers want the organization to take a positive stand against abortion, and the reply of the March of Dimes people is that this is beyond the organization's purpose.

Maronite Rite

What is the Maronite Rite? How is it different from other Roman Catholics? Can one easily move from one to another? — Name withheld, Richmond, Va.

The Maronite Rite is one of the branches of the Eastern Church that differs from the West in language, calendar, and liturgical celebration. The Maronites are part of the Antiochene Rite, which devolved from the liturgy of St. James of Jerusalem. This particular rite was founded by St. Maron and has always been united to the Holy See in Rome. There are almost two million Maronites in jurisdictions in Lebanon, Cyprus, Egypt, Syria, the United States, Brazil, Australia, and Canada. Maronite liturgical languages are Syriac and Arabic. Roman Catholics can legitimately fulfill the Sunday obligation at a Maronite service and when necessary receive Maronite sacraments. One is a member of the rite into which he or she has been baptized. It is not easy to change rites, since the Holy See wishes to protect the integrity of each rite. Canon law allows three ways of changing rites: (1) by application to the Holy See, which can grant permission if the cause is justified; (2) by interritual marriage, when either spouse may transfer to the rite of the other; and (3) by reason of age, that is, children of the first two cases, who are under fourteen years of age, may change rites.

Marriage

My husband and I have always told our children that if they left the Church to marry someone, we would not come to the ceremony or pay for the wedding. Are we wrong? My sister says she could not do that to her children. Should our nephews and nieces expect us to go? — *Name withheld, Springfield, Minn.*

You are perfectly within your rights for the position you have taken. Many people, like yourself, feel that they should not cooperate in the wrongdoings of another. If your nieces and nephews know that this is your position, they should not expect you to attend a wedding outside the Church. Sometimes I think that the position your sister has taken is what leads to trouble. Children get the impression from parents that Church teaching is not important and hence put up little resistance when they are asked to go against it. With the regulations that exist today there is no reason for anyone to be married outside the Church. A dispensation can be obtained to be married in a non-Catholic church by a non-Catholic minister and a Catholic priest can even be present to bless the marriage.

UNWILLING ANNULMENT • My husband got an annulment that I didn't want. That was over a year ago. I didn't sign any papers. I was baptized, raised a Catholic, and received sacramental marriage. Now I have lost all that and I have two children. To me that is like denying our children, as if they were born out of wedlock. I still feel we are married in the eyes of our Lord. We have been divorced over thirty years. Now I feel that I am not worthy to go on with my Catholic faith. — *Name withheld, Fort Wayne, Ind.*

This is a matter you should talk over with your priest, for I have no details on which to make a judgment and I do not know the grounds on which the annulment was obtained by your husband. I can make some general observations. First, even though an annulment was granted, this does not make your children illegitimate. Church law (Canon 1137) provides that children born in a marriage contracted in good faith, though invalidly, are to be considered legitimate. The fact that an annulment was granted to your husband in no way separates either of you from the Church and you should continue to share in the life of the Church. The fact that you have been divorced for thirty years shows that the marriage, for any practical purpose, has long since ended. In an annulment, it is not necessary for both parties to agree or for the nonpetitioning partner to sign papers. What is important are the grounds on which the annulment is based, and there I do not know the circumstances. I advise you to contact a priest familiar with the case.

ANNULMENT REASONS • Please tell me some of the reasons for a marriage annulment. I would like to find out if I am eligible for one. I would like the Lord to give me another chance. I really don't have anyone to talk to about this. — *Name withheld, San Antonio, Fla.*

This is a matter you must discuss with a priest, preferably your pastor. It is a technical matter that will require interviews and cannot be done by mail. What you are speaking about is properly called a decree of nullity, that is, a declaration that no marriage existed in the first place. The decision that what was presumed to be a valid marriage is really invalid is made by the diocesan marriage court. The reason for such a finding is the concealment of a diriment impediment from the beginning, an essential defect in consent, radical incapability for marriage, or a condition placed by one or both parties against the very nature of marriage. In recent years much greater attention is paid to maturity and the psychological state at the time of the original marriage. Since your letter contains no specifics of your own case, I cannot comment specifically. That is why I urge you to see a priest who can go into details and advise you. Once the case goes to the marriage court, there are fees for preparing and organizing testimony, but these fees are modest. There is no fee for discussing this matter with a priest and learning where you stand.

EASY SOLUTION • I have not been to confession in over twenty years, since I have been married twice, both times outside of the Church, divorced once, although my first wife is still living. My question is: Am I qualified for Holy Communion? — *Name withheld, Hyattsville, Md.*

Would that all marriage problems were as simple as yours! Since both of your marriages were outside the Church, in the view of the Church you have never been married. You do not mention if your second wife is still alive, but I am presuming so, and that you are still together. The simplest way to resolve your situation is by having your present marriage blessed. This can be arranged privately without any fuss, if that is what you wish. If, however, your present wife would be opposed to such a ceremony, you can ask for a *sanatio in radice*, which is a dispensation from the impediment of mixed religion and a declaration that the present marriage is to be considered valid from the beginning. Before the marriage ceremony or after receiving the dispensation, you would have to go to confession, after which you would be able to receive Holy Communion and enjoy the full life of the Church. Go to the pastor of the parish in which you live and he will take care of this matter for you. If by chance your second wife should be dead or separated, you can return to the sacraments at once by going to confession.

BASIC VALUES • I am a young Catholic girl about to get married. My parents brought me up to believe that abortion is murder and that using oral contraceptives is a sin. I'm mixed up, now that I have grown up and listened to other Catholic views on these subjects. I'm desperate. — *Name withheld, Elkhart, Ind.*

Your dilemma is that of many young Catholics who have grown up in a society that has become secular and pagan and of Catholics who have often accepted the values of this society rather than those of the Church, which teaches with the authority of God. Abortion is wrong because it is murder. Once the child begins forming in the womb, human life has begun and no one has the right to end it, no matter the popular slogans about women's rights, free choice, etc. Just because we cannot see the baby we kill, murder is not a solution for failed contraception. Oral contraception is wrong because it is sometimes an abortifacient; it is also wrong because it is contrary to the Church's teaching that the sexual act must remain open to human life. Oral contraception prevents this. I do not know if you are taking a marriage preparation course that many parishes now give, but that is the place to bring up these questions. If not, you and your fiancé should sit down with a priest and discuss these problems. Also, you should seek out classes in natural family planning. But a caution. Natural family planning is not a do-it-yourself project. It must be learned through competent instruction if it is to be effective. You are to be congratulated for questioning values contrary to those which you have been taught. Do discuss these matters with a priest.

NO BARRIERS • I was married by a justice of the peace. Some months ago my husband died. What is my position in the Church? I have received Holy Communion several times and am wondering if I am wrong. — *Name withheld, Lafayette, Ind.*

Once your husband died you were free to return to the full life of the Church, including the sacraments of penance and Eucharist. There was nothing wrong in what you did. While you were married outside the Church, there were restrictions on you. But with the end of your civil marriage by the death of your spouse, these no longer applied and the Church regards you as it does any unmarried Catholic.

FAILING MARRIAGE • I am not a Catholic but am married to a fervent one, and after many years of a power struggle between my wife and me I have decided to give up. I have no control over finances (she works, has her own bank account, and does not see the necessity of pooling resources to better use money). There is no "positioning" of children, parents, and husband in her mind. Present canon law gives the wife total control. I have seen much written for the single religious woman but little for the married. — *Name withheld, Sandy, Oreg.*

Something is definitely wrong with the marriage you describe, starting off with a lack of communication. Vatican Council II described marriage as an "unbreakable oneness." It called for "equal and total love" in marriage. While a mixed marriage has inherent difficulties, they can be overcome through mutual love. Someone has given you a bum steer on canon law because there is nothing there that favors a wife over a husband. It is difficult to be specific in your case because I do not have enough facts. One thing I learned years ago is that in marriage problems one should never try to settle them with one party alone, but to only discuss them when both parties are present and each can tell his or her own story. The Church has active programs to help married people, and there is probably a Marriage Encounter group in your area. This organization brings married couples together for a weekend directed by a team of several married couples and a priest for the purpose of developing their abilities to communicate as husband and wife. The National Marriage Encounter office is at 4704 Jamerson Pl., Orlando, FL 32807, and a letter there can tell you what units are in your area. Another organization, called the Cursillo Movement, also has weekend programs for married couples. I would suggest you try to line up a weekend at either one of these. The only other recourse is a Christian marriage counselor, but this can take an extended time and possibly be expensive. I think you want to save your marriage or you would not be writing. Call a parish priest in your wife's parish and see if he can give you information on the above movements.

DIVORCED AND REMARRIED • I would like to know what "a divorced and remarried Catholic" is. Since when is there such a category? "Let no man put asunder" is as plain as you can make it. For whatever reason Catholic couples split up, that is their hang-up. — *Mike Rapchak, Hammond, Ind.*

You are correct in your view of Catholic marriage. Once a legitimate Catholic marriage has taken place and is consummated, no earthly power, including the pope, can dissolve it. However, a couple can be legally married and still not be married in the eyes of the Church (for example, a Catholic who attempts marriage before a justice of the peace). Such a person can get a legal divorce and be remarried in the Church. Also, a marriage that has taken place in the Church can be annulled if the proper conditions are present. A party in such a marriage can get a divorce and remarry. So it is quite possible to be a divorced and remarried Catholic.

RECTIFYING MARRIAGE • I am a woman who has been married almost forty-nine years. I was married outside the Church and into a family that was prejudiced. I have seen to it that my girls were brought up Catholic and all my grandchildren and great grandchildren. I have walked to Mass every Sunday. Do I have to go through a marriage ceremony? If I took Communion would I be a terrible person? — *Name withheld, Long Beach, Calif.*

The Church has a remedy for a situation such as yours and you do not have to go through a marriage ceremony. Go at once to your pastor and tell him you wish to have a *sanatio in radice* ("healing at the root") applied to your marriage, according to Canon 1161. Through this canon a retroactive dispensation is given to your marriage, which makes it valid from the beginning. It takes effect the moment the bishop grants it. Your pastor will prepare the necessary papers to send to the bishop. Once you have received this dispensation you are restored to the full life of the Church.Until that time, however, you may not receive Communion. This, too, is Church law. Incidentally, as regards the dispensation, you do not have to tell your husband you are applying for it. I urge you to do this at once.

RETURN TO CHURCH • Thirty years ago a Catholic friend of mine married a non-Catholic in a civil ceremony. The two children from the marriage were raised secularly. Now my friend would like to attend Mass and other functions but feels she is not allowed to even enter a Catholic church anymore, so she visits a nearby Protestant church for the "comfort" of being able to pray and sing. Please comment. — *Thelma Douglas, Denver, Colo.*

There is no reason why your friend cannot attend Mass and other Catholic ceremonies. You should invite her to go with you to Mass to help ease her return. She should also speak to a priest, either anonymously in confession or even better in a call at the rectory, to find out how she can return to the sacraments. She may be a little nervous about such a visit, but it will be an act of Christian charity on your part to help her and assure her that priests handle such cases frequently and it is his vocation to be of help. Your friend may think she is excommunicated. That was true years ago, but the penalty has since been abolished. It would be a great blessing to her if you could bring her "home." You should also speak to her about having her marriage validated by seeing a priest.

MINISTRY TO DIVORCED • We have a son who was married in the Church and is a practicing Catholic but got divorced about ten years ago. He has not received an annulment from the Church for his marriage, although his former wife did apply for it a year ago. He is planning to get married in June in a civil ceremony. My question is: Will he be excommunicated from the Church or will he still be a Catholic? What will his standing be? — *Name withheld, Fort Wayne, Ind.*

While formerly there was a penalty of excommunication for one who attempted marriage outside the Church, this is no longer in effect, so your son will not be excommunicated but remain a Catholic. However, if he goes through with this civil marriage, he will not be permitted to receive the sacraments of penance and Holy Eucharist. He will be free to attend Mass and take part in other church activities. Also, any children born of such a marriage can be baptized and raised in the Catholic faith. If his wife has not received an answer to her annulment petition by now, it could be coming at any time and if it is granted he would be free to marry. Most parishes today have a ministry for the divorced and separated, and you should encourage your son to look into this. Pope John Paul II addressed this growing problem in his apostolic letter on the Christian family. He commanded pastors and Catholics: "Help the divorced with solicitous care to make sure that they do not consider themselves as separated from the Church, for as baptized persons they can and must share in her life. They should be encouraged to listen to the Word of God, to attend the Sacrifice of the Mass, to persevere in prayer, to contribute to works of charity and to community efforts of justice, to bring up their children in the Christian faith, to cultivate the spirit and practice of penance and thus implore, day by day, God's grace."

FORCED MARRIAGE • I hope you can explain what the Catholic Church can do regarding my problem. My fifteen-year-old daughter is pregnant by a seventeen-year-old boy. Both are Catholics. The father of the boy will not sign for his son to marry because he says the boy is not capable of taking care of himself, let alone a baby. He mentioned giving up the baby for adoption, which is out of the question for us. The father is supposed to be a devout Catholic, which really surprises me. Will the Catholic Church marry them when the time comes and can she have the baby baptized if she doesn't get married right away? — *Name withheld, Indianapolis, Ind.*

Your daughter and her boyfriend are of canonical age and therefore can be married in the Church, provided civil requirements are met. Also, the baby not only can be baptized but should be baptized as soon as possible. Parishes now require some prebaptismal instruction, so you should contact your pastor and make the necessary arrangements, even before the child is born. I would not condemn the boy's father. He may know his son and be acting prudently. In cases such as this, it is very easy to fall into a second mistake by a premature marriage. The divorce rate for teenage marriage is exceptionally high and that of "forced" marriages even higher. You and your daughter should talk the whole matter over with your pastor. He is experienced in such cases. You are to be congratulated on wanting to keep and raise the child and for avoiding the terrible solution of abortion. God will bless you for these decisions. There may be some difficult days ahead, but with God's help you will get through them. Do see your pastor and follow his advice.

Martyrs

I believe that you are mistaken in your answer that an intelligent decision is necessary for one to be a martyr. In the liturgy, the Holy Innocents are considered martyrs, and this has been taught for years. Your answer is confusing. — *Thaddeus J. Kozicki, Jr., El Dorado, Kans.*

The term martyr comes from the Greek meaning "witness" and was so used in the very early Church. However, the term came to mean, in succeeding centuries, one who voluntarily suffers death because of his beliefs. It is in this sense that the term is used today and the word "voluntarily" presupposes an act of the will that was not present with the Holy Innocents, whom the Church regards as martyrs. There are a number of reasons given for this. Because these children died in the place of Jesus, they were given special consideration. A few theologians have speculated that the use of their free will was accelerated, but St. Thomas Aquinas disagrees with this conclusion and says in the *Summa*, that "it is better to say that these children in being slain obtained by God's grace the glory of martyrdom which others acquire by their own will." Thus Thomas looks upon the Holy Innocents as an exception to the general rule.

Mary

I know we adore God, but do we adore Mary? — *Name withheld, Greenville, Pa.*

Adoration is an act of honor due only to God. To adore any other than God would be idolatry and a serious sin against the First Commandment. We venerate (or respect) Mary and the saints because of their service to God. The greatest regard we can show for Mary and the saints is to imitate the virtues that made them holy. Theologically, the terms used for the reverence given God and the saints are "latria," "dulia," and "hyperdulia." Latria is the worship given only to God, dulia is the veneration and homage given to saints, and hyperdulia is the greater reverence paid to Mary because she is the Mother of Jesus.

MOTHER OF GOD • In saying the Hail Mary I cannot reconcile the phrase "Mother of God." Logically, how can she be the Mother of God when she is the Mother of Jesus Christ? God has always been and has no human mother. — *Name withheld, Mishawaka, Ind.*

It is Christian belief that Jesus Christ is God, the Second Person of the Blessed Trinity, and since he is God, Mary, his Mother, is the Mother of God. Jesus taught that he and the Father were one, and he told the apostle Philip that "he who sees me, sees the Father." While the Trinity is a mystery we will never understand, we must believe that each person of the Trinity — Father, Son and Holy Spirit — is the one God, revealed to us by Jesus himself (Matthew 28:19). Mary was the Mother of the Second Person of the Trinity, not the Father or Holy Spirit.

BIOLOGICAL LAW SUSPENDED • Since the only human parent of our Savior was the female one, Mary, why did the Holy Spirit keep Mary's child from being what the biological law of reproduction called for, namely a female? — *Tim Dunn, Baton Rouge, La.*

Biological laws were suspended in the case of Jesus. Biological laws call for a male parent, and scientists tell us that it is the male that determines the sex of the child. Why Jesus was born a male and not a female is something only the providence of God can answer. He was born into a society that was male-dominated. Also, the Scriptures when speaking of the Messiah always spoke of a male. This seems to have been God's plan from the beginning. In Scripture, Adam was created before Eve, and the role of women in the Old Testament (with but a few notable exceptions) was that of support of the man. The fact that Jesus was born as a male is one of the main arguments for a male priesthood.

DIFFERENT FROM VIRGIN BIRTH • What is the difference between the Immaculate Conception and the virgin birth? What is the basis of belief in each? With regard to the Immaculate Conception, are we to think of Mary as "full of grace" from conception, rather than "conceived without original sin" in view of the present understanding of the scriptural Adam and Eve? — *Dorcas Zimmerman, Billings, Mont.*

The Immaculate Conception refers to the fact that Mary was conceived without any attachment to sin, including original sin. The virgin birth refers to the fact that she conceived and

148

birthed Jesus without loss of her virginity. The dogma of the Immaculate Conception was defined as a doctrine necessary for Catholic belief by Pope Pius IX in 1854. It was not based on any scriptural teaching but on the long tradition of the Church, the teaching of theologians, and the fact that it was not contrary to reason but was a truth being revealed to the Church by God. The virgin birth is a truth established in Scripture (Matthew 1:23, etc.). Original sin is a doctrine of the Church and finds its scriptural basis in 1 Corinthians 15:21ff and Romans 5:12ff. I believe by "present understanding" you mean the view of some modernists that there were no such persons as Adam and Eve. This is not the view of the Church nor of Scripture. The Church teaches that Adam and Eve were historical persons, and that some time in the history of the world God infused souls into two creatures who fell from God's grace, and because of this fall all their human progeny shared in this loss of grace. The two great heresies on original sin, taught by Pelagians and the Reformers, still find expression today among some who challenge the teaching of the Church.

EVER-VIRGIN • How can I answer my Protestant friends about Mary being forever a virgin when they quote Matthew 1:18 where it says "before they came together," meaning I suppose that they lived as husband and wife. — *Name withheld, Manhattan, Mont.*

The verse you refer to is rendered in the new Catholic and Protestant versions as: "Now this is how the birth of Jesus came about. When his mother Mary was engaged to Joseph, but before they lived together, she was found with child through the power of the Holy Spirit." Your friends are doing an injustice to Scripture and Jewish custom to read a sexual meaning into these words. It was the Jewish custom that a man and woman who intended to marry were betrothed (engaged) for a period of a year. The Scripture means that a marriage contract had been drawn up between Joseph (or his parents) and the parents of Mary. At the end of the year of espousal the marriage would be accomplished when the groom took the bride to his home. That is what "coming together" means and has nothing to do with sex. The verse you quote should be interpreted along with verse 24, which uses the same expression. When Joseph found that Mary was with child, he intended to end the espousal, until God intervened. So "coming together" means nothing more than the bride going to the groom's home. While this formal act was usually followed by a sexual union of the newly married, this did not occur with

149

Mary, who was already pregnant with the Child Jesus and pledged to virginity.

VISITATION • What is the teaching about Mary and Elizabeth's visit? We know that John was six months older than Jesus. Was Mary with Elizabeth when John was born? Did Mary and her family visit with Elizabeth when the boys were growing up? — *Norma I. Sims, Osterville, Mass.*

All we know definitely is what is contained in Chapter 1 of Luke's Gospel. When Mary learned that Elizabeth was six months with child, she hurried to see her cousin who lived in the hill country near Jerusalem (about a four-day journey). She had a joyous and spiritual meeting with Elizabeth during which Elizabeth prophesied about Jesus and Mary composed her Magnificat. Mary remained with Elizabeth for three months. Anything else is speculation, and although there are apocryphal writings these do not have to be believed. Evidently, Mary had high regard for Elizabeth to make a journey so far and remain so long from home. Since she remained three months, it can be presumed she stayed until John was born. If Mary and Elizabeth were so close it seems probable that she would stop and see her cousin on trips to Jerusalem. Jesus and John probably met before Jesus began his public life because John recognized him when Jesus appeared at the Jordan, and John directed his own disciples to Jesus.

CHILDREN OF MARY • My granddaughter joined a Bible study class at college. I asked her how they explained the quotation that the Blessed Mother had several children. She said: "Could be." I told her they were cousins of the Lord but don't think I impressed her. Is there a better explanation? — *Name withheld, Whitehall, Pa.*

It has been the tradition of the Church from the earliest times that Mary was always a virgin. This teaching was never challenged seriously until the Protestant Reformation. For Catholics, it is basically a matter of faith founded in the teaching of the Church, which cannot teach error. The rationale of this teaching is more complex. While Scripture indicates Mary's perpetual virginity, the fact cannot be proven from Scripture. It is true that Aramaic had no word for "cousin" and the words used in Scripture for brothers and sisters of the Lord can mean sons and daughters of the same parent or varying degrees of blood relationship. Scripture never says that they were sons and daughters of Mary. Protestants say that Scripture calls Jesus the "firstborn" and this means other children. This is also incorrect. The word used here is a technical term for the child that opens the womb and is so used on tombs of women who died during or immediately after their first childbirth. The indication of the Gospels is that Mary had only one son, Jesus. The account of the Finding in the Temple reads naturally of one child of a widow. On the cross Jesus entrusted his mother to John, which would have been unnatural if there were other sons and daughters. For Catholics, however, it is a closed matter. It was defined as an article of faith by the Lateran Council in 649 and is therefore a doctrinal matter to which Catholics must give belief.

Masons

> What is the historical cause for the antagonism between the Catholic Church and Freemasonry? Is it allowable for a Catholic to join the Masons? — *Michael McBride, Orlando, Fla.*

Masonry developed out of the medieval guilds of Europe. The stonemasons who built the great cathedrals of Europe moved from place to place to pursue their trade. To protect their jobs and recognize fellow stonemasons, they devised a system of passwords and signs, and their worksheds were known as lodges. As cathedral-building diminished, these lodges began admitting nonmasons. In time these free masons outnumbered the working masons, and the lodges took a new character that was greatly affected by the ideas put forth in the Enlightenment, a philosophy that exalted Deism and was in opposition to Catholic doctrine. Deism was a naturalist religion that made human reason its mistress and guide. It allowed of no dogma or religion that was not wholly the product of human intelligence. Thus there was a denial of revelation, and Masons defined God as the Great Architect of the Universe. Deism proclaimed universal doctrines to which any Buddhist, Muslim, or Jew could subscribe. This retreat from the Gospels brought it into conflict with Catholicism and led to punitive strictures of Catholics who joined the Masons. While Masonry in the United States was originally that of the Enlightenment to which many of our founding fathers belonged, in time many of the American lodges became more fraternal groups than philosophical advocates. However, even today the Grand Orient and Latin American lodges are strongly anticlerical. This is true of English Masonry and in some American branches, particularly the Scottish Rite, Southern jurisdiction. While American Blue Lodges are not noted for anti-Catholicism and are regarded more as fraternal associations with extensive charities, and because there was a period of confusion about Catholic membership in these lodges during the late 1970s (during which some Catholics in good ecumenical faith joined), the most recent ruling of the Church forbids Catholic membership. This ruling recognizes the fact that the new Code of Canon Law removed direct mention of the Masons and only penalizes those who join an association that "plots against the Church" (Canon 1374). The Congregation for the Doctrine of the Faith declared in 1983 that it would be seriously wrong for Catholics to join the Masons, since the principles on which Masonic associations are founded are irreconcilable with Church teachings. The practical question of what must converts do who are Masons, or what must those who joined during the 1970s in good faith do, does not have a clear solution, but there is a consensus among canonists and moral theologians that those who joined lodges not openly anti-Catholic may continue passive membership as long as they do not take part in internal rituals.

Mass

Is it not official doctrine of the Church that, at the Mass, Christ dies in an unbloody manner and is offered for our sins? I have always been taught that his dying and Holy Communion were the essential parts of the Mass. Please state the canon law number and what its says. — *Nancy Bekeleski, Chicago, Ill.*

It is not correct to say that Christ dies each time Mass is offered. Christ died once and for all time on Calvary. The Mass is offering once again to God that sacrifice. Canon 897 describes the Mass this way: "The Eucharistic Sacrifice [is] the memorial of the death and resurrection of the Lord, in which the sacrifice of the cross is forever perpetuated." The Council of Trent declared: "There is in the Catholic Church a true Sacrifice, the Mass instituted by Jesus Christ. It is the Sacrifice of His Body and Blood, Soul and Divinity, Himself, under the appearances of bread and wine. The Sacrifice is the same as the Sacrifice of the Cross, inasmuch as Christ is the Priest and

Victim in both. A difference lies in the manner of offering, which was bloody on the Cross and is bloodless on the altar." Vatican Council II, in its *Constitution on the Sacred Liturgy*, stated: "At the Last Supper, on the night when He was betrayed, our Savior instituted the Eucharistic Sacrifice of His Body and Blood. He did this in order to perpetuate the sacrifice of the Cross throughout the centuries until He should come again." The Consecration of the Mass is the essential act of sacrificial offering that takes place in the changing of the bread and wine into the body and blood of Christ.

LITURGY VARIATIONS • I have the occasion to go to various parishes and I am shocked to find so many variations in the liturgy. So many priests seem to be doing their own thing. Why doesn't the Church do something about this? — *Name withheld, Largo, Fla.*

A great deal of mail that comes to me contains complaints from the faithful, usually about something specific that some priest is doing. Most of them I do not use here, since there is nothing I can do and I am not the person to whom complaints should be made. The Vatican II document that was the occasion for the renewal of the liturgy gives the rules and specifies very clearly that no priest "may add, remove, or change anything in the liturgy on his own authority" (*Constitution on the Sacred Liturgy*, No. 22, Para. 3). This is a clear and concise directive. That it is often being ignored is obvious, but the person to whom the complaint should be made is the one who is violating it. If this does not correct the matter, the complaint then should be made to his bishop, who is the local custodian of the sacred liturgy. I do think the regulation quoted above should be stressed in seminary training, and that perhaps then new priests entering the ministry can show some who have gone before that the liturgy is an official action of the Church not open to personal whim, and that when a priest or deacon is celebrating the liturgy, he is doing so as an official of the Church and not in his own right. Years ago everything was very precise and the language and actions were the same no matter where one was in the world. Today we have the vernacular, and the introduction and conclusion of the Mass are variable and perhaps this has given the impression to some that they are free to make other changes, but no one has the right to go beyond the rubrics that the Church has specified.

WHAT CANNOT BE MISSED • My question is prompted by what I read in *Our Sunday Visitor*. Father Walter

Burghardt wrote: "If you came to me in confession and said you missed the Liturgy of the Word, I think I'd have to say that you did not hear Mass. So the Liturgy of the Word, including the homily, is an integral part of the Mass." Before Vatican II, when we had a shortened form of the Liturgy of the Word, I don't think the penalty was quite that grievous. — *Name withheld, Aurora, Ill.*

Your understanding is correct, but that was one of the things that liturgical renewal sought to correct. Prior to the council, moral theologians taught that anyone who omitted a notable part of the Mass committed grave sin. The "notable part" was defined in two ways: from the dignity of the parts and from length of time. Thus theologians said anyone who missed the Consecration and Communion did not attend Mass, and anyone who missed a third part of the Mass missed a notable part. One manual I have before me says that missing the beginning of the Mass up to the Offertory exclusively could be considered a slight omission. It should also be noted that theology in those days was more legalistic than it is today. The Vatican II liturgical renewal has changed our outlook. As the *Sacramentary*'s "Structure, Elements, and Parts of the Mass" (No. 7) teaches: "Although the Mass is made up of the liturgy of the word and the liturgy of the eucharist, the two parts are so closely connected as to form one act of worship." Then, in speaking of the Liturgy of the Word, which is called "a principal element of the liturgy," the instruction says: "When the scriptures are read in the church, God himself speaks to his people, and it is Christ, present in his word, who proclaims the Gospel." Hence, I would agree with Father Burghardt whom you cite. The introductory and concluding rites would, in my opinion, be considered in pre-Vatican II terms as "slight omissions" and if unavoidably missed would not compel a person to attend another Mass to fulfill the Sunday obligation.

MASS NOT SYMBOLISM • In a recent response you stated that Jesus took bread and wine and said, "This is my body" and "This is my blood" and that he didn't say they were symbols but meant it literally. This is true. But it is also true that in John 15:5 he says, "I am the vine, you are the branches." He didn't say that was a symbol either, yet we know by common sense that he is not literally a vine. — *Paula F. Criscione, Seattle, Wash.*

Two important points must be remembered when interpreting Scripture. One is to consider the verses being interpreted in their full context and in conjunction with other Scriptures. The second is the understanding of those who heard Christ and the opinion of the Fathers of the early Church who were close to the witnesses (tradition). The Last Supper has to be interpreted in the light of the eucharistic discourse and its consequences in John 6. When the Jews question the literalness of eating the flesh of Jesus and drinking his blood, Jesus reiterates his teaching (verse 53). Even some of his disciples broke away (verse 66) because they could not accept this literal interpretation. St. Paul takes Christ's symbolism or analogy of the vine and branches and develops it into the doctrine of the Mystical Body in 1 Corinthians 12 and elsewhere. It was so understood in the early Church. Moreover, when we read John 15 carefully, we can see that Jesus is using analogy in comparing himself to a vine, his Father to the vinegrower, and ourselves to the branches. Finally, St. Paul and the Fathers stress the importance of the Sunday Eucharist, which clearly shows their understanding of the literalness of Christ's teaching on this subject.

STIPENDS REGULATED • When I request a Mass to be said by the missions for someone deceased or alive, are the benefits the same as if I had requested it to be said by my pastor? The Mass in my parish has but one intention, while I am sure that the missions lump many requests together. — *Carol Fender, Fowler, Ind.*

If a mission society lumps Mass intentions together, it is doing something very illegal. Mass stipends set up a sacred trust between the donor and the acceptor. Canon 948 rules that even if the stipend is very small, a separate Mass must be said for that intention. Because of the nature of the obligation created, canon law has a whole series of laws governing the handling and fulfillment of Mass intentions. The Mass has infinite value because of the nature of the sacrifice, hence all benefits would be the same whether your Mass is offered by a priest in your parish or a priest in Africa. The advantage of a Mass in your parish is that you know when it will be said and you can be present. The advantage of a Mass said in the missions is that your stipend is helping to support a missioner who needs it because he gets few intentions. Of course, it is possible that some unscrupulous operator might lump intentions together, but in doing so he would be in grave violation of a serious law. However, I would think this to be remote. Canon law requires that the priest accept only one stipend Mass a day (except for Christmas) because the Church wishes to avoid any trafficking in Masses or appearance of commercialism. Canon law also requires that when a person gives a sum of money with a general request, "Say some Masses for my intention," the number of Masses are to be decided according to the local stipend offering. Thus, if such a request was accompanied by twenty-five dollars and the local offering was five dollars, the priest would be obliged to offer five Masses (Canon 950). A priest can refuse to accept a Mass intention, but once he does accept, he must then fulfill it according to the intention of the donor.

> **MORTAL SIN TO MISS MASS?** • Since Vatican II, is it still taught in seminaries and to the laity that it is "a mortal sin" to miss Mass on Sunday (or Saturday evening) for trivial reasons such as: I'm too busy, not in the mood, too tired, have company, etc.? I don't need qualifications or explanations, just "yes" or "no." — *Ada L. Baumgartner, Raytown, Mo.*

Like it or not, this is not a question any priest can answer "yes" or "no." If I were in a court of law and forced to make a direct response, I would have to say "yes," but that would not necessarily be correct. Sin has two dimensions, objective and subjective, and that is why a priest sits in the confessional: to judge. Objectively, through the power of the keys, the Church can bind. It does so in the matter of Sunday Mass and makes this a serious (mortal) obligation. Therefore, missing Sunday Mass is objectively a mortal sin. However, a subjective judgment must also be made both by the person and by the confessor. Were all the conditions for committing a mortal sin present? Were there any compensating reasons? Under ordinary circumstances the reasons you give in your letter would not be compensating. However, even here, a judgment must be made. A doctor or a nurse working on accident victims would have an obligation to continue that work even if it caused him or her to miss Mass. A wife who had housework to do would not be so excused. Many people have a misformed conscience about this obligation, which must be corrected but which also must be taken into account. People want black and white answers about sin, but in reality sin exists in all shades of gray.

> **READINGS IMPORTANT** • Our parish bulletin had this to say: "We are instructing the ushers not to seat any persons during the proclamation of the Scripture reading. The word of God is as important as the eucharistic prayer." Surely the Church is not going to tell us that the Consecration is not better than the readings. You can't

have a valid Mass without the Consecration. — *John N. Igo, San Antonio, Tex.*

I sympathize with what your pastor is attempting to do, but I would have phrased it a bit different. The instruction in the *Roman Missal* tells us that the Mass is made up of two parts, the Liturgy of the Word and the Liturgy of the Eucharist. They are so closely connected with each other that they constitute one act of worship. When the Sacred Scriptures are read, God himself is speaking to his people. The instruction calls the readings "among the most important elements in the liturgy." It refers to the eucharistic prayer as the "most important," and "the heart of the Eucharistic celebration." The Mass is not to be seen as a series of acts but as a whole. Since the Liturgy of the Word is so important a part, your pastor wants all the people present and seated. I feel sure he would agree with what I have written.

VENIAL SINS FORGIVEN • During the Penitential Rite at Mass the priest says, "May Almighty God have mercy on us, forgive us our sins, and bring us to everlasting life." Is this an actual absolution, the same as if he were to use the formula for private confession: "I absolve you from your sins, etc."? Having received the communal absolution, can we receive Holy Communion again if we don't go to private confession and confess our mortal sins? Why do we seldom hear our priests encouraging us to go to confession? And why don't they encourage us to pray? — *Name withheld, Laurel, Md.*

The Penitential Rite is an acknowledgment by members of the community of their sinfulness and their need for God's forgiveness. It is not the rite of reconciliation (confession). It is the general teaching that through the Penitential Rite *venial* sins are forgiven, not mortal sins, which must be confessed. There is no communal absolution given in this rite; it is a prayer for mercy. We can always receive Communion as long as we are not in the state of mortal sin. I do not know why we do not hear more on the need for reconciliation and the nature of the sacrament of penance. I personally believe an extensive catechesis is needed on this subject. I think priests often encourage their people to pray, but again I believe we need some good homilies, frequently repeated, on the nature and purposes of prayer. Too much prayer is "gimme" prayer and not enough adoration and reparation.

DRESS FOR MASS • What do you think of the habit of some parishioners, usually young men and women, of attending Mass wearing shorts? And I mean short shorts. I know this is not the norm because I only see two at a Sunday Mass, so evidently the majority show reverence for our Lord. Is this prevalent throughout the country? — *Robert P. Groves, La Mesa, Calif.*

Just as it is not prevalent in your parish, it is not prevalent throughout the country. Sometimes at resorts and beaches you find people dressing more informally than they would at home. Most people still "dress up" for church. In almost any crowd you will find a few with bizarre sartorial styles. I don't think the few people in your parish who come in shorts mean disrespect for the Lord. They simply have poor taste and sense of place.

BYZANTINE RITE FULFILLS OBLIGATION • I find myself in a city where there is both a Latin Rite and Byzantine (Catholic) Rite church. As a Latin Rite Catholic am I obliged to go to the Latin Rite church on a day of obligation? — *Ward J. Kanouse, Ludington, Mich.*

You would be fulfilling your obligation by attending the Byzantine Mass. Under ordinary circumstances one should attend Mass in one's own rite and one's own parish; however, the obligation can be fulfilled in either rite.

VALID FORM • I just can't go to Mass anymore and go to Communion because the priest does not say the Consecration words he is supposed to. I approached him and he said that as long as you say, "This is my body. This is my blood," all is okay. All my life I have believed that the priest must say the exact words of Consecration or the Consecration does not take place. — *Name withheld, Terre Haute, Ind.*

For the Mass to be valid, the priest must say the exact words of Consecration approved by the Church. These are printed in the *Sacramentary* in large type. For the bread: "Take this all of you, and eat it: this is my body which will be given up for you." For the wine: "Take this, all of you, and drink from it: this is the cup of my blood, the blood of the new and everlasting covenant. It will be shed for you and for all so that sins may be forgiven. Do this in memory of me." Some theologians hold that a slight change, such as forgetting a word or inverting a phrase, would not invalidate the Mass, although it would be illicit. I know of no one who would hold that retaining only the eight words you mentioned and supplying other words is not invalid. The third instruction on the *Constitution on the Sacred Liturgy* says specifically: "The liturgical texts composed by the Church also deserve the greatest respect. No one on his own authority may make changes, substitutions, additions or deletions in them. . . . This rule applies to the *Ordo Missae.*"

Masturbation

I thought all this nonsense about masturbation had been laid to rest years ago. Now as the result of a Vatican statement it looks as if everyone will be made to feel guilty over hormonal surges that he or she cannot control. Everyone masturbates at one time or another. It is a simple answer to a real physical and emotional need. — *Name withheld, North Branch, N.Y.*

You state your case strongly in modern terminology, but I must disagree with the humanistic approach of your letter. It is the teaching of the Church that every act of masturbation is gravely sinful in itself as an act of self-centeredness that is an aberration of God's plan for human sexuality. I also strongly disagree with your statement that these urges cannot be controlled. Any confessor has ample experience to the contrary of people who lead chaste lives. The Vatican's statement on sexual ethics tells us: "The traditional teaching of the Catholic Church that masturbation is gravely sinful is frequently doubted nowadays, if not expressly denied. It is claimed that psychology and sociology show that, especially in adolescents, it is a normal concomitant towards sexual maturity and for this reason no grave fault is involved. . . . This opinion, however, is contrary to both the teaching and pastoral practice of the Church." The statement concludes: "Masturbation is an intrinsically and gravely disordered action." The arguments are based on the Church's consistent teaching that any use of the sexual faculty outside of marriage is wrong. Your argument that "hormonal surges . . . cannot be controlled" is a denial of free will and contrary to pastoral experience. It is true that the sexual urge is strong, particularly in adolescents, but to say that it can't be controlled is to reduce man to the level of an animal without reason. It is also true that in the amoral world in which we live, our young people are subject to many sexual pressures through peers, television, movies, songs, etc. But Christ foresaw this when he said that the Christian could not be part of the world. Christianity is a way of life, not a Sunday morning diversion. To live as a Christian is to strive always to overcome the temptations of the world, the flesh, and the devil. Christ knew it would not be easy and for this reason gave us the sacraments and a life of grace. Unfortunately, too few Christians understand this and give themselves over to the philosophy of the world: The easiest way to get rid of a temptation is to give in to it. We have lost the sense of God, vice has become commercialized, and chastity is scorned. I suggest that you read 1 Thessalonians 4:3-8 and Ephesians 5:3-8 to learn what St. Paul said on this subject. To obtain the full discussion of the Church's position on this and other sexual matters you might read the documents *Declaration on Certain Problems of Sexual Ethics* and *Human Sexuality*, which can be found in the documents of the Second Vatican Council.

Medjugorje

I have more than an impression from reading your answers that you are opposed to our Lady's message at Medjugorje. How can a priest stand in opposition to the Mother of God? I will pray for you. — *Kathleen Kelley, Chicago, Ill.*

I am not in opposition to Mary and her messages. However, regarding Medjugorje I have counseled caution until the Church makes a definite pronouncement on the validity of what is going on there. Until that time, Catholics should respect the wishes of the bishop of the diocese who is the lawful authority. He asked for a cessation of pilgrimages; he asked that priests not bring groups there, and that priests refrain from saying Mass there — all of which are ignored. Claims about apparitions of the Virgin Mary are coming from many parts of the world, both outside and behind the Iron Curtain. Some of these are obviously spurious, some may be genuine; but this is a decision Church authority must make. There was a woman in Italy who claimed Mary told her that on a certain date the sun would dance around the sky and at night Mary would write a message across the skies. An estimated one hundred thousand people turned out to see the phenomenon, but nothing happened. That woman was not only discredited, but her pastor, who supported her, was removed. There are all kinds of self-appointed seers both here and abroad, and prudence alone advises caution. It took thirteen years for the message of Fátima to be approved, and since the visitations of Mary are claimed to be continuing in Medjugorje, the Church will probably not take final action until told that these apparitions have ended. There are many good things about the Medjugorje events, a few disturbing. All I have ever said is that we should withhold final decision until the Church renders a verdict and that in the meantime we should obey legitimately appointed authority. I do not believe the Mother of God would find that advice defective. Mary's advice to the wine stewards at Cana about Jesus, "Do whatever he tells you," is the same advice she would give about Jesus' Church: "Do whatever it tells you."

Mexico

Although I have been in the United States many years, I am from Mexico. Our church building back home has not been totally finished. I believe I'll get some money from a sale of a piece of land and I'd like to do something for the church, like a nice altar. I just learned that the churches in Mexico belong to the federal government. What does this mean for us Catholics? Does it mean that if the government in Mexico decides to take a church building, it will do so? What can we do about it?
— *Baldomesa Gómez, Long Beach, Calif.*

The Mexican Constitution of 1917 completely severed the relations between church and state and made the Catholic Church a nonentity. Priests are prohibited from conducting schools; religious processions and religious acts outside the church are forbidden; the Church and all religious organizations are forbidden to hold property; priests lose political rights and exercise of citizenship; and all buildings that housed institutions of the Church are declared the property of the state. These and other discriminatory articles are still part of Mexican law. In recent years there has been some relaxation of hostility against the Church, and today the laws are interpreted mildly (although they could all be enforced strictly at any time). There is little that we can do in this country. It is up to the Mexican people to change these laws.

Miracles

In a book by Rev. Charles Mortimer Carty a paragraph reads: "A miracle to be accepted by the Church must be instantaneous, such as: to resuscitate a corpse, to cure a sickness on the spot, to restore a missing limb. . . ." Has the restoring of a missing limb ever been recorded by the Church? If so, when and where and by whom? Where can I look up this information? — *Ellis O. Fortune, Waco, Tex.*

Your question should properly go to the publisher of the book. I know of no case where a missing limb was restored to someone, although I don't deny the possibility that some saint might be reputed to have done so. The nearest thing that comes to mind is the incident in Luke 22:51, in which Christ restored the ear Peter had cut off one of the men who had come to arrest Jesus. A number of saints are reputed to have restored life to the dead, but these cases were not subjected to the scientific scrutiny that could be done today. Moreover, I do not agree with the Carty definition. A miracle is an observable effect in the moral or physical order that is in contravention to natural laws and that cannot be explained by any natural power but only by the power of God. It is opposed to the law of nature for one dead to be restored to life, to walk upon water, to be in two places at once. It is opposed to the law of nature to make a sudden and immediate cure without medical care. The Church admits a miracle only when every natural explanation has been exhausted. Then there are miracles of grace in which God operates in an unusual way to make a conversion. While not miracles in the literal sense, these remarkable changes in a soul can only be attributed to God.

Morality

A lot of young priests will say there is no absolute wrong or right. It is just as though you are half wrong and half right. Am I not right in saying that as a Catholic you are either wrong or right? — *Name withheld, Dundas, Iowa*

The answer to your question is yes and no, which brings us back to your original problem of absolute right and wrong. It would be simple if everything was black and white, but that is not the way things are and why a priest must be a judge in the confessional. Truth is of two kinds: objective, that is, what it really is in fact; and subjective, how a person perceives that truth. Therefore, in making a judgment, a spiritual adviser or confessor must determine the subjective state of a person. For example, many young people have been taught that it is not a serious sin to miss Mass and as a result have stopped going. This attitude objectively becomes seriously sinful, since it violates both divine and Church law. However, subjectively there may be no sin present at all because the individuals involved believe what they were taught. What must be done in such cases is to show how such an attitude violates the First and Third Commandments of God and the first precept of the Roman Rite ("Assist at Mass on Sundays and holy days of obligation"); it must be stressed that both God and the Church expect these commandments to oblige gravely. What the confessor must do is lead the person from the subjective misapprehension to the objective truth. One of the difficulties in a column like this, where answers must be short, is in always making the distinctions. When people ask a question it is presumed an objective answer is wanted, yet at the same time it is realized that the objective or actual truth may not always correspond to the subjective state of the questioner.

Mormons

Our daughter and her children have joined the Mormon Church and we are sick about it. If they ever want to come back to the Catholic Church can they? I have always heard the Mormon Church is just another cult. Is this true? Can you tell me why it is not considered a Christian religion? — *Name withheld, Deer River, Minn.*

Mormonism is a very missionary-oriented religion that attracts many by its strong family concerns, its internal fellowship, and its convincing sense of purpose. Few people who join are competent to examine its doctrines. The Church of Jesus Christ of Latter Day Saints was begun by Joseph Smith, a farm laborer in New York state. He claimed he had a revelation through the angel Moroni to establish a church. The result is a confusion of spiritualism, materialism, Freemasonry, Judaism, Protestantism, etc. Some of the Mormons' claims include: God the Father is a material being, a perfect man, and a polygamist. God did not create matter; he organized it.

Christ, after his resurrection, set up his church in North America among the Indians who were remnants of the lost tribes of Israel. God the Father procreated many souls destined to be gods after they received Mormon baptism. In addition, the Mormons teach, "What man is now, God once was; what God is now, man may become." The Mormons have one doctrine that they preach, and another that they explain to initiates. Doctrines are subject to change (the practice of polygamy, the barring of blacks from Mormon priesthood). Mormons are distinguished by large families, a church-related social life, a high esteem of education, love of culture and music. Smoking and drinking alcoholic beverages are prohibited; so is the use of coffee and tea. Mormons pay tithes to the church, which also engages in profitable business enterprises. Mormons, while insisting on strong centralism in authority, have had divisions and schisms, and have had some dark spots in their history (the Danites, the Mountain Meadow Massacre, blood atonement). However, through strong propaganda and missionary activity, the sect is experiencing rapid growth throughout the world. Despite the fact that it proclaims itself the only true Christian church on earth, Mormonism, because of its syncretism of doctrine and confusion as to the person of Christ, cannot in the strict sense of other Christian denominations be called Christian at all. Converted Mormons do leave the church and some have entered or come back to the Catholic Church. Your daughter and her children could do so.

Mystical Body

I am disturbed when I hear Catholics say, "We are the Church." Is this theologically correct? I have always been taught that the entire Church on earth is the Mystical Body of Christ. Christ is the head of this body, the Holy Spirit is its soul, and the faithful its members. — *Gene Dougherty, Biloxi, Miss.*

The faithful are not the Church in themselves, only part of the Church. I think what you hear has come about by misunderstanding the Second Vatican Council's reference to the laity as the "People of God." Your understanding of the Mystical Body is accurate. However, the Church is somewhat different. The Church consists of three parts: the Church Triumphant (all those in heaven), the Church Militant (those on earth), and the Church Suffering (souls in purgatory). There is also a juridic way of looking at the Church in which there is a hierarchy of persons: pope, bishops, priests, deacons, religious, laity. Moreover, there are other ways of looking at the Church, but in none of them can the laity say that they are solely the Church any more than can the pope say he is the Church or priests say they are the Church.

Novenas

From time to time some Catholic newspapers carry very short novenas in which Catholics are asked to say the novena nine times a day for nine days and the favor they request will be granted. What is your opinion on that type of novena? — *Name withheld, Los Angeles, Calif.*

While it is good to pray and pray often, no novena can assure a particular result and to do so is presumption. I believe a great deal of superstition is involved in the type of ads you mention. I have no difficulty in urging people to pray to a particular saint or for a particular reason, but often these suggestions are surrounded by promises that I find offensive to God's liberty and providence. I think some Catholic newspapers should be more discriminating in what they allow to be advertised.

Occasion of Sin

I'm sixteen and, like a lot of adolescents, I have a crush on someone. Is a crush sinful? I know that dreamed-up sexual orgies are sinful, but what about other thoughts — a kiss, an embrace, or other things that seem harmless? — *Name withheld, Lockeford, Calif.*

No, a crush is not sinful. It is something natural that most people begin to experience about your age. It is God's way of telling you that you are getting to that age when marriage becomes possible. Neither are thoughts about a kiss or an embrace sinful, as long as they are not deliberately done to arouse the passions. However, thoughts are powerful and develop rapidly and can lead to trouble. That is why the Church teaches us to avoid the occasions of sin, which are not necessarily sins in themselves but can lead us that way. Keep a wholesome outlook on life, trust God, and do not worry over things that arise spontaneously.

Occult

I have noticed that the occult is very big and information on it easy to get. How does the Church feel in such matters, and as Christians what can we do about it? — *Joseph J. Zegzdryn, Camp Lejeune, N.C.*

Following the occult is a form of superstition, which in itself is wrong because it assigns to creatures or things power that belongs solely to God. There exists in many people a strong desire to explain the baffling mysteries of life, to escape life's insecurities and anxieties, and to control one's destiny. Because such control is beyond one's abilities, some people turn to the occult as an answer to their problems, thus failing in either belief in or trust in God. The Bible — both Old and New Testaments — is strong in its condemnation of occultism and superstition. The occult is a natural preying place for Satan because in entering the occult, people have already taken the first step away from God. The devil, who is the Father of Lies, uses the occult to increase his hold upon people and perpetuate evil in the world. The sacrifice of Christ accomplished the liberation of mankind from all principalities and powers, and the devil is exorcised in baptism. Therefore, it is gravely sinful for a person to create a situation where Satan can regain his power over an individual. As Christians we have the obligation to educate ourselves to the nature of Christian life and to develop our faith so that it is strong enough to endure fear and doubt, and to remain true to the belief that our salvation comes solely through Jesus Christ.

Organ Donations

Is it okay for a Catholic to donate his body to science? I understand after use the remains are cremated. — *Name withheld, Elmhurst, N.Y.*

One may donate his or her body to scientific research, provided the remains are treated with reverence. The ad you enclosed with your question is from a New York teaching hospital, and I presume the body is dissected and the organs studied. The advancement of scientific knowledge that can improve health is a valid reason. However, I personally believe it is much more useful to donate one's organs to organ banks that can give life and health to specific individuals in need. Organs removed at death — corneas, kidneys, the heart and liver — can make a great difference to those in need of them. This seems to me to be more laudable than having the body dissected to show students what a heart or liver looks like. I suppose some people give a body to a teaching hospital to avoid the cost of a funeral, but I still recommend organ donation.

Original Sin

My question is on original sin. I was taught that it is the stain of our first parents' sin. I was taught that I had this sin on me until I was baptized. Now I am going to an "information class" and I am being taught that original sin is a break in the love relationship I could have had if it were not for Adam's sin. Could you clear this up? — Leroy W. Stotle, Joseph, Oreg.

Original sin is the actual sin of Adam (Genesis 2:8 — 3:24), which was personal to him and which was passed on to all his descendants as a deprivation of grace. The basis for the teaching on original sin is scriptural (for example, Romans 5:12-19, 1 Corinthians 15:21ff). The effect of original sin on each of us is that we are born without sanctifying grace and without the special gifts that go with that grace. The spiritual life of sanctifying grace is restored to us through baptism. What you were taught is not incorrect nor is what you are being taught now. The life of sanctifying grace might be called a love relationship with God that can be broken by sin. However, we must be careful to interpret this correctly. God loves us, even when we sin against him. It is we who break the relationship, preferring the sinful act to God. In the case of original sin, we inherited this break from Adam.

Orthodox

Would you please inform me as to what the basic truths are in the Greek Orthodox Church that differ from the

Roman Catholic Church? Would members of either Church be fulfilling their Sunday obligation by attending one another's liturgy? Are members from both churches permitted to partake of the Eucharist at such a liturgy? — *Sister Mary Justus, Milwaukee, Wis.*

The main difference is on the primacy of the papacy. The Orthodox seem willing to concede the pope a primacy of honor but not jurisdiction. There are some other differences, such as the Orthodox permitting divorce for reasons of adultery. Under ordinary circumstances Sunday obligation cannot be fulfilled by attending the other's liturgy. Both churches forbid intercommunion, which is regarded as a sign of total unity. On one of his trips Pope John Paul II attended an Orthodox liturgy but did not participate in the Eucharist.

EXCOMMUNICATIONS LIFTED • In 1965 Pope Paul VI lifted the excommunication of a Greek Orthodox patriarch who was excommunicated about one thousand years ago. What was the name of the patriarch? On what month and day did Pope Paul do this act of good will? — *Dionisio Berrios, Grand Rapids, Mich.*

In 1054 Cardinal Humbert and legates of the Holy See excommunicated Patriarch Michael Cerularius of Constantinople. In return the patriarch and the Synod of Constantinople excommunicated the cardinal and his legates. Thus the break between East and West was made permanent. In a joint ceremony held both in Rome and Istanbul (formerly Constantinople) on December 7, 1965, Pope Paul VI and Patriarch Athenagoras I formally removed these excommunications.

Our Father

Shouldn't the language used in the Mass be modernized? I am thinking of the archaic *King James* English used in the Lord's Prayer: "Who art in heaven . . . hallowed be thy name." — *Name withheld, Champaign, Ill.*

At the time that the Latin of the new liturgy was being translated into English the Committee for English in the Liturgy debated this very point about the Our Father. It was finally decided that because of the great respect that this prayer and the Hail Mary held with the ordinary faithful, it would be too upsetting to change the traditional formulas. There are many who feel as you do and others who disagree strongly. Personally, I like the archaic "thee" and "thou" when referring to God. It sets him above our ordinary language.

DOXOLOGY ENDING • Why isn't it traditional to say the last part of the Our Father ("For thine is the kingdom, the power, and the glory, for ever and ever, Amen") as the prayer is worded in the Gospel of Matthew? I have always used it. Is it improper to do so? — *Joe Kovalioff, Carteret, N.J.*

The doxology you quote is found in some Greek manuscripts but was not in the manuscripts used by St. Jerome in translating the Bible into the Latin *Vulgate*. You will not find those words even in the modern translations, such as the *New American Bible*, because they are not found in what are accepted as the most reliable manuscripts. A somewhat similar doxology is found in the *Didache*, written before the year 100, because Jews ended most prayers with a doxology and this was the custom among some Christian groups. The best opinion is that the words were not those of Jesus but were inserted by a copier and later adopted by the Greeks as part of the Lord's Prayer, a usage adopted more than a thousand years later by Protestant churches. Because of the venerability of these words they were placed in the revised Mass liturgy we now use, but so that they will not be confused with the Our Father they are separated from it by one prayer. I do not find any difficulty in adding this doxology to your Our Father, as it is an ancient ending for any prayer. However, it would not be correct to conclude that these were the actual words of Jesus.

Papacy

I would like to know what procedure is used in the election of a pope. — *Stephen Kelly, Peoria, Ill.*

Upon the death of a pope, all cardinals under the age of eighty are summoned to Rome for a meeting (conclave) that is held between fifteen and twenty days after the death of the pope. This meeting is held in the Vatican behind locked doors and its members are pledged to secrecy. Two votes are taken each morning and afternoon until a candidate receives a two-thirds plus one majority. If the meeting becomes deadlocked, the cardinals can, by unanimous vote, do one of three things: (1) appoint a committee to select the pope, (2) vote to elect by a majority plus one, or (3) select between the two candidates who have received the largest numbers of votes. When the election is completed, the dean of the College of Cardinals asks the one elected if he accepts. If he does so and is already a bishop, he immediately becomes pope and gives the name by which he will be known. If he is not a bishop, he is immediately ordained and accepts the election. The pope is elected for life. If he should resign, the above procedures are followed to elect a successor.

PROTESTANT ACCUSATION • Recently I heard a Protestant theologian on the *John Ankerberg Show* state that there were no popes prior to the Council of Nicaea in A.D. 325. There are two hundred sixty-two popes listed in *The Catholic Encyclopedia*, beginning with St. Peter. It is noted, however, that two are listed for the same period in several instances. Please explain. — *Ernest A. Morgan, Norfolk, Va.*

Some Protestant groups try to claim that the Catholic Church did not exist before 325 or that there were no popes before then. There has been an unbroken series of bishops of Rome from St. Peter to our own time. To deny this is to deny recorded history. It is true that the Church did not exist legally until the fourth century, when it was recognized by Constantine and was able to emerge from the catacombs, but it had been a presence before then, as its list of popes and martyrs can testify. There have been at times two popes, each elected by his own faction. It is the task of historians in such cases to decide who was the true pope and who was the antipope. There have also been other reasons. Pope Martin I was pope from July 649 to his martyr's death on September 16, 655. Because Martin was in exile, Pope Eugene I was elected pope in 654, and thus two popes would be listed for the years 654-655. After Martin's death Pope Eugene continued in office. There is also the case of a pope being deposed and the question of whether his successor was a true pope or antipope. The history of some of the popes of the first millennium is not always clear in deciding who was the legitimate claimant to the chair of Peter.

Parish

We have a number of people from other parishes attending our small debt-free church. This causes a crowding problem and a false urgency to build a bigger church. These outsiders serve on the parish council. Should this be allowed? — *James E. Howrey, Wylie, Tex.*

Since this matter is evidently bothering you, it is really something you should discuss with your pastor. Canon 107 states: "Each person acquires a proper pastor and ordinary through both domicile and quasi-domicile." Domicile, according to Canon 102, is acquired by having a residence where one intends to live. Parishes are territorial divisions within a diocese; thus by living in a certain area one acquires a parish and pastor. One is obligated to support the parish in which one lives. Thus by law, rather than by attraction of a certain church, pastor, or liturgy, one is assigned to a particular parish. However, having said all this, one may attend Mass in a parish or oratory that is not one's own. Because of the easy mobility of Americans, many Catholics do choose a place to partake in the liturgy that may not be theirs by law. This can sometimes create problems when marriages, sick calls, funerals, etc., arise. One's proper pastor does have certain rights. It can also cause friction between parishes and pastors. Nevertheless, one is free to go elsewhere to fulfill the Sunday obligation. Canon 536 speaks of the establishment of parish councils, over which the pastor presides and the members have only a consultative vote. Canon law does not give qualifications for membership, and unless the bishop has laid down parameters, the pastor determines membership. Some canonists in their commentary on this law define membership as "representative members of the parish," but this is not stated in law. The canon does mention that those who share in the pastoral care of the parish should belong to the council by virtue of their office. Frequently such people (director of music, director of religious education, etc.) live outside the parish itself. Thus membership in the council does not have to be limited to the parish itself. Problems such as you have stated should not be left to rankle, and that is why you should talk to your pastor about what bothers you.

Passion

The Lord once said to Catherine of Siena, "All my saints are passionate." The definition of passion: "An intense impulse or longing which leads to physical indulgence; proclivity to sensuality." How can they say Jesus was a lover of chastity when lust, temptation, and sensuality come from God? — *Theresa Garlo, Brooklyn, N.Y.*

There are a half-dozen different meanings to the word "passion" and almost an equal number for "passionate." The student has to find out the sense of the author. St. Catherine used the term in the sense of ardent or as Webster defines it: "Capable of, affected by, or expressing intense feeling: Enthusiastic." The Lord wants us all to be ardent for him. It is incorrect to say that lust, temptation, and sensuality come from God. They arise from our own fallen nature. While God permits these emotions, he does not will them. Only good is the object of God's will.

Peace Greeting

I find the peace greeting at Mass to be very distracting. At a time when we should be preparing to receive our Lord we go through this racket and movement through the congregation and then turn back to the Eucharist. Why can't it come after Communion? — *Martin D. Edger, Clearwater, Fla.*

Of all the letters that come to this column concerning the liturgy, music and the peace greeting receive the most complaints. One of the reasons for the latter is that it has never been properly explained to the people, either historically or theologically. The peace greeting, originally a kiss, extends back to apostolic times — St. Paul and St. Peter mention it in their epistles. It was introduced into the early Mass as a reconciling act in accordance with Christ's admonition in Matthew 5:23-24: "If you bring your gift to the altar and there recall that your brother has anything against you, leave your gift at the altar, go first to be reconciled with your brother, and then come and offer your gift." In the old days the Mass was divided into two parts — the Mass of Catechumens and the Mass of the Faithful. Those preparing for baptism were admitted to the first part but had to leave after the Gospel and homily when the second part began. The Mass of the Faithful began with the kiss of peace, according to the admonition found in Matthew. The Christians made peace among themselves and only after this did the Offertory procession begin. In time this action was moved to where we now find it, as a preparation for Communion. Also, in time it became limited to the ministers at the altar, and then only at a Solemn High Mass. Following Vatican II, the liturgical revision restored it to the people, and while I can see the reasons for its present position, I do think it would be more suitable after the Prayer of the Faithful where it originally was found. I suspect that one of the reasons it fell into disuse among the people was its placement.

Peer Pressure

How does one cope with people who feel they must tell you dirty or off-color jokes? I try to pass them off in a casual manner but become scrupulous and feel I have committed a mortal sin by listening to them. — *Name withheld, Denver, Colo.*

First, objectively I do not think the conditions are present for mortal sin. While sins against chastity are always serious, those against modesty admit venial matter. You do not will the joke to be told to you and would prefer the teller to stop, so full consent of the will is not given. Then the matter is not necessarily grave. However, Jesus tells us that we must be pure in heart; therefore, we must avoid what could be an occasion of sin. One of the most difficult things in life is resisting peer pressure. This is particularly acute in our teens, but it lasts through all ages. We have to be strong enough to let people know that we do not like certain things. The person who tells you such jokes should be informed that you do not appreciate such stories and do not want to hear them.

Penance

I do not know what sins to confess for a good confession. I am a widow and my children are all grown. I attend Mass regularly, observe the holy days, say prayers, observe abstinence, etc. — *Mrs. Floyd Porter, O'Fallon, Ill.*

The only sins we are obliged to confess are grave (mortal) sins that separate us from God's grace. However, we should not look on the sacrament of penance solely as a means of getting rid of punishment due to serious sin. We should approach the sacrament positively, as a way of growing in grace. Confession should be a means of spiritual development, a point at which we pause and check how we are growing in sanctity. We are called by God to be holy. We either work to become saints or must be purified in purgatory, since only the pure can enter heaven. Most people who use the sacrament do not commit grave sins to separate themselves from God; however, many are guilty of deliberate venial faults. In our examination for confession, we look at these faults and try to root them out. Then come sins of frailty — the thoughtless word in anger, the too quick and unkind judgment of another, and so on. We tell these to our confessor. It is not enough, however, to confess, for example, "I was distracted in my prayers." We tell why we were distracted: for example, "I failed to compose myself properly at the beginning." The reason itself will suggest the remedy and the resolution to be taken. Using confession in this manner will keep it from being routine and will enable us to grow in virtue with greater success.

Permanent Deacons

We will soon have in our church two permanent deacons. What will their duties be and how many priestly duties can they perform? — *Frank Bremei, Downey, Calif.*

The permanent diaconate was restored by Vatican Council II and it has been very successful in the United States, which now has more than eight thousand permanent deacons. Ordained deacons are clerics along with priests and bishops. Pope John Paul II, in his visit to the United States, called these deacons "living signs of the servanthood of the Church." They are ordained to serve the People of God in various capacities. The pope told the deacons that their ministry was threefold: a ministry of the word, a ministry of the altar, and a ministry of charity. As ministers of the word, they read the Gospel at Mass (formerly reserved for the priest) and are also allowed to preach the homily. As ministers of the altar, they have a role at Mass, speaking several times to the people; they can baptize and witness marriages; give out ashes on Ash Wednesday; expose the Blessed Sacrament and by right give out Holy Communion, etc. As ministers of charity, their services to the Church vary according to needs — some serve as catechists, some fill official roles in the diocese, some have special ministries to the sick, etc.

ROLE DEFINED • I have heard that a deacon can perform a marriage and read Mass prayers, but he cannot consecrate or hear confessions. Is this true? — *Name withheld, Fowler, Ind.*

Vatican Council II in restoring the permanent diaconate stated in its *Dogmatic Constitution on the Church* (No. 29) that the deacon is ordained to a ministry of service. The council defined his role in these terms: "To administer baptism solemnly, to be custodian and dispenser of the Eucharist, to assist at and bless marriages in the name of the Church, to bring Viaticum to the dying, to read the Sacred Scriptures to the faithful, to instruct and exhort the people, to preside at the worship and prayer of the faithful, to administer sacramentals, to officiate at funeral and burial services." The deacon cannot celebrate Mass or hear confessions, nor can he anoint the sick.

Place of Honor

Since a priest is "another Christ," when he is invited to dinner by a Catholic family, Catholic etiquette requires that he be given the place of honor at the head of the table. Right? — *Donato G. Valente, Buffalo, N.Y.*

I imagine etiquette would require that any guest — priest or otherwise — be given the place of honor. Where that place is depends upon the customs of the family. In most places it would be the right hand of the host.

Porno Phones

What can be done about those porno phone numbers (direct dialing) that are being distributed among the students at school? The phone company knows about them but claims it can't do anything. — *Name withheld, Cincinnati, Ohio*

These are phone numbers that are answered by sultry voices giving a sexual message and attempting to sell pornographic literature. Although the police have received complaints from parents who found themselves charged with a lot of long-distance calls, neither they nor the phone company can legally do anything. It would involve costly First Amendment (free speech) suits. The onus is on the parents who must teach responsibility to their children and establish some controls on telephone use, particularly long-distance calls.

Possession

Would you please enlighten me? Is there really such a thing as being possessed by the devil? The person I am referring to is trying to pray and live normally, but it seems like something has hold of her. She has terrible thoughts just about always. Please advise on what to do. — *Name withheld, Chicago, Ill.*

Yes, one can be possessed by the devil, but such instances are quite rare and exhibit such signs as the use of unknown tongues, making known hidden things, and exhibiting strength completely out of proportion to one's abilities. Also, a person, although not possessed, may be subject to greater temptations by the devil than another. The more probable explanation is psychoneurosis, or what we commonly call an emotional disorder, or nerves. However, this should be determined by someone who is an expert, such as a priest psychologist. What your friend probably needs is some professional counseling and you should encourage her to seek it.

Prayer

I have several questions concerning prayer. I was told in Catholic school that prayers should be said with movements of the lips to obtain the graces they obtain. I am in doubt about this because I have prayed many times mentally. Must one always kneel to recite the Rosary? I sometimes say the Rosary at work but sometimes cannot remember the mystery for the particular day and I use whatever mystery comes to mind. Is my Rosary valid? Must one have the rosary in the hand to benefit from it? — *Carmen J. Lenzo, Gary, Ind.*

While one might tell a child to form prayers with his or her lips because of the difficulty a child has with mental concentration, this advice would not apply to most adults. Mental prayer is a high form of prayer, and contemplation, which is pure mental prayer, is the highest. So you need not pray with your lips, although in some circumstances this helps with concentration. One need not kneel to pray the Rosary. It can be said sitting, standing, walking, or, as many do, in bed. One need not even have beads, although many rosaries have indulgences attached, which are gained when the beads are used. Many people use their fingers to keep count. Also, while certain mysteries are suggested for certain days, one can substitute or change the order. Prayer is raising the heart to God and this can be done in various ways, all of them good. So continue to pray the Rosary without worrying about legalisms.

PRAYER EFFECTIVE • I am disturbed because I read recently that Masses and prayers for the dead are only a pious practice; they cannot help the dead. Are the Masses I have read for my beloved dead for naught? — *Catherine G. McDonald, Gloucester, Mass.*

There is nothing wrong with a pious practice. While prayers for the dead may be called a pious practice, so, too, are the Rosary and the Stations of the Cross. I suppose someone might try to use the term disparagingly, but it literally means a regular work of piety, and that is something good. The Bible tells us (2 Maccabees 12:45-46) that it is a holy and pious thing to pray for the dead. Since God hears every prayer we offer, your own prayers and Masses for the dead have not been wasted.

PRAYING FOR OTHERS • Is it possible for me to offer good deeds and sacrifices to help someone who is living? My friend is mentally ill and hurting deeply. The only way I can help her is by prayer. What is the Church's teaching on this? — *Name withheld, Gary, Ind.*

Yes, you may pray and sacrifice for your friend, asking God to be merciful toward her. There are two Church doctrines that touch on this. The first is the communion of the faithful (saints) wherein all the People of God on earth, in purgatory, and in heaven affect one another by faith, grace, prayer, and good works. The second is the doctrine of the Mystical Body in which we are all united with Christ, and what one does or fails to do affects all members of the body. There are cloistered orders whose members spend their days praying for the needs of others, and certainly other Christians can imitate them. It is a great act of charity to pray and sacrifice for others and you are to be commended for your concern for your friend.

Predestination

This is really a scary question to ask, but it has nagged at me off and on for many years. Since God knows everything from always, doesn't this mean that even before God created a damned soul that he knew it was damned? How could he do such a thing? — *Natalie Anderson, Hollywood, Calif.*

Your question is one that has been asked many times through history. It was the stumbling block for John Calvin, the founder of Swiss Protestantism. Calvin taught absolute predestination of some persons to heaven and others to hell. His elect were incapable of losing grace and those who were destined for hell were going there no matter what they did. His mistake came from the misreading of Romans 8:28-30 when he applied to individuals what Paul was writing of groups. In dealing with this question we must make a distinction between predestination and preknowledge. One of the attributes of God is that he is omniscient, that is, all-knowing. He knows everything that has happened, is happening, will happen. This does not mean that he wills it. He knows people will commit sins that are against his will, yet he allows this to happen because he gave mankind its great gift of free will. He wants us to use that will to choose himself and he is ready to forgive those who depart from his will if they but repent.

Prisons

I have searched the Bible for an answer on how we are to deal with crime as Christians. All I can find is either restitution or retribution as God's way of dealing with crime. I find no mention in the Bible of a prison system.

Is it sinful for a Christian to send someone to prison? — *William Baehr, Valley Park, Mo.*

There are a hundred mentions of prisons and prisoners in the Bible, the first appearing in the Book of Genesis when Potiphar put Joseph in prison (39:20) Prisons have been around almost as long as man. In the days when society was in clans, an offender would be driven out of the clan; this is what we find happening to Cain after his murder of Abel. But as tribal life became more stationary and complex and offenders more numerous, prisons came into being to remove offenders from society. In his servant prophecies, Isaiah sees the servant (Christ) rescuing prisoners from dark dungeons (42:7). Jesus in his parable of the merciless official seems to approve of prisons for injustice (Matthew 18:35). God's justice has also created hell, in which the evil are separated from the rest of humanity. At the same time, Jesus counseled that we should still love those who offend us (Matthew 5:43-44), and in his description of final judgment he made kindness to prisoners a means of salvation. We must also remember God is both a God of justice and mercy. Thus in rendering justice to those who violate the laws of society, we punish them and remove them from society. At the same time we show mercy if there is repentance and reformation (through parole), and always we should treat prisoners with fairness and show them love in the hope that they will change.

Problem of Evil

What part does God play in the deaths of young adults involved in accidents? I belong to a compassionate bereaved parents' group. Some say it is God's will, others that God had nothing to do with it. What is your answer? — *Name withheld, Clawson, Mich.*

This is a complex question involving the problem of evil in the world that has troubled so many humans over the centuries. The psalmist and other biblical minds pondered it and so have many others, but no one has come up with a wholly satisfying answer. It is a spiritual axiom that everything that happens in this world, sin excepted, happens because of the will of God. But we must immediately distinguish between the will of God and the desire of God. God does not desire evil to befall us, but he knows that it will come our way, either through the abuse of free will or the imperfection of human nature. Having established certain laws of nature, God allows them to operate without interference, even though they can bring harm to us by abuse. Take a carload of teenagers, driving home early in the morning after an all-night party. The driver has had too much to drink and as a result he drives too fast, misses a curve, and the car crashes into a tree. God knows this will happen and permits it. But what has really happened is that the driver abused his free will by getting intoxicated, abused it again by driving under the influence, and again by driving too fast. Perhaps you think God should interfere, but that is not his way. Free will is our greatest gift and if we abuse it, it is not God's fault. God is the only absolute perfection and goodness. It is man's lot to suffer because this is lacking in himself. Evil is not a substance in itself but the absence of good. Hence evil will always be part of our lives because we lack the supreme good, God himself.

Protestants

I often wonder why Protestants call themselves Protestants. I have asked many Protestants of different persuasions what they are protesting against. Some didn't know and some said they were protesting against Catholics. I asked why, and they said, "Simply because they are Catholics." I hope you can answer this riddle. — *John Stefanuk, Susanville, Calif.*

The name Protestant goes back to the *Protestatio* ("A Protest") that was delivered by a minority of delegates to the Diet of Speyer (1528), which had ruled against further innovation in the Church. The name came to be applied to those who disagreed with the teaching of the Church and broke away from it. It was never used for any particular church until the title was assumed by the Protestant Episcopal Church (1783) as the name for the American branch of the Anglican Church. The characteristics of Protestantism were the acceptance of the Bible as the sole rule of faith, rejection of the papacy and tradition, and belief in the universal priesthood of the laity. In most Protestant churches there was also a downgrading of liturgy. When your friends said they were protesting against Catholics, they were not exactly right. They are protesting against the Catholic Church, particularly certain of its teachings. However, few Protestants today have a sense of actual protest.

They are merely following a creed in which they have been raised.

Purgatory

We have a convert to Catholicism in our RENEW group who needs proof from the Bible that purgatory exists. — Name withheld, Longview, Wash.

Purgatory is one of the most frequent arguments used against the Church by fundamentalists seeking to convert Catholics. If you are looking for the word purgatory in the Bible, you will not find it because it does not exist there. Neither will you find the word Trinity, although the Trinity is a basic Christian belief. You will find a place of purgation mentioned in the Bible. However, for Catholics there are two sources of faith: the Bible and the Church (tradition). Nowhere in the Bible does it say that this inspired book is the sole source of faith. But the Bible does tell us that Jesus founded a Church, that he promised to send the Holy Spirit to guide this Church, and that he himself would be with this Church until the end of the world. Thus the Church founded by Jesus is guided by him and the Holy Spirit, protecting it in matters of faith and morals from error. It has been a consistent teaching of the Church that purgatory exists. The most recent teaching on this matter was twofold. Pope Paul VI in his "Credo of the People of God" (1968) taught: "We believe in eternal life. We believe that the souls of all those who die in the grace of Christ — whether they must still make expiation in the fire of Purgatory, or whether from the moment they leave their bodies they are received by Jesus into Paradise like the good thief — go to form the People of God which succeeds death." In 1979 the Congregation for the Defense of the Faith issued an instruction, "The Reality of Life After Death." In it the Sacred Congregation teaches: "In fidelity to the New Testament and Tradition, the Church believes in the happiness of the just who will one day be with Christ. She believes there will be eternal punishment for the sinner. . . . She believes in a possibility of a purification for the elect before they see God, a purification altogether different from the punishment of the damned. This is what the Church means when speaking of Hell and Purgatory." Jesus taught that only the pure can see God. Very few people die wholly pure. Most of us have some attachment to sin. If it is not serious sin that separates us from God, we have an opportunity to be purified (purged) of that sin. This is what the Church calls purgatory. Contact Our Sunday Visitor for the book *Life After Death*, which goes into this matter in greater detail and will answer many questions for which space is lacking here.

HELPING POOR SOULS • Please tell me of the Church's belief regarding praying for the souls in purgatory and gaining indulgences for them. How often can we gain plenary indulgences for them? Years ago we were told we could gain plenary indulgences for them every day, provided we had gone to confession and received Communion. Now I am confused. — *Mrs. Julia Garbarino, Brooklyn, N.Y.*

The Church's present teaching on indulgences was defined in an apostolic constitution issued by Pope Paul VI in 1967. An indulgence is a remission, wholly or in part, due for sins already forgiven. It can be gained by a Catholic for performing a good work and is granted by the Church because of the superabundant merits gained by Christ and his saints, and because of the power of the keys (that is, the papal jurisdiction over the Church) when Christ told his Church that what it bound would be bound in heaven and what it loosed would be loosed in heaven (Matthew 16:17-19). An indulgence is full (plenary) if all punishment is removed, or partial if some is removed. Either indulgence can be applied to the dead by way of suffrage. While many partial indulgences may be gained in a day, only one plenary indulgence a day is now allowed. To gain a partial indulgence one must perform the good work, be free from serious sin, and have the intention of gaining the indulgence. To gain a plenary indulgence, one must be free of attachment to sin, perform the work to which the indulgence is attached, and fulfill the conditions of confession, Communion, and prayer for the pope. There are many practices and prayers to which indulgences are attached and they are listed in the official book, the *Enchiridion*. Some popular devotional practices to which plenary indulgences are attached are: (1) adoration of the Blessed Sacrament for at least a half hour; (2) reading of Holy Scripture for at least a half hour; (3) saying the Way of the Cross before the Stations; and (4) reciting the Marian Rosary in a church, or in a family group, religious community, or pious association. There are a few plenary indulgences applicable only to souls in purgatory and not oneself. An example would be the plenary indulgence granted on November 2 (or on the following Sunday), which is gained by a visit to a church to pray for the dead.

NECESSITY OF PURGATORY • We were always told that when we go to confession, no matter how grave the sin, God forgives us and forgets. Why then must we atone for the temporal punishment in purgatory or by doing good works? — *Mrs. Paul Schaefer, Austin, Minn.*

God forgives, but God does not forget. What God knows, he knows for all eternity. We have to distinguish between forgiveness and atonement. It is like a boy who hits a ball through his parents' window while playing baseball. He tells his mother he is sorry. She replies, "I know you didn't mean it, so you're forgiven. However, I expect you to pay for a new window from your allowance." She does this because it is just and she wants to teach her son responsibility for his acts. Atonement for sin is one way God teaches us responsibility. Moreover, few of us die perfect, and that is what is needed to enter heaven. We still have attachment to sin. We die with our pride, our failures in charity, our lack of prayerfulness. Certainly these are small defects, not great enough to cause eternal separation from God, but they are still defects that must be removed if we are to enter the heaven of saints (those without imperfections). These faults must be purged and the place for this cleansing is purgatory. God is not only a God of mercy but also a God of justice — and justice demands reparation for acts against his will.

Race

There is something that has been bothering me for a long time. I can find no logical explanation why God, our Creator, saw fit to create some humans black. We also have the yellow race and Indians, but they are not as totally different from the white. Blacks have two strikes against them from the start. — *Mrs. Lucy Nead, Thiensville, Wis.*

First, God did not necessarily create anyone black. Color is the result of environment. What color were our first parents? No one knows. Some anthropologists believe our first ancestors were brown-skinned. They believe mankind originated somewhere in Asia, perhaps the Middle East. As people separated and lived apart, differences began to appear. Peoples in equatorial lands became darker and darker while those who went north became lighter and lighter. Today the darkest people are found in equatorial West Africa and the lightest in Scandinavia. Skin color is determined by two chemicals, carotine and melanin. The former gives a yellow tinge while the latter browns the skin. People who are darker than others simply have more melanin. It is better not to speak of people on the basis of color but of race. Many people of the Caucasian race are darker than many blacks. Color is only an accident and has nothing to do with basic humanity, in which all peoples are the same. It is unfortunate that the American experience was colored by slavery. Africans were brought to this country as slaves, kept uneducated and in poverty. Thus they were looked down upon as the lowest class of society. Unfortunately, this attitude carried over even after the end of slavery. We are all descendants of common ancestors and are all children of the same heavenly Father. The fact that the sun burned some people darker than others or that the lack of sun left some people pale and blond is purely an accident of history. In our souls, which God directly creates, we are the same — without color or physical traits. If people from all parts of the world were put in the same darkened room, and provided they all spoke the same language, no one could tell anyone's color or notice any physical differences. God loves us all equally. It is the bigotry of people who must have someone to look down upon that creates the problems in this world.

BLACK PUZZLEMENT • I am a black Catholic and a traditionalist at the young age of twenty-seven. Could you please tell me why a lot of white Catholics (laity, nuns, priests) are so hateful toward blacks but are the first to have in their petition of prayer, "Please pray for all men, of all races"? Also, I notice many blacks go to Holy Communion but not to confession. Are we not teaching my people the importance of the sacraments of the Church? — *Name withheld, Kansas City, Mo.*

I cannot answer your question directly, since I do not know the cases to which you refer. I realize there are remnants of bigotry still among some white Catholics, but I would attribute these more to family conditioning in childhood than to positive adult decisions. I have found the same thing to be true on the part of some blacks toward whites. Also, "hateful" is a strong word. I have never met a priest or nun who "hated" black people, and all those I know would accept the teaching of Christ that there are no distinctions of race before God who loves every human being equally. I do not deny that discrimination still exists in this country, and that on the part of many there are suspicions about people who are different from them, discriminations based not only on color but also nationality of parents, religion, social stature, or any difference from themselves. But these have no place in the Christian community that worships a God who created all and who died that all might be redeemed and saved. It is possible, too, that you are reading more into something than is there, perhaps from impressions picked up in your past. As for confession, I do not think blacks are any different from whites, who also are not using the sacrament. I am at a loss to explain the reversal that has taken place in confession since my own youth. I do suspect that it may be due to faulty education and preaching, which some years back decided to always stress the positive. Sin is a negative thing, but we should be taught its evil and our personal responsibility for it and the need to not only have it removed but be led to know how to overcome it. Too much of our teaching and preaching is in the abstract. It may be satisfying to preach on love toward all people, but this can ignore the family down the street whose members really need a positive expression of that love. Jesus once asked how we could say we love people at a distance whom we do not see, when we do not love those whom we can see. Love must be proven in deeds, not in words.

Rape

What can a victim of rape legitimately do to protect herself against pregnancy? — *Name withheld, Clarks Summit, Pa.*

Since the woman is a victim of an unjust aggression, she may defend herself from the effects of such attack by seeking immediate medical attention to prevent pregnancy. This includes the neutralization of the assailant's sperm, the presence of which is a continuation of such attack. Recently, the bishops of England and Wales published a statement that said that postcoital (morning after) pills may be administered, provided the victim has not ovulated, and the pills are taken urgently (within twenty-four hours). The bishops said, "Such efforts to prevent conception following rape need not be, morally speaking, acts of contraception, such as have been excluded from Christian life by the constant and very firm teaching of the Church." The statement also warns that many persons taking such pills have adverse side effects. Rape, however, never justifies the taking of innocent life (abortion), no matter how incipient.

Rapture

I recently read a book by Hal Lindsey called *The Rapture*. Why doesn't the Catholic Church address this subject along with the tribulation associated with this period, which I believe is going to occur? — *Emil J. Sereda Jr., Fresno, Calif.*

The rapture refers to Paul's description of the end-times when the Lord will return from heaven, when the dead will rise again, and the living "will be caught up with them in the clouds to meet the Lord in the air" (1 Thessalonians 4:17). Although many fundamentalist writers and preachers are predicting that the end-times are at hand, the Church teaches, according to the words of Jesus, that we do not know the day or the hour and that we should always be prepared for the Parousia, or Second Coming. There are Catholic books that treat this subject, but they avoid the fundamentalist mistakes. Probably no other Christian teaching is surrounded by as much nonsense as is the end of the world. Apocalyptic literature must be carefully interpreted and much of it cannot be taken literally, as it is often contradictory. If Christ is to come as a thief in the night (1 Thessalonians 5:2), how can he also come, as claimed in 1 Thessalonians 4:16, with blaring trumpet? We must seek to understand the writer's intention and not always his literal expression. Most homilists treat the end-times at the beginning of Advent, but when all is said and done, we simply do not know the exact when and how. Write or call Our Sunday Visitor for the booklet *Is the End Near?* by Father Edwin Daschbach.

Reincarnation

Over the past several years within my personal experiences and those of friends, several experiences are leading us to wonder about reincarnation. To the best of my recollection, Catholic doctrine leaves little room for reincarnation. Is there a way to reconcile reincarnation and Christian dogma? Can you share your thinking on these points? — *Name withheld, Kent, Wash.*

Reincarnation is the inhabiting of the soul in a new body after the death of the former body. Reincarnation is the product of eastern religions, which differ on whether the soul reinhabits the body in the same species or can take a higher or lower form of life. Reincarnation is opposed to Christian teaching because, as Hebrews 9:27 points out, "men die only once, and after that comes judgment." Death, after which there is no time to repent, and judgment, which is final, are almost thematic in the New Testament. The experiences you are referring to are a sense of *déjà vu*, a feeling of having been some place before or having experienced the same thing before. These feelings arise from the subconscious and have a natural explanation. However, there is still much we have to learn about parapsychology and the supernatural. There are scientists engaged in the study of extrasensory perception (ESP) and prevision. At the same time there is a great deal of pseudoscientism around. There is a type of person who seems drawn to the occult and paranormal, but most people have enough difficulty with the normal things of life and do not care to go exploring in fields of uncertainty.

Religious

When did the Church start using the terms clergy and laity or Religious and laity? I tend to feel this causes a division among the people of the Catholic faith. Isn't any Catholic who practices the faith a Religious? — *Daniel L. Merrick, Carmel, Ind.*

It is true that a person who lives up to his or her faith is religious (adjective with small *r*), just as the same person through baptism into the Mystical Body shares in the royal priesthood of Christ. However, the terms as you use them are precise legal terms as used in canon law. It was Jesus himself who established the hierarchical nature of the Church with Peter as head and the apostles as leaders of Christ's disciples and other followers. We find this hierarchy developed in the apostolic Church with bishops, priests, deacons, and laity. The term laity has both juridical and theological meaning, which derives clearly from Scripture. Canon law uses it in the sense of *Christifideles*, those who believe in Christ as God's revelation to mankind and who have been baptized into the People of God in his name and under the leadership of the Church's hierarchy. A cleric is one who by a particular state of life is consecrated to divine service to the People of God. A Religious is one who belongs to a religious society of men or women living in common, under a common rule, observing the vows of poverty, chastity, and obedience, and approved by legitimate ecclesiastical authority. I do not see how this structure is divisive any more than a family is divided by having a mother and father as the heads of the house.

Restitution

I bought some merchandise and the goods were guaranteed by the manufacturer, not the merchant. With no questions asked, the merchant replaced what I thought were defective goods. Later I discovered that the goods were not defective. In order to make restitution to the manufacturer, I need information as to address, etc., and that is somewhat embarrassing to ask the merchant. Am I obliged to do this? — *Name withheld, Washington, D.C.*

Restitution is an obligation arising from justice to repay another for an injury done. This injury is caused by taking or retaining what belongs to another or by damaging either the property or reputation of another. Presuming that you returned the original merchandise, there is no such obligation on you. You have what you paid for; the merchant or manufacturer has back the equivalent that can be sold again. You did cause some inconvenience, but this is not grave enough to be subject to restitution.

Right to Die

A state court recently ruled that a comatose man should be denied food and water and be allowed to die. What does the Church say about such a case? — *Name withheld, Cleveland, Ohio*

The case you mention is another example in the growing permissiveness of our legal system to allow euthanasia by starvation. The Church teaches that we must use ordinary means to preserve life but are not required to use extraordinary means. Ordinary means requires that we provide food and water; however, it does not require that a patient be connected to machines. Courts are ruling more and more that those who are no longer able to care for themselves need not be cared for by relatives or the state, yet these helpless individuals are the ones who most need the care of the state. To condemn anyone to death by starvation or dehydration is the most cruel of punishments upon people who do not deserve punishment. The crusade against "nonmeaningful" life is gathering strength all over the country, led by such antilife groups as the Hemlock Society. At the moment it is directed at the comatose, but there is no question in my mind that it will eventually include the elderly, the disabled, and the retarded on the grounds that they are no longer productive to society. The time to stop this is now, before it gains irreversible momentum as happened with abortion.

Rosary

Please publish the regulations governing the recitation of the Rosary. It is recited with many variations, omissions, and additions. — *Name withheld, Irvington, N.J.*

The Rosary is a form of mental and vocal prayer that revolves around events in the lives of Jesus and Mary. The complete Rosary consists of fifteen decades, each decade being an Our Father and ten Hail Marys. Each decade represents a mystery of the Rosary. There are three divisions, each of five mysteries: *Joyful:* the Annunciation, the Visitation, the Nativity, the Presentation, the Finding of Jesus in the Temple; *Sorrowful:* the Agony in the Garden, the Scourging at the Pillar, the Crowning with Thorns, the Carrying of the Cross, the Crucifixion; *Glorious:* the Resurrection, the Ascension, the Descent of the Holy Spirit, the Assumption, the Coronation. Usually a third, that is, five decades, is said each day (one set of mysteries). While the prayers are being said, the mind meditates on the mystery being considered. This is the essential Rosary. Custom and varied usage add other prayers, such as concluding each decade with a Glory Be to the Father, introducing the Rosary with an Our Father, three Hail Marys, and a Glory Be. In many areas it is customary to conclude the Rosary with an Our Father and three Hail Marys for a particular intention and to add the Hail, Holy Queen. So outside of the basic description there are no fixed rules, and custom is usually the deciding factor in how the Rosary is said.

WHY MYSTERIES? • When we recite the Rosary we say the mysteries appropriate for the particular day. Why are they referred to as mysteries? A more appropriate term would be events in the life of our Lord. — *Name withheld, St. Louis, Mo.*

It is true that the mysteries of the Rosary are events in the lives of our Lord and our Lady. The Church uses the word mystery in a theological sense; that is, a mystery is an event of a sacred character whose full significance is veiled. Thus while we accept the event, we do not fully understand it. For example, in the mystery of the Annunciation Mary conceives by the Holy Spirit, but we do not fully understand how this takes place. In the Incarnation we have the great theological mystery of how God becomes man. The Assumption is a mystery because we cannot explain from human experience how a human body can be assumed into heaven.

ROSARY BEFORE MASS • In our parish we were in the habit of praying the Rosary before Mass began. Now that has been stopped because we have been told that the Rosary is not a good preparation for Mass. If meditating on the life of Christ isn't good preparation, could you tell me what is? — *Margie Wethington, Louisville, Ky.*

I see nothing wrong in saying the Rosary before Mass. It is a custom in many parishes. Moreover, a plenary indulgence is granted when the Rosary is prayed and meditated upon in a church. Perhaps you misunderstood your pastor or he has another reason for not allowing the Rosary to be said before Mass. Why not talk the matter over with him?

Sabbath

Why was the Sabbath changed to Sunday and called the Lord's Day? I've been studying the Scriptures and it seems clear to me the commandments of God are not to be changed. — *Name withheld, Ramsey, N.J.*

First, there is no commandment that Saturday should be the Sabbath. The six days when we labor and the seventh when we rest (Deuteronomy 5:13) is the commandment. The Jews chose what we now call Saturday to be their Sabbath. This tradition can be traced back to the Mosaic era, but whether Moses took it from the Kenites, among whom he lived, we do not know. At the time of Jesus, Saturday (Saturn's Day) was looked upon by the Romans as a day of evil omen when nothing important should be done. The Jews made many laws about the Sabbath that led an exasperated Jesus to exclaim (Mark 2:27): "The Sabbath was made for man and not man for the Sabbath." Then he added: "The Son of Man is lord even of the Sabbath." Because of the attitude of Jesus to the Sabbath, he gained the hostility of the Jewish priests. It was not that Jesus was opposed to a day set aside to honor God, but the day had become so involved in legalisms and red tape that its true meaning was being lost. The Sabbath was a day of the Old Law and Jesus had come to fulfill that law with the New Law. So after the death and resurrection of Jesus, the apostles decided that the Christians would worship on the first day of the week. As the Church Father St. Justin Martyr explained to Emperor Antoninus, "It is on what is called the Sun's Day that all who abide in town and country come together, and we meet on the Sun's Day because it is the first day on which God formed darkness and mere matter into the world and Jesus Christ our Savior rose from the dead. For on the day before Saturn's Day they crucified him, and on the day after Saturn's Day, which is the Sun's Day, He appeared to His apostles and disciples and taught them." The observance of the first day dates from the beginning of the new Church (Acts 20:7). For some who might object that the apostles had no authority to do this, we must remember that Jesus gave Peter great power: "Whatever you declare bound on earth shall be bound in heaven: whatever you declare loosed on earth shall be loosed in heaven" (Matthew 16:19). Thus in their decision the apostles clearly showed that the New Law had replaced the Old Law and that the New Law was centered in Jesus Christ.

Sacred Vessels

I watch a local Sunday Mass on TV and notice that some of the priests use chalices and patens made of pottery. I thought these had to be of silver and gold and nothing else. — *John F. Agness, Washington, D.C.*

The present rule on sacred vessels states only that they "should be made of materials which are solid and esteemed as valuable in the region where they are to be used." The chalice cup must be impervious to liquids. The rules say that if the chalice is made of metal that could become tarnished, then the inside of the cup should be of gold. The rules allow artists to use regional cultures in their design. Some priests do have chalices made of heavy pottery as being closer to what Jesus used, rather than a gold cup, which normally only wealthy people would have owned. The rules do say that "preference should be given to materials that do not easily break or deteriorate." So while gold and silver are no longer required, the sacred vessels should be artistic and in good taste.

Saints

Years ago when I was teaching confirmation classes I had a small book of saints' names with their derivatives. I lost my book and do not know where it was published. Could you help me out? — *Sister Mary Andrew Roy, Rutland, Vt.*

The only such work at present in print that I know of is a double volume published by Our Sunday Visitor: *A Saint for Your Name.* There is one volume for boys and another for girls. The books give biographies of each saint, feast day, and names derived from that of the saint. The books are also illustrated. An index in the back of each gives quick reference.

ANDRÉ BESSETTE • At one time, in the old Church, there was widespread devotion to St. Joseph. There was a Brother André, somewhere in Canada, who was building a basilica in honor of St. Joseph. What is the address of this center of devotion? What happened to Brother André? — *Name withheld, La Lux, N. Mex.*

Brother André Bessette, a Holy Cross brother, known during his lifetime as "the miracle man of Montreal," died in 1937 and was beatified in 1982 by the Holy Father and is now called Blessed André. He had great devotion to St. Joseph and built a magnificent basilica in his honor on Mount Royal. The address is: Basilica of St. Joseph of Mount Royal, Montreal, Quebec, Canada. It is a place of pilgrimage and has a reputation for miracles. For a book on this remarkable individual, write or call Our Sunday Visitor and ask for *The Life of Brother André,* by C. Bernard Ruffin.

ANGELS AS SAINTS • People refer to St. Michael the Archangel. We were taught to pray to Blessed Michael the Archangel. Since Blessed Michael the Archangel is a spirit and never had a body, could he be a saint, too? A Presbyterian friend of mine thinks the title is irreverent. — *Name withheld, Clearwater, Fla.*

I don't see any irreverence in the term "saint," but then I do not know how your Presbyterian friend understands the word. "Saint," like many other words, can have various meanings. St. Paul, for example, used the word to mean the "holy people of God" and thus he addresses his epistles to the saints in Philippi or the saints in Rome. The Mormons refer to all members of their sect as "saints," calling their church the Church of Jesus Christ of Latter Day Saints. The Catholic Church uses the word in a double sense. One is technical and refers to the final step in the process of canonization, which advances through the stages of Venerable, Blessed, and Saint. But in the general sense in which the Church uses the word it means one who is in the presence of God in heaven. Thus all angels are saints as well as those who lived on this earth. The Church has always referred to Michael, Gabriel, and Raphael as saints, both in its liturgy and prayers. If you are old enough you may remember that formerly at the end of Mass a prayer was said to St. Michael that began, "St. Michael the Archangel, defend us in battle. . . ." Likewise, there is nothing wrong in referring to angels as Blessed, just as we refer to the Blessed Virgin or Blessed Joseph, although we also call them St. Mary and St. Joseph. Blessed in this sense means one who has found favor with God.

BENEDICT THE BLACK • We frequently hear about St. Martin de Porres. Are there no other black saints? — *Rita Johnson, Chicago, Ill.*

Yes, there are quite a few. Before Martin de Porres was canonized, one of the most popular was St. Benedict the Black. His parents were African Negroes who were taken in slavery to Sicily, where they converted to Catholicism and where Benedict was born. Benedict served his master so well that he was given his freedom and allowed to work for wages. He saved his money, bought a pair of oxen, and rented himself and his team out as a day laborer. Attracted by the lives of some hermits near Palermo, he sold his few possessions, gave the money to the poor, and became a hermit, following the rule of St. Francis. He was elected superior of the group. When he was about forty years old, Pope Pius IV ordered that all solitaries following the Franciscan rule should join a Franciscan monastery. St. Benedict entered a Franciscan community near

Palermo. His prayerfulness, charity, and good sense led to his election as superior of the community, despite the fact he could neither read nor write. When his term ended, he asked that he be allowed to go back to his work in the kitchen. He fasted for forty days, seven times a year. He slept on the floor and performed other penances. Because of his reputation for holiness, people from all over Sicily came to him for advice and direction. He died on April 4, 1589, on the date and hour he had predicted. He was then sixty-three years old. Several years later when his body was moved, it was found incorrupt.

CHRISTOPHER • I work in a gift shop where we carry medals and chains with the image of St. Christopher. Almost every day there is someone upset over what they consider to be the fact that the Church has "thrown St. Christopher out." Can you give a brief explanation of just how the Church regards St. Christopher so that I could post it and relieve the anxiety of our visitors about a saint they love? — *Mrs. Fredericka Agins, West Sedona, Ariz.*

St. Christopher was an early Christian martyr. The *Roman Martyrology* says he suffered in Lycea under Decius by being shot with arrows and beheaded. The earliest recorded church dedicated to him was in the year 452. His feast is celebrated on July 25. He is the traditional patron of travelers. This is all we know about him with any certainty, although Caxton's *Golden Legend* contains many stories. In the revision of the universal Church calendar, after Vatican Council II, some of the older saints whose feasts were mainly celebrated regionally were supplanted by newer saints of more universal appeal. St. Christopher was among those. Newspapers sensationalized the story, making it appear that St. Christopher had been "decanonized" or declared a mythical person. This simply was not true. The Vatican newspaper *L'Osservatore Romano* had to print an article pointing out that there were only so many days available on the universal calendar and that removal of some to make way for others in no way implied that those who had been replaced had somehow become unworthy of veneration. Christopher's popularity, particularly for American travelers, remains constant.

DISMAS • The Church teaches that those in heaven are saints. Does this mean that the thief who died on the cross alongside Jesus at his crucifixion (and whom Jesus promised would be with him in paradise) is a saint? If so, what is his name? — *Mrs. Joseph G. Bowling, Lawton, Okla.*

Yes, the good thief is considered a saint and is known by the name St. Dismas. His feast day is March 25. While Luke, who recounts this incident (23:39-43), does not give names to the two who died with Jesus, apocryphal literature names them as Dismas and Gestas, and for want of greater certainty these two names are used, Dismas being the defender of Christ and Gestas his unfortunate companion.

DYMPHNA • At a garage sale I bought a small statue of St. Dymphna but cannot find her listed in my book of saints. I would very much like to know about her. — *Julienne B. Horeser, Dolgeville, N.Y.*

St. Dymphna is a saint whose tomb is in Gheel, near Antwerp, Belgium. According to popular legend she was the daughter of a Celtic chief, but it is unclear whether he was Irish or Briton. Dymphna was a Christian, and after the death of her mother her father made indecent proposals to her. To preserve her chastity she fled with her confessor and two companions to Antwerp. Later the group moved to Gheel, where they built an oratory and lived as hermits. Her father, with some henchmen, tracked her down, killed the priest (St. Gerebernus) and the two women, and when Dymphna refused to return home with her father, the enraged man killed her. When the bodies of Dymphna and Gerebernus were discovered, in the thirteenth century, the tomb became a place of pilgrimage and many cures were reported among epileptics and people suffering mental illnesses. As a result, Dymphna was made patroness of epileptics and those afflicted with mental disease. Her feast day is May 15.

GABRIEL POSSENTI • I would like a summary of the life of St. Gabriel, Passionist. — *Thomas A. Griffin, Phoenix, Ariz.*

St. Gabriel Possenti was born in Assisi, Italy, in 1838, the eleventh of thirteen children of Sante Possenti, a lawyer. He was educated at a Jesuit school in Spoleto and sought to join the Jesuits but was prevented by poor health. When his health improved somewhat, he entered a Passionist monastery at Morrovalle in 1856 and was given the name of brother Gabriel of Our Lord of Sorrows. He was known for his self-denial, humility, and devotion to the Passion of our Lord. He was stricken with tuberculosis and, after great suffering, died on February 27, 1862, in a Passionist community in Abruzzi. He was canonized in 1920 by Pope Benedict XV.

INEZ • I would like to know more about St. Inez. It was my mother's middle name and now my daughter has used it for her little daughter. I heard it is the name of a saint well known in Mexico. I could not find any information in a book on the lives of the saints. Can you help me? — *Carol V. Weber, Bellevue, Wash.*

St. Inez (also spelled Ines) is the Spanish form for St. Agnes. St. Inez, or St. Agnes, was martyred as a teenager in Rome about the year 304. She is commemorated in Eucharistic Prayer I. When she refused to compromise her chastity, she was condemned to be burned at the stake by the prefect of Rome. When this failed, she was ordered beheaded. She was buried on the Via Nomentana and later the daughter of the Emperor Constantine had a church built over her grave. Devotion to the young martyr spread throughout Europe and the Spanish brought this devotion to the New World. Her feast day is January 21.

JOSEPH • A book (*History of Joseph the Carpenter*) claims that: 1. Joseph was married before Mary. 2. Joseph had children by that first marriage. 3. Some of Joseph's children were alive when Jesus lived. 4. When Joseph died, the archangels Michael and Gabriel took his soul to heaven, and his body did not decay. Is any of this accepted as belief by our Church? — *William G. McCormick, Jamaica, N.Y.*

The book you mention sounds quite imaginative. Scripture tells us very little about the background of Joseph other than that he was a just man of the family of David. Some writers on Sacred Scripture explain "the brothers and sisters" of Jesus (see, for example, Matthew 13:55) by giving the opinion that they were children of Joseph by a previous marriage and hence half-brothers and half-sisters of Jesus. However, this cannot be proved or disproved from Scripture. There is an ancient tradition in the Church that Joseph was always a virgin, but again there is no evidence of this in Scripture. The only thing we can be sure of is that these "brothers and sisters" were not children of Mary. As for Joseph being taken to heaven by Michael and Gabriel and remaining incorrupt, this is pure speculation on the part of the author and has no basis in Church teaching.

KEVIN • For our grandchildren's First Communions we have always presented them with the medals of the saints they are named after and have the name and date engraved on the back. Our grandson Kevin Paul will have made his First Communion by the time you receive this. I thought I would have to go with St. Paul because I had never heard of a St. Kevin, nor had anyone else. To my amazement, I found a St. Kevin medal in one of our religious goods stores. Who was this saint? — *Eleanor K. Erb, Fort Wayne, Ind.*

St. Kevin (baptized Coemgen by St. Cronan) is one of the patron saints of Dublin. He was born into a royal family at Leinster, probably in the early 500s. Educated by St. Petroc, he studied for the priesthood and after ordination became a hermit. Others gathered around him for his wisdom and he founded a monastery at Glendalough. He went to Rome and brought back relics for his monastery. Prominent Irish families trusted him with the education of their sons. One such pupil was the son of King Colman. Kevin lived to a very venerable age (one hundred twenty by one account) and in his last years he retired to a hermitage near his monastery. His feast is celebrated on June 3.

LUCY • Could you please send me the address of a shrine for a patron saint for people who have bad eyesight? — *Michael Redmon, Antioch, Tenn.*

The patron saint for people with eye troubles is St. Lucy. I do not know of any shrine to her in the United States. According to tradition, St. Lucy (who died in 304) was born to noble parents in Syracuse, Sicily. When she refused marriage to a suitor, she was denounced to authorities and was ordered to be burned to death, but the flames did not consume or harm her. She was then stabbed through the throat. Another tradition has her eyes torn out. Perhaps because of this or because her name means light, she has been traditionally invoked by those with eye troubles.

MEXICAN, INDIAN SAINTS • Are there any Mexican or Indian saints? I am familiar with the names of Spanish saints from Spain, but have any natives been canonized? — *M. C. Rodman, Los Angeles, Calif.*

A Mexican who comes immediately to mind is St. Philip of Jesus (Philip de las Casas), who was born in Mexico City on May

1, 1571. His life was stormy during his teens, and to keep him out of trouble his father, an importer-exporter, sent him to the company office in the Philippines. There he became engaged to be married, but before the wedding could take place his fiancée died of fever. This caused Philip to examine his life, and he then entered the Franciscans in Manila. When it came time for him to be ordained, it was decided to have the ceremony in Mexico. The ship carrying him home was caught in a storm and driven to the coast of Japan, just as a persecution against Catholics was beginning. When he went ashore to visit Franciscans there, he was arrested and crucified (1596) at Nagasaki, along with twenty-five other Christians. His feast day is February 6. Other Mexicans have had their cause introduced in Rome, among them the Indian Juan Diego, to whom the Virgin of Guadalupe appeared. Recently beatified was Father Miguel Pro, S.J., executed during the Mexican persecution of the Church. No American Indians have yet been canonized, but Blessed Kateri Tekakwitha is close to that honor. Born in an Indian village in New York state, she was converted by a Jesuit missioner. Persecuted for her new faith, she was forced to seek safety in a Catholic Mohawk village in Canada, where she died in great holiness. Known as the Lily of the Mohawks and celebrated for miracles, she was beatified in 1980 by Pope John Paul II. Also, Rome has been sent the names of three other Indians who were martyred in New York for the faith: Stephen Tegeananokoa, Frances Gonannhatenha, and Margaret Garangouas.

PAUL • How did Saul of Tarsus, who became St. Paul, get to be a saint? What did he do to merit that title? — *Melvin Le Blanc, New York, N.Y.*

St. Paul got to be a saint because of his total service to Jesus Christ. From a persecutor of the Church he became its greatest defender, ultimately suffering martyrdom by beheading for his devotion to Jesus. Paul, more than any other apostle, gave form and direction to the infant Church. He underwent great suffering to spread the new religion, as he wrote in 2 Corinthians 11:24-27: "Five times at the hands of the Jews I received forty lashes less one: three times I was beaten with rods; I was stoned once, shipwrecked three times; I passed a day and night on the sea. I traveled continually, endangered by floods, robbers, my own people, the Gentiles; imperiled in the city, in the desert, at sea, by false brothers; endured labor, hardship, many sleepless nights, in hunger and thirst and frequent fastings; in cold and nakedness." Any study of Paul's theology reveals that he was totally Christocentric. There is no question in my mind that Paul was the greatest figure that the Church has produced.

PETER CLAVER • Do you know of any religious order that is devoted to St. Peter Claver, the patron of blacks? I have always wondered about the apostles, mainly their ages. I had always assumed that they were all around Jesus' age, with the exception of Peter who always impressed me as being older. Is there anything in tradition about this? — *Melvin L. Williams, Chicago, Ill.*

I know of no religious order exclusively devoted to St. Peter Claver. Since he was a Jesuit, the Society of Jesus would pay him particular honor. So, too, I imagine, would the Josephite Fathers, who are devoted exclusively to work among our blacks. You might write the Josephite Fathers for further information: 1130 N. Calvert St., Baltimore, MD 21202. We know nothing definite about the ages of the apostles, but many scholars think they were all about the age of Christ, including St. Peter. Peter was martyred during the persecution of Nero, around the year 64. This would be about thirty-one years after the death of Christ. This would put him in his sixties, which seems reasonable.

PROTESTANT SAINTS • I am a convert of several years. I am very interested in saints who were unheard of in my previous Protestant church. Have there ever been any Protestants who have attained the status of sainthood? I have also been reading about saints with incorruptible bodies. Have any devout Protestants had incorruptible bodies? — *Eugene Wiemer, North Platte, Nebr.*

A saint (holy one) is anyone who has attained heaven and is enjoying life with God. Certainly there were many baptized Protestants who have lived holy lives, doing their best to follow the will of God as they knew it, and who thus won heaven after death. These people are saints. However, a second meaning of "saint" and the way it is usually used in the Church means "canonized saint." This is a person who has not only led a holy life but whose life has been examined in minutiae by canonical process to be sure that there is nothing contrary to holiness and whose holiness is testified to by the accomplishment of several miracles after death. The Church reserves this process only for its own members and has thus never canonized a Protestant. I do not have any knowledge of Protestants who remained incorruptible after death. Incorruptibility is often used as an argument for sainthood, particularly when this is opposed to laws of nature. For example, when St. Francis Xavier died on Sancian Island trying to enter China, Portuguese sailors who helped bury him put lime on the body to speed its disintegration. However, later when the remains were exhumed to be taken to India, it was discovered that the lime had had no effect and the body was the same as the day it was buried. This was interpreted as a mark of God's favor.

TIMOTHY • In our Maryknoll Missal there are two St. Timothys — one a martyr at Antioch and another who was stoned to death at Ephesus. Recently I heard from a friend attending a new church in Arizona, St. Timothy's, who says her pastor claims there is only one St. Timothy. Can you clarify this? — *Gertrude Netzel, Chula Vista, Calif.*

Only the Lord himself knows how many St. Timothys there are. One book of saints I have lists twelve, another six. Your friend's confusion may have arisen since the Church calendar was revised to include only one feast of St. Timothy (January 26) for the universal Church. That does not mean that the others are not saints; rather, their feasts are no longer celebrated universally, only locally. The St. Timothy feast that was retained honors the second saint you mentioned. He was a disciple and confidant of St. Paul, to whom Paul wrote two letters that are now part of the New Testament. He became the first bishop of Ephesus.

VALENTINE • I was doing a crossword puzzle and it asked for the patron saint of preachers and the answer was Paul. I have never heard of St. Paul as the patron of preachers, have you? And does the Church recognize St. Valentine as the patron saint of lovers? — *Helen M. Bennett, Orlando, Fla.*

I know of no list that has St. Paul as the patron of preachers and I would guess that this was an invention of your crossword-puzzle maker. St. John Chrysostom was named patron of preachers by Pope Pius X. He was famed for his preaching in the early Church and was called the Man with the Golden Mouth because of his eloquence. Before that, St. Catherine of Alexandria was listed as patroness of preachers because, according to a not-too-reliable tradition, she once converted by her oral arguments a whole school of pagan philosophers who were then put to death by the Emperor Maxentius. She is also said to have converted the emperor's wife, an officer, and the soldiers of the empress's guard by her preaching. However, neither event can be proved historically. Valentine was a Roman priest and physician who was beheaded in Rome under Claudius the Goth. His feast day is celebrated on February 14. People in medieval times believed birds began to mate on that date and the custom began of sending greetings to a loved one, which were called Valentines, after the feast day. Thus St. Valentine became regarded as the patron of lovers.

Salvation

My daughter thinks a person doesn't have to believe in Jesus to go to heaven, only be a good person. I tell her that Jesus said, "No one goes to the Father except through me," which proves her idea is wrong. — *Marge DeWitt, Santa Barbara, Calif.*

The ordinary means for salvation that God the Father wills is through his Son, Jesus Christ, and his teachings. Jesus in turn founded his Church, which Vatican Council II calls his "sheepfold, the sole and necessary gateway." Anyone who knew this and refused to enter the Church or to follow him and his teachings could not be saved. However, what of people who do not know this? The same document (*Dogmatic Constitution on the Church*, No. 16) says: "Those who, through no fault of their own, do not know the Gospel of Christ or His Church, but who nevertheless seek God with a sincere heart, and moved by grace, try in their actions to do His will as they know it through the dictates of their conscience — these too may achieve eternal salvation." Some writers have called these people "anonymous Christians" — that is, they would be Christians if they knew that this was what God wanted. In short, it is the teaching of the Church that God wishes everyone to be a Catholic, but those who do not know that the Church is the ordinary means of salvation can be saved as long as they follow their consciences and seek God's will.

PROTESTANTS SAVED • You stated that there were Protestants in heaven. Please explain what you mean. Hasn't the Church issued a de fide statement saying that there is absolutely no salvation outside the Catholic Church? The only possibility the Church gives to those outside relates to the invincibly ignorant. Surely, you don't think that a baptized Protestant is invincibly ignorant. — *Jeffrey M. Talbot, Monterey Park, Calif.*

I suggest that you read Chapter 2 of Vatican II's *Dogmatic Constitution on the Church* in which it is said: "Basing itself on scripture and tradition, it [the council] teaches that the Church, a pilgrim now on earth, is necessary for salvation" (No. 14), adding, "Hence they could not be saved who, knowing that the Catholic Church was founded as necessary by God through Christ, would refuse to enter it or remain in it." Thus the council reaffirmed your statement that there is no salvation outside the Catholic Church. However, the *Constitution* goes on to consider other Christians who are joined in a greater or lesser degree to the Church, even unknowingly; and finally, the council considers that even those who have not yet received the Gospel can be related to the People of God in various ways. The council Fathers then conclude: "Those who, through no fault of their own, do not know the Gospel of Christ or His Church, but who nevertheless seek God with a sincere heart, and moved by grace, try in their actions to do His will as they know it through the dictates of their conscience — those too may achieve salvation" (No. 16). For these reasons the Church sees those who serve God and try to live according to their conscience as joined to the Church in varying degrees. Whether individuals, not of the Catholic communion, are in invincible or vincible ignorance, is something else to be determined. Protestants can be both vincibly and invincibly ignorant of the true nature of the Catholic Church. Certainly there are good Protestants and non-Christians who try to do the will of God as they know it, and who believe their particular church is the true church of God. The council is saying that these people are not necessarily cut off from salvation. The desire to do God's will is the primary consideration. Catholics who fail in this will be lost while Protestants and others who succeed will be saved. Having said all this, I also affirm that the Catholic Church is the ordinary means ordained by Jesus for salvation and that it is the mission of all Catholics to work to bring those outside into the Church.

Satan

Does an ubiquitous Satan really exist? Who originated the concept of his existence, and when? — *Joseph A. McGuire, Baltimore, Md.*

There is no doubt of the Bible's and the Church's conviction of the presence of Satan and other evil spirits in the world. Satan entered human history at the dawn of humankind when in the guise of a serpent he tempted our first parents and caused original sin to enter the world (Genesis 3). Jesus called Satan "a liar and the father of lies" (John 8:44) and said (Luke 10:18): "I watched Satan fall from the sky like lightning." Satan is known by other names: the devil, Lucifer, Belial, Beelzebub, etc. Satan is a Hebrew word meaning enemy or adversary, and that is how Scripture depicts this evil being. Since God is the author of all creation, Satan and his cohorts are also creatures of God. God created angels as spiritual beings with free will. Some used this free will to rebel against God and for this offense were driven from the presence of God. The Old Testament depicts Satan as the opponent of God's plan for humanity and the New Testament as the prime enemy of Christ and then of Christians. St. Peter presents him as a greedy lion roaming among Christians seeking whom he may devour. Paul depicts him as the tempter, striving to lead all into sin. St. John in his epistle says that the Christian must choose between God and Satan, between Christ and Belial, and concludes that on the last day the Christian will be with one or the other. The Book of Revelation, particularly from Chapter 12 on, gives a biblical summary of this adversary of humanity: Although Satan is powerless against Mary and her Child, he turns his enmity toward Christians. Revelation ends with the triumph of the Lamb, with Satan and those who have succumbed to him being thrown into "the pool of fire, which is the second death" (20:14).

Scapular

The Blessed Virgin Mary promised St. Dominic that anyone who died clothed in the scapular would not suffer eternal fire. In 1920, everyone at their First Communion was enrolled in the scapular. They haven't done this for years. Why? I think that Mary would be displeased. I also asked three priests if the red scapular has the same benefits as the brown scapular. None could answer my question. — *James C. McKellips, Lodi, Calif.*

There are some twenty scapulars in use. The five most popular ones are those of Our Lady of Mt. Carmel (brown scapular), the Holy Trinity, Our Lady of the Seven Sorrows, the Passion, and the Immaculate Conception. These scapulars (two small decorated squares of woolen cloth, joined by strings and worn over the shoulders) are adaptations from the scapulars worn as part of the monastic habit. They were worn for devotional purposes and are often given in a ceremony of enrollment. In 1910 Pope Pius X authorized a scapular medal that could be worn or carried in place of the cloth scapular. The Church has never made any official decision on the promises attached to the various scapulars, and only encourages their use as a reminder that the wearer should live a truly Christian life. You may have been enrolled in a scapular when you made your First Communion, but this was not a general practice even then. Many did not feel it was proper to enroll seven-year-old children into obligations they did not fully understand. One must also be careful that superstition does not enter into the use of sacramentals or religious objects. For this and other reasons, I do not think it is wise to try and rate scapulars one against another. Each serves the same purpose: to remind us to live up to the obligations of our religion.

Scripture

Scripture scholars tell us that all the original Old and New Testament writings are either lost or not extant. The oldest Scriptures that do exist are copies of copies of copies. With the exception of the Qumran scrolls and others found around the Dead Sea, where are the oldest Scriptures to be found? — Vern Eldridge, Janesville, Wis.

This is a complicated question that would take a book to answer because there are different languages, different versions, and bits here and there in the Vatican, Near East monasteries, the British Museum, museums in Jerusalem, etc. It is true as you say that no manuscript of an author of any biblical book is still extant. What we have is the work of scribes. First, the Old Testament: Hebrew manuscripts until recently only went back to medieval times. Scholars placed great trust in these because Hebrew scholarship insisted on accuracy by copiers. Then the Qumran scrolls were discovered, which took scholarship back to the pre-Christian era, and proved the accuracy of the medieval texts. The Qumran manuscripts are now the oldest Hebrew texts extant and are in a special museum in Jerusalem. There are Greek texts (*Septuagint*) that antedate Christ. Others were made in the early Christian era. The

Codex Vaticanus dates to about A.D. 350 and is complete, with the exception of some of Genesis, thirty Psalms, and some verses in 2 Samuel. The Codex Sinaiticus (one hundred fifty-six leaves in the British Museum, forty-three leaves in Leipzig) has some lacunae and is also fourth century. The Codex Alexandrinus (fifth century) is also in the British Museum and is quite complete, but with verses in Genesis and 1 Samuel missing. Some papyrus manuscripts dating to the second century have been found in Egypt. The Latin *Vulgate* text began in 389, but there are Latin bits existing before that date. These manuscripts are in the Vatican. There are also Coptic and Aramaic texts in existence. Second, the New Testament: The Greek text of the New Testament exists in various forms. The Codex Vaticanus is missing Hebrews 9:14 on, the pastoral epistles, and Revelation. The Codex Sinaiticus contains all the New Testament and several books not admitted as canonical. Of interest to Americans is the Codex Washingtonensis, the most important biblical manuscript in the United States. It dates to the late fourth century or early fifth and contains the four Gospels. There are other texts in various places too numerous to mention here.

SINS AGAINST THE SPIRIT • In Matthew 12:30-32 it states that men's sins will be forgiven, but sins against the Holy Spirit will not be forgiven. In Mark 3:28-30 it conveys the same message. What are the sins against the Holy Spirit and why would they not be forgiven? — *Name withheld, Tucson, Ariz.*

Your quotation is not exact. In both passages Jesus does not speak of sins (plural) but of blasphemy against the Holy Spirit. The sins against the Holy Spirit are despair of salvation, presumption of God's mercy, envy at another's spiritual good, obstinacy in sin, and final impenitence. I suppose in a broad sense any one of these could be called blasphemy of the Holy Spirit because each reveals a contempt for the action of the Holy Spirit and the influence of the Spirit's grace. Such sins are obstinate sins and as long as they exist they resist the working of grace in the soul and are thus unforgivable. It was this obstinacy to which Jesus was referring in the passage you cite. The Pharisees attributed the miracles of Christ to the devil. This attitude revealed their closed mind and such opposition to the Spirit of God that it made them very difficult to convert and, if they would not repent such sin, it would never be forgiven. All sins except final impenitence can be forgiven as long as they are repented in this life. Final impenitence (resisting the Holy Spirit's call to repentance) cannot be forgiven because that is the way we die and we are judged on our relationship with God at the moment of death. Thus the ultimate blasphemy of the Holy Spirit is rejecting the Spirit's urging to reform and repent at the moment we die.

PRAYER HEARD • Recently a bishop in our parish, following the homily, stated: "We really believe, Jesus, that you meant it when you said, 'Whatsoever you shall ask the Father in my name will be granted you.' We pray the following." Since anyone over the age of reason knows this statement by Jesus Christ (if he made it) to be untrue, isn't this passage better forgotten? — *Robert C. Jones, Narbeth, Pa.*

This statement (John 14:13) was made by Jesus in the course of his Last Supper address to the apostles. Some exegetes hold that the words refer solely to the apostles to whom they were addressed, others that they were meant for all Christians. In Semitic usage, "name" is equivalent to the person. Thus faith is not a simple belief in a proposition but a deep commitment to the person. Even with the apostles, Jesus was not guaranteeing that prayer will be granted simply by the invocation of a name but because of an abiding faith, implying communion with Jesus and an obedience to the will of God. John spells this out more clearly elsewhere (1 John 3:21-22), when he writes: "Beloved, if our consciences have nothing to charge us with, we can be sure that God is with us and that we will receive at his hands whatever we ask. Why? Because we are keeping his commandents and doing what is pleasing in his sight." So it is a passage better not forgotten because I have seen it operate too many times when the conditions were present.

CELIBACY • I would like an explanation of Matthew 19:12: "Some men are incapable of sexual activity from birth; some have been deliberately made so; and some there are who have freely renounced sex for the love of God's reign. Let him accept this teaching who can." — *Francis J. Dion, Willimantic, Conn.*

In this section of the Gospels, Jesus is advocating celibacy, a style of life that was his own. He realizes that it is not a lifestyle for everyone, since he says in verse 11: "Not everyone can accept this teaching, only those whom it is given to do so." In rabbinic teaching eunuchs were divided into two classes: the impotent and the castrated. Jesus then makes a statement, surprising and out of keeping with the times, that there is a third class: those who give up marriage for the reign of God. Celibacy was not unknown in Palestine in the time of Christ. It was practiced at least temporarily by the Essenes. Both John the Baptist and Paul were celibate. Jesus is recommending it to his followers who are able to embrace such a life as leaving them freer to follow him than those in a married state who have obligations to wife and children.

MAGI • Is it true that the Bible account of the three wise men is a myth and that it is not based on fact? I heard this recently from a member of the Catholic clergy and I was shocked. — *Bernard Beauchesne, Chicopee, Mass.*

There is no evidence to disprove the story of the magi. This account is exclusive to Matthew and fits in with a theme of his Gospel — the appeal of Jesus to the Gentiles and the claim to his royal messiahship. We have many iconoclasts these days who do not hesitate to undermine the simple faith of people. Biblical criticism is a complex science, and simply because a person is a priest does not mean he is equipped for it. The Bible has stood the tests of many centuries, and you should believe *it* rather than some skeptic who likes to shock people.

TWO QUESTIONS • I have two questions to which I never received a satisfactory answer but which Protestants occasionally ask me. The first concerns Exodus 20:4-5, which makes Protestants wonder about our many statues and people kneeling before them. The second concerns Matthew 23:9, about addressing no one on earth as "Father." Has this something to do with translation? — *Patricia B. Howorth, Biloxi, Miss.*

As you know, Chapter 20 of Exodus is part of the Decalogue. Verse 4 forbids the carving of idols and verse 5 worshiping them. Most Scripture scholars hold these two verses to be later accretions to the original that read simply: "I am the Lord your God. You shall have no other gods besides me." These verses warn the Hebrews not to fall into the error of the pagan tribes that surrounded them and who made idols and worshiped them as beings of power. As for statues in church, these statues are not idols or gods but merely representations of actual people, just as the statue of some famous person in the town square is not an idol or a god but a representation honoring that individual. Catholics do not pray to the statue but to the person it represents, asking that person to pray to God for them. All this is quite different from what Exodus had in mind. As for calling our priests "Father," the verse from Matthew has always been interpreted by the Church in its restricted literal sense. Jesus was rebuking scribes and Pharisees who sought titles — *rabbi* (master), *abba* (father), and *moreh* (teacher) — to give importance to their own state. Jesus indicates that such people were unworthy of such titles. He did not mean that we shouldn't call our own parent father, or one who teaches us in school, teacher. We Catholics use the term "Father" because through baptism the priest gives us spiritual life. Jesus was reminding us that we should be humble and should not be seeking honors for our own gratification. Protestants also use titles such as Reverend (Revered One) or Pastor (Shepherd).

Scruples

I pray you can help me. I am a widow living alone. I feel I am a lost soul because of the sinful life I led when I was young. Later in life I made general confessions and I am sure I confessed everything and even then I'd go back to the priest to be sure. I receive Holy Communion every time I go to Mass and plead that the Holy Communions are not the condemnation of my soul. — *Name withheld, Cincinnati, Ohio*

Your letter reveals that you are badly afflicted by scruples. This is a very real trial and the only remedy for it is to be completely obedient to your confessor or spiritual director. You must have faith in Jesus and his Church. Jesus passed on to his priests the power to forgive sins: "Whose sins you shall forgive they are forgiven them." The Church long ago forgave you your sins. They are in the past. Live for today and not for yesterday. Say often the Serenity Prayer: "God, grant me the serenity to accept the things I cannot change, courage to change the things I can, and the wisdom to know the difference." Jesus told us that though our sins be scarlet they will be made white as snow. You have repented the past and you must not make your own purgatory. Believe Jesus and put the past out of your mind, trusting only in his mercy and love.

Seal of Confession

How can I find out the truth about the seal of confession? I was recently shocked when a priest — after hearing schoolchildren's confessions — as part of his homily revealed a problem brought him by one of the children. I couldn't believe what I was hearing. I have tried to discuss this with several priests, but none has the same answer. Is it any wonder lay people are confused today when priests cannot answer a question with uniformity? This priest was only ordained a year and a half ago, so maybe seminarians are not getting all they should be given. — *Name withheld, El Segundo, Calif.*

Canon 983 declares that the sacramental seal is inviolable. A decree of the Sacred Congregation of the Holy Office that has the effect of law states that confessors are to avoid all public talk about what they have heard in confession, whether it be in public sermons and instructions or in private conversations. Canon 1388 says that a confessor who directly violates the seal automatically incurs excommunication reserved to the pope. Woywod's *Commentary on Canon Law*, a standard reference work for priests, declares: "When a missionary, a teacher of religion, or a professor of moral theology wishes to teach the proper confession of sins, it is unnecessary and highly improper to tell how somebody confessed, for that somebody may be present and, if he is not there, others will fear lest this missionary, teacher or professor may one day speak similarly of their confession." The wisdom of these directives is shown by your reaction and the scandal that could have been given if the penitent was present. The case you mention shows a lack of common sense and a failure to understand the teaching of the Church on this matter.

Secular Humanism

Could you give a brief explanation of secular humanism? — *Frank J. Ostendorf, Aurora, Ill.*

I once heard a speaker define secular humanism as "religionless Christianity." However, this is not accurate. Secular humanism is "religionless" but also "Christianless," recognizing neither God nor creed. Secular refers to worldly or temporal concerns. Humanism refers to a way of life that asserts the value of the human being and his ability for self-realization through reason alone, with neither regard nor acceptance of the spiritual. Father John Hardon, S.J., calls it "the deification of man to the exclusion of a transcendent God." We do good to others because it is the "nice" thing to do, not because God commands it or because there is punishment (other than civil law) if we fail to do so. Ethical culture and ethical cultural societies are a form of secular humanism and these groups are promoting their philosophy in the schools as a replacement for God-centered morality. Secular humanism is a form of idolatry in which man is worshiped instead of God.

Servile Work

My husband and I are in our late twenties and have three children. Being very religious we are much bothered by the fact that my husband works on Sundays. What is a young and struggling family to do to scrape by financially and keep true to God's word at the same time? — *Name withheld, Manassas, Va.*

The Church understands this problem. Not only are there necessary services that must be maintained on Sundays, but people also have to work to keep their jobs. Our Lord himself faced this problem when Jewish officials complained to him that his disciples were not properly observing the Sabbath. After giving the example of esteemed Jewish ancestors who broke the laws of the Sabbath because of necessity, Jesus said to them: "The Sabbath was made for man, not man for the Sabbath." We therefore approach Sunday with reason and common sense, giving to God the honor we can while also taking care of those things that are necessary. You do not state your husband's working hours or the specific problem these hours cause. Keep the Sabbath as far as you are able and be assured that God understands why your husband has to work on Sundays.

Sex

I would like to know if premarital sex is no longer considered a sin. There is so much of it these days, yet we never hear this preached from the pulpit. In fact we never hear anything preached in regards to sin. Why is this? — *Mary Harrington, Chartley, Mass.*

Premarital sex is a serious wrong and it has been condemned in numerous allocutions by the Holy Father and by the U.S. bishops in their letter on sexuality. All of these condemnations have been reported in the Catholic press. I do not know why we do not hear more about this sin and other sins from the pulpit. I do know some priests talk about them, but many others are silent. In part it may be due to training. Vatican Council II was a positive council, stressing virtue over sin. This has, to a certain extent, influenced theological outlook. However, we must remember that the Ten Commandments are both positive and negative, and while virtue is to be praised, sin must also be condemned.

OCCASION OF SIN • When does an act involving a single girl and a married man become a mortal sin? What is the best way for the girl to stop this when she is in love with the man? — *Name withheld, Phoenix, Ariz.*

You do not specify what you mean by "act." If you refer to sexual intercourse, that is always a mortal sin of adultery. But even placing oneself in the occasion of sin can be mortal. It is also quite futile, since nothing can come from such a relationship. The girl is treading on forbidden ground that she must get off of at once. In such a relationship the married man is taking what he can get for nothing. The only solution for this problem is to stop seeing the man and to put oneself in a position where he is not even met. The traditional resolution to avoid the occasions and near occasions of sin is still valid.

Sign of the Cross

Can you tell me the origin of the sign of the cross? — *Charles M. Crowder, Manchester, Ga.*

The sign of the cross refers to that manual act in which two intersecting lines are drawn with the hand to symbolize the cross on which Jesus died. There are various ways of making it, such as a small cross traced with the thumb on the forehead; the large cross which goes from forehead to breast and shoulder to shoulder; and the cross made with the hand in blessing such as the priest makes at the end of Mass. It evidently arose as a spontaneous act on the part of early Christians. That it existed in the second century is testified to by the writer Tertullian, who says that in all actions "we mark our foreheads with the sign of the cross." St. Cyril of Jerusalem writes: "Let the cross be our seal, made with boldness by our fingers on our brow; over the bread we eat and the cups we drink; in our comings and goings; before our sleep and when we awake." The larger sign of the cross (which is the one most commonly used nowadays) seems to have arisen as an answer to the Monophysite heresy and was popular by the ninth century.

Sign of Peace

Did the sign of peace originate during the Second Vatican Council? If not, what was the original? — *Charles J. Sippel, Cherokee Village, Ark.*

No, it is of very ancient usage. Formerly, it was called the kiss of peace. St. Paul exhorts the Romans (16:16), "Greet one another with a holy kiss." He gives this same command in both his epistles to the Corinthians and 1 Thessalonians. The same command is given in 1 Peter 5:14. This greeting came to be used at the beginning of Mass. With the passage of time it began to disappear until it only survived among the ministers at Mass. If you are old enough, you should recall that before the changes of Vatican II, at a High Mass after the Agnus Dei, the ministers and clergy exchanged the kiss of peace by the one giving the greeting placing his hands on the shoulders of the other and saying, *"Pax tecum"* (Peace be with you), and the minister or others receiving the greeting replying, *"Et cum spiritu tuo"* (And with your spirit). This is the way the ministers should still do it. In revising the liturgy the desire was to return to older forms. Hence, the peace greeting was inserted for the laity. The celebrant's prayer for peace was removed to precede the Agnus Dei and the rubric called for the sign of peace according to local custom, which in the United States was interpreted as a handshake. Personally, I would prefer a revision of this rite, moving it to precede the penitential rite at the beginning of Mass and have the people bow to one another rather than shake hands and to use the words, "Peace be with you" and "And with your spirit" or something similar. One conclusion I came to after Vatican II is that we shouldn't freeze changes too quickly but should make them temporary for a period of five to ten years before carving them into stone.

Sin

I understand God forgives sins when we are truly sorry and confess them. But does this mean that we will never have to suffer or atone for these forgiven sins? I know someone who does commit sin and she enjoys herself and is always happy. She will be forgiven when she is ready to confess these sins. Why should I be good? — *Name withheld, Pittsfield, Mass.*

While it is common today to stress the mercy of God, to be honest we must give equal importance to the justice of God wherein every person will get his or her due. So while your friend might seem to be getting away with sin, there will one day be a balancing of the books and fair judgment given. Some people believe they will always have time to reform and straighten out their lives, but as Jesus told us, not one of us knows the day or the hour he or she will be called to God. There is an old spiritual axiom: "As you live, so shall you die." One who lives in sin will probably die in sin. How foolish to deliberately take such a risk! But even if one does have time to have one's sins forgiven, the temporal punishment remaining must still be purged. St. Augustine says the "fire" of purgatory will be "more severe than anything a person can suffer in this life." There a person will come to understand how sin separates one from God and that this terrible loss, even though only for a time, is the result of one's own misspent life.

MORTAL SIN • My friend and I have had a number of discussions over what is and what is not a mortal sin. He said you can have an immodest thought and not realize it and that is not a mortal sin. Please elaborate. — *Name withheld, St. Louis, Mo.*

A mortal sin is one that brings spiritual death. It is refusing obedience to God or the Church in a serious matter. Three conditions are necessary to commit a mortal sin: (1) it must be a serious offense in thought, word, or deed; (2) one must know it is a serious matter; and (3) one must freely choose the action. It is easy to say that this or that action is seriously wrong, but it is not as easy to say that a person doing the action is doing a serious wrong because one of the conditions may be lacking. Immodest thoughts often arise spontaneously. It is only when one realizes that the thought is wrong and then continues to dwell on it that one commits sin.

PENITENT SINNERS • I have always been taught of God's infinite mercy and his forgiveness for penitent sinners. However, Hebrews 6:4-6, 10:26-28, and 12:16 seem to contradict this belief. One of the verses seems to imply that, after once having the faith and then falling away, it is impossible to repent again. I am worried because at one time I had cast my faith aside and then came back. — *Name withheld, New Brunswick, N.J.*

What you have been taught is correct. There is only one unforgivable sin — final impenitence. This is unforgivable because the sinner dies rejecting God. All other sins are forgivable because we can seek and receive God's mercy before death. What Hebrews is talking about in the three passages is apostasy, and the last gives the example of Esau who sold his birthright for a meal. Apostasy is the complete repudiation of Christian belief after it has been accepted freely. Such apostasy incurs excommunication. In the early Church Christians were under governmental pressure to apostatize and give worship to Roman gods. This is the denial Hebrews is considering. Apostasy must be differed from neglect of one's faith, which, even when total, is not apostasy. This neglect often results from laxity or doubts. There is no formal act of denial. Apostasy must also be distinguished from heresy, which is only partial abandonment by denying certain teachings.

Soul

Can you give me the Catholic Church's definition of the human soul? Is one endowed with a soul at birth or is the soul acquired at baptism? — *Name withheld, Benton Harbor, Mich.*

Catholic theologians define the soul as the everlasting principle of life, infused into the body at the moment of conception. On the basis of this teaching, the Church stands firmly against abortion, holding that there is a continuum of life beginning at conception. The Church's teaching derives from the classical Greek philosophers who taught that there are three aspects of the human person: *sōma* (body), *psychē* (soul), and *pneuma* (spirit — the knowing and willing self of man). Modern philosophers hold that the *pneuma* is an operation of the *psyche* and not an entity in itself. The essence of the human being is the soul, created by God, which continues in existence after the death of the body. The body will be reunited with the soul in the general resurrection, not as we know it now but in a glorified state.

Stations of the Cross

My church does not have any Stations of the Cross. When the new young priest came he had them removed. I am a senior citizen and have always said the Stations, especially during Lent. What has happened to our Church? No prayers, no profession of faith, no confession, no Rosary. I look at my grandchildren and wonder how much they are missing. Shouldn't the Stations be on the wall as they always were? — *Mrs. V. K. Mayer, Virginia Beach, Va.*

There is no requirement in Church law that the Stations of the Cross be in any church. The Stations that were designed as a substitute for a pilgrimage to Jerusalem were popularized by the Franciscans. It became a customary devotion to erect them in churches, either as simple crosses or as statues or pictures. The Church endorsed this devotion by granting rich indulgences to saying the Stations. The formula for their erection was written into the Roman Ritual, and the Code of Canon Law gave both cardinals and bishops the right of erecting them. I suppose your pastor was within his right in removing them, but it would have been more prudent to consult with the parish. The only thing I can suggest is that if enough people feel strongly about their loss, they approach the pastor about restoring them, or else go to another parish that still has them.

Statues

In the new changes in the Church, we are not to have statues because they distract us. In their place are banners of colored material. The statues were always a help in reminding us of the saints and bringing us closer to God in prayer. Banners don't enhance our prayers at Mass. — *Name withheld, Faribault, Minn.*

The *Constitution on the Sacred Liturgy* (No. 125) says: "The practice of placing sacred images in churches so that they may be venerated by the faithful is to be maintained. Nevertheless their number should be moderate and their relative position should reflect right order." The removal of all statues is an excess that the council never intended. It is true that in the past some churches overdid statues so that it seemed that the altar and Mass were secondary and some people approached the statues without ever heeding the Blessed Sacrament. This was as much an excess as has been the complete stripping of some churches. The key word of the decree is "moderate." Banners can be useful liturgical aids, but they should not replace other sacred art.

Suffering

St. Thérèse of Lisieux wrote that God must have greatly loved her father because he had so much to suffer. I do not understand what the saint meant. I find it difficult to accept suffering for which I am not responsible. I become very bitter, resentful, and angry at God. Am I sinning? How do I cope with suffering that comes to me because of my physical abnormality? — *Name withheld, Chicago, Ill.*

Suffering is something that has occupied the mind of the philosophers down through the ages. The Bible frequently treats of suffering, and the whole Book of Job concerns the suffering of a just man. Job was spoken to by God through suffering. It was sent to keep him humble, and when it came, it was because of his pride. The Book of Wisdom also sees suffering as a discipline from God, a correction and a testing of fidelity that God gives only to those worthy of him. The hope of the suffering is in a blessed immortality. We must remember that we are imperfect beings and because of that imperfection things go wrong in body, mind, and spirit. The worldly mind looks upon suffering as evil and thus the modern seeks to escape it through drugs, alcohol, and revels. But to God suffering is not evil, otherwise Christ could never have endured suffering, since he could do no evil. There is an old spiritual maxim: "Whom God loves, he chastises." The saints saw suffering as a way, a shortcut, to heaven. Hence they sought out suffering when it did not come through nature, by scourgings and fastings and other severe penances. As in the Bible, they saw suffering as proof of God's love — thus St. Thérèse's remark about her father. Suffering comes to us all, in one form or another, to some more severely than others. We cannot escape it. For some, the suffering is in body, as in your case. For others, it is hidden within, in mind and soul. The important thing is what we do with suffering. We can accept it and use it to become morally stronger and closer to God, or we can reject it and grow bitter within, resentful of God. Hebrews 12 speaks of God's treatment of his sons. St. Paul tells his readers that suffering is God's paternal discipline to perfect us and he exhorts them to imitate the example of Jesus who suffered all that men can endure both in body and soul. Paul himself suffered, for he tells us he carried a defect in his body; on top of this he was beaten and tortured and imprisoned. His sufferings only made his faith stronger. Who knows what we might have become if we had not suffered, even that we might be lost for eternity? So we can use suffering as a gift from God for our spiritual growth or resent it and become inwardly stunted.

Suicide

If a person commits suicide does that person go directly to hell or does our Lord sometimes overlook this matter? — *Chester Waz, Chicago, Ill.*

This is a question that God alone can answer, since he alone knows a person's disposition at death. Suicide is a very serious sin, closely allied to final impenitence. It is a rejection of God's domination over life and a denial of his providence. But no one knows how clear these facts are in a person's mind, how confused thought is (thus diminishing responsibility) when the suicidal act is committed, or even if there is repentance after the act has taken place and before death occurs. We have to leave the fate on such people up to God's justice, mercy, and all-understanding wisdom. While the Church can prohibit Catholic burial because of notoriety or the scandal involved, even such a decision does not presume God's judgment.

Sunday Obligation

When there is no priest available in our parish, is a Communion service conducted by an ordained deacon a valid way to satisfy one's Sunday obligation? Would one be obliged to drive to a neighboring town thirty miles away to attend an actual Mass? Also, can a deacon perform a funeral or would it be better to call in neighboring clergy so that there can be a Mass? — *Name withheld, Delta, Colo.*

One does not satisfy the Sunday obligation solely by the reception of Holy Communion. In a meeting with U.S. bishops Pope John Paul II urged them to lead Americans "to an even greater conviction of the sacredness of the Lord's Day" and to "full and active participation" in Sunday Mass. Unless there is inclement weather or some other substantial reason, I do not consider a thirty- to forty-minute drive unreasonable in fulfilling the Sunday obligation. In mission countries many, many people walk for hours to get to Mass. It comes down to a question of values. People think nothing of driving for an hour to go shopping but find that same distance an excuse to avoid Mass. When Mass cannot be offered or attended, a eucharistic prayer service is the next best thing. This can be led by a deacon or an extraordinary minister of the Eucharist. A deacon can officiate at wake services and funerals, and even when priests are available, deacons are frequently given this responsibility. However, for the full funeral liturgy (Mass) a priest would be necessary. Still, if a priest is not available at the time, the deacon can conduct the interment service and the funeral Mass may be offered at a later time.

Sunday Work

I live in a farming community and I am writing you about the commandment to "keep holy the Lord's Day." Here the vast majority of the people work on Sunday, especially at planting and harvest time. Would you please explain how much work can be done on Sunday? — *Name withheld, Seneca, Kans.*

According to Canon 1247, Catholics are to abstain from such work or business that would inhibit the worship to be given to God, the joy proper to the Lord's Day, or the due relaxation of mind and body. Sunday is supposed to be a day of worship of God and a day of rest. However, the Church approaches this regulation with the example of Jesus in mind (Matthew 12:1-8, Luke 6:6-11), namely, that which is necessary can be done on the Sabbath. This leaves it up to the conscience of the individual. Because there are critical periods in farming — sowing at the right time, getting the harvest in during a limited period of time — it is permitted to work at these times, as are people allowed to work who are performing essential services. The Church also implicitly recognizes this fact by allowing the Saturday Vigil Mass. This change was originally sought by Latin American bishops, whose people traditionally have Sunday markets to sell the produce they raise during the week, and which is necessary for them to live. I know that there was once a great deal of legalism connected with Sunday work, people measuring work in minutes that would not break the law. But we are expected to approach the law with reason, moderation, and good judgment. In the end it is our conscience that must decide this matter.

Tithing

I want to contribute my fair share for the financial support of our parish. However, I do not have any guidelines to go by regarding how much to give. Is church tithing an acceptable practice? — *Name withheld, Martinsburg, W. Va.*

It is one of the commandments of the Church that Catholics are bound in conscience to contribute to the support of their parish, but the amount and manner are not fixed by law, leaving it up to the conscience of each parishioner. In recent years the movement toward tithing has been growing, and many Catholics now follow this practice. Tithing is biblical in origin and the practice is mentioned forty-six times in the Bible. It involves setting aside one-tenth of one's income for the work of religion. The earliest example in the Bible is Abraham giving one-tenth of his gains to the priest Melchizedek. The Jews did not always pay their tithes to the priests in money but often in cattle, farm produce, or wine. The early Church followed this practice as a continuation of Jewish custom, and there was Church legislation on the matter in the fourth century. The practice fell into disuse but as noted is now being voluntarily restored. Those who advocate the practice suggest that five percent be set aside for one's parish and five percent for such special needs as the missions, Peter's Pence, and special collections. It is an old axiom that God will not be outdone in generosity, and those who do tithe are very enthusiastic about it.

Tradition

You have written several times that, unlike Protestants, Scripture is not the sole rule of faith for Catholics because the Church gives equal rank to tradition. Can you explain this further? — *Robert Newbold, Cincinnati, Ohio*

The two sources of Catholic faith are Scripture and tradition. St. Paul in 2 Thessalonians 2:15 instructs his converts, "Therefore, brothers, stand firm. Hold fast to the traditions you have received from us." So from the earliest days of the Church, tradition has had importance. Moreover, Jesus promised to be with his Church for all time and that the Holy Spirit would guide it and keep it from error. Thus what the apostles and Church Fathers did takes on tremendous importance. It is from this teaching that infallibility and inerrancy flow. The Second Council of Nicaea in 787 said that its actions followed "the divinely inspired teaching of our Holy Fathers, and the tradition of the Catholic Church, for we know that this is the Holy Spirit who certainly dwells in it." The same council describes tradition as "the doctrine of our Holy Fathers." It is the teaching of the Church that the apostles received more from Christ than is contained in the Gospels. As Vatican II puts it, "The apostles, handing on what they themselves had received, warn the faithful to hold fast to the traditions which they have learned either by word of mouth or by letter, and to fight in defense of the Faith handed on for once and for all." The same council explains, "The tradition which comes from the apostles develops in the Church with the help of the Holy Spirit." Thus the mystery of Christ remains present in history.

Transfiguration

In the Transfiguration (Matthew 17, Mark 9), Peter said to Jesus, "How good it is to be here. With your permission, I will erect three booths here, one for you, one for Moses, one for Elijah." What is meant by erecting three booths? Are they temporary or permanent places of habitation or shrines? I would like a true explanation. — *William A. Ruspantine, Beverly, N.J.*

The Israelites had a feast called *Sukkoth*, which can be translated as tabernacles, booths, tents, or places of meeting. This feast took place in the fall, after the harvest, when there would be a gathering of the clans who came together and would go around meeting relatives and friends in tents that were set up. When the Jews became less nomadic, this feast was celebrated annually in Jerusalem for seven days. You may also remember in Exodus how the Jews had a portable tent (tabernacle), which was set up whenever they camped and which held the Ark of the Covenant. There the priests would go to commune with God. This is what Peter had in mind when he made his offer to Jesus. He thinks the last days have come and he would like to celebrate from that moment on the Feast of Tabernacles. He would erect his tents as places of eternal meeting with Jesus, Moses, and Elijah. However, Jesus ignores his request, indicating that the days of trial are not yet over and that the last days are not yet at hand.

Transubstantiation

Please tell me a few things about transubstantiation. I know it is dogma. What is the changing of the bread and wine based on? Why do Lutherans and other denominations not accept this? Does the Anglican Church accept this dogma? Is there any biblical passage about this? — R.E. Marsh, Salem, Oreg.

Transubstantiation is the theological term for the change of the substance of bread into the body of Christ and the wine into the blood of Christ, which is accomplished at the Consecration of the Mass. While this teaching is as old as the Church, the actual word was not used until the Fourth Lateran Council in 1215. In response to Protestant challenge to this doctrine, the Council of Trent issued authoritative treatment on the subject, which was reaffirmed by Vatican Council II. Pope Paul VI in his "Credo of the People of God" summed up Catholic teaching: "We believe that, as the bread and wine consecrated by the Lord at the Last Supper were changed into His Body and Blood which were to be offered for us on the Cross, so likewise are the bread and wine consecrated by the priest changed into the Body and Blood of Christ now enthroned in heaven. We believe that the mysterious presence of the Lord under the appearance of those things which, as far as our senses are concerned, remain unchanged, it is true, real, and substantial presence. Consequently, in this sacrament there is no other way in which Christ can be present except through the con-

221

version of the entire substance of bread into His Body and through the conversion of the entire substance of wine into His Blood, leaving unchanged only those properties of bread and wine which are open to our senses. This hidden conversion is appropriately and justly called by the Church transubstantiation.'' This doctrine is based on the Catholic interpretation of Scripture. Jesus announced this doctrine after his multiplication of loaves in his discourse on the Bread of Life (John 6:22ff) in which he declared: "Let me solemnly assure you, if you do not eat the flesh of the Son of Man and drink his blood, you have no life in you." Most of his Jewish listeners could not accept these words and turned away from him. The apostles believed and remained. Then on the night before his death Jesus assembled his apostles at the Last Supper (Luke 22:14-20) where he instituted the Holy Eucharist and commanded his followers to perpetuate the sacrifice. It was the fulfillment of the earlier discourse. The Church has always taken these words of Christ literally. When the Protestant revolt came, this interpretation of the Church was rejected and it was taught that the words of Christ should not be taken literally but only symbolically. To counteract this erroneous teaching, the Council of Trent restated and explained the ancient doctrine. Today, some Anglicans agree with the teaching of the Catholic Church, and some Protestants are seeking explanations that go beyond symbolism, coining new words to explain their theories but not yet prepared to accept Catholic teaching.

Tubal Ligation

What is the Church's stand on married women having their tubes tied? Is it a mortal sin? Is it forgivable? Can one still receive the sacraments? I am still a single woman, but I know married Catholic women who have done this because they say they can't afford a large family. — Name withheld, Newark, N.J.

Tubal ligation is a grave sin. It is opposed in fact to the Fifth Commandment and in intention to the Sixth Commandment. Like all sins it is forgivable in confession, provided there is sorrow for it, atonement, and purpose of amendment. Some moralists believe that generally in cases of tubal ligation there is no true sorrow for the sin and that purpose of amendment is lacking. If such is the case then the sin would not be forgiven even though the person went to confession. As long as one is in serious sin, one cannot receive the sacraments, but once that sin has been properly forgiven, full Catholic life is restored. Tubal ligation is a popular form of birth control, but its use seems to be diminishing.

Ukrainians

I was told by a friend of mine who is a Ukrainian Catholic that he was both baptized and confirmed as an infant. Is this actually so? If so, as an adult could he choose to be confirmed again? — *Sheila A. Mellick, Syracuse, N.Y.*

Your friend is correct. It is the custom of the Eastern churches to give both baptism and confirmation (holy chrism) at the same time. This custom is recognized by the Holy See. There are three sacraments of initiation into the Catholic faith: baptism, confirmation, and the Eucharist. In the Eastern Rites the first two are given to infants at the same time. In the Western Church these first two are separated for infants. However, the *Rite of Christian Initiation of Adults* specifies: "According to the ancient practice maintained in the Roman Liturgy, an adult is not to be baptized unless he receives confirmation immediately afterward, provided no serious obstacle exists. This connection signifies the unity of the paschal mystery, the close relationship between the mission of the Son and the pouring out of the Holy Spirit, and the joint celebration of the sacraments by which the Son and the Spirit come with the Father on those who are baptized." This ceremony is usually followed by Mass, so the newly baptized receives baptism, confirmation, and the Eucharist in a continuous ceremony. Since confirmation imprints an indelible character on the soul, it cannot be repeated. An infant who is confirmed could not have the sacrament repeated when he or she gets older.

Virginity

I wish you could help me explain to my young people why they should remain virgins until marriage. I am told I am not "with it." I will not permit them to bring their dates home to bed down at my place. The young people think nothing of spending their vacations with their boy friends or girl friends. Marriage was sacred in our day. Today most TV programs have everyone hopping in and out of bed at random. This even applies to the oldsters such as *The Golden Girls*, so how can we expect our young people to think it is not all right? The Church doesn't discuss it anymore but just goes along. What is your opinion? — *Monica Rockwell, So. San Francisco, Calif.*

There are two discoveries that came into being shortly after World War II that have wrought a profound social change in the United States. One was the creation of "the pill," which was intended to be a means for controlling family size but which has become a passport for easy sex. The pill has given women a feeling of security in sex without fear of pregnancy, which formerly was a great restraint. It has made today's easy sexual mores possible. The second was the development of television as an entertainment medium. The industry quickly fell into the hands of producers and writers who were, at best, amoral and scornful of religion. There were exceptions, but they were rare. While general audiences appreciated moral quality and made such shows as *The Waltons* and *I Love Lucy* popular, the TV establishment began introducing free sex into situation comedies until today almost anything goes, and in most dramas a bedroom scene is mandatory. There is never a question of moral values on the part of the characters and never a problem of conscience. This amorality cannot help but affect viewers, Catholics included. The Church teaches two sexual commandments: virginity before marriage and monogamy in marriage. If these commandments were followed, the problem with AIDS and other social diseases would be almost nonexistent. If your children were living a fully Christian life, they would be following these commandments. Instead, like many other Catholics, they have adapted to the common social culture, which is post-Christian. The Church to be successful must appear as a counterculture. What your children and so many others need is conversion, and this is what the Church in the United States must preach. Many are concerned at the inroads that fundamentalist groups are making, even among Catholics. The reason is that the fundamentalists preach conversion and a new way of life. Our young people have to be challenged to accept the teachings of Christ and change their values. Baptism and even a Catholic education are no proofs that this has been done. The fundamentalists speak of being born again. We must challenge our youths to be "born again" to the values of Jesus and not those of the world. God's grace is still operative in the world and it is not God who has failed but ourselves.

Vocations

There is no question in my mind that both religious orders and the diocesan priesthood are sick. Religious communities of women are aged and dying; those of men have closed their training houses. Diocesan seminaries are at an all-time low. What do you think God is telling us? — *Hilda Rochdale, Los Angeles, Calif.*

First, I think you are drawing a long bow, and, second, you cannot judge the entire Church by what is happening in the United States or Europe. And even there you cannot make universal conclusions. While many of the old orders and women's institutes have come on hard days, others are prospering. Mother Teresa's order, the Missionaries of Charity, is getting more than ample vocations. The male Legionaries of Christ order is growing rapidly. The Church is burgeoning in the Third World and vocations in such places as Africa and India are at an all-time high. Major seminaries in the Church reached their low point (60,142 seminarians) in 1975 and since then have been rising steadily and in 1984 passed the 80,000 mark. In this period seminarians from North America shrank from 12,264 to 8,894. But in the same period seminarians in South America went from 5,587 to 13,768, and their numbers in Central America and the Caribbean almost doubled. It may be that in years to come the United States instead of sending missioners abroad will be on the receiving end from Asia and Latin America. So I don't think God is telling us anything by what is happening in this country, other than that he will take care of the needs of his Church. A more apt question might be: Why are we suffering a vocational crisis in the United States? I know many reasons are given: the breakdown of the family, affluence, materialism, the question of celibacy, and on and on. Undoubtedly, all of these play a part, but my own theory is that our religious societies and our seminaries have become a mirror image of their own civilization: They no longer really diverge or stand apart from their times. In short, they have lost their polarity. When Francis of Assisi left his materialist world, put on a coarse robe, and established a strict way (that is, adherence to poverty, chastity, and obedience), the contrast he presented drew those who questioned the values of the world in which they lived, and the Franciscans — both men and women — grew rapidly. Today, a great deal of this polarity has disappeared and the challenge of contrast — a way of life different from the world — has been lost and blurred. I believe those institutes that remain true to the visions of their founders will prosper, while those who water down those visions to adapt to the world as "a sign of the times" will only create problems for themselves. We don't need a mirror image of the world — what we need is a reverse image. That is what Mother Teresa presents and why so many are drawn to follow her.

LATE VOCATION • I've noticed a lot of older men being ordained. Are women afforded the same privilege of entering religious life in their forties and fifties? Also, if one has been divorced but had an annulment through the Church, does that exclude her from religious life? — *Name withheld, Bayville, N.J.*

That depends upon the religious community. Some do accept older women. Years ago the accent was on young women, but with the shortage of religious vocations, many communities now accept older applicants in order to keep up their membership. Inquiry would have to be made of each individual group. As for the second part of your question, there is no law invalidating the admission of a woman whose marriage was annulled, since an annulment is a ruling that there was no marriage in the first place, and that she is the same as she was before the attempted marriage. The only thing in canon law is found in Canon 643, which makes one of the invalidating impediments to acceptance in a religious community that of being a spouse in a current marriage. But that is not the case here.

War

Please tell me why during war Catholics fight Catholics, such as in World War II? Priests would bless Catholics before battle and send them to fight other Catholics. Is it more important to follow the law of the land or God's command "Thou shalt not kill"? — *Joseph Rocco, Northford, Conn.*

The question you ask is one that has troubled many people over the centuries, during which Christian nations have fought Christian nations. While one has the right to self-defense, it must be proportionate to what one would lose. Thus you could defend your own life, even at the cost of an aggressor's life. You could not take an aggressor's life if only a few dollars are involved. But Jesus gave counsels that called for a more disinterested action: "But what I say to you is: Offer no resistance to injury. When a person strikes you on the right cheek, turn and offer him the other. . . . Should anyone press you into service for one mile, go with him two miles" (Matthew 5:39, 41). And again (verse 44): "My command to you is: Love your enemies, pray for your persecutors." These counsels of Jesus are the ideal form of action. However, in times of war this is sometimes quite difficult. While the United States makes provisions for conscientious objectors, Nazi Germany, for example, did not. If a person refused service, he was executed. In World War II many Americans felt an obligation to oppose Nazi tyranny. As for a priest sending soldiers out to kill other Catholics, this is a distortion. Priests (chaplains) did bless soldiers, asking God to keep them safe and giving them absolution in case death took them. But the chaplain does not send them into battle, as that is the doing of military officers who are carrying out in turn the orders of their superiors. What your question implies is that we live in an imperfect world and even among Christians, beliefs do not always run deep.

Wealth

Is the Catholic Church, as an institution, anti-wealth and against making a profit? All the sermons I have heard for the past forty years are anti-wealth and pro-giving away everything. Where in the Bible does it say that we must be poor? — *Lawrence Dziedzic, Norwalk, Calif.*

Jesus did not condemn wealth, but he told his followers that they were to be poor in spirit (Matthew 5:3). Jesus saw that wealth could lead its owners from God and cause injustice to the poor, and he warned against allowing wealth to control its owner because "where your treasure is, there is your heart also" (Matthew 6:21). Jesus made himself the Messiah of the poor and was himself a poor man. The Church, in being faithful to Jesus, must support the poor, succor them, and see that the Gospel is preached to them. The difficulty with wealth is that it is often gained at the expense of the poor, that too many people turn it into an idol or a god to be served, and that as such it takes people from the true God. A rich man can be saved, but it is not easy for him (Matthew 19:16ff). There are rich and powerful people who have become saints (St. Louis or St. Casimir, for example), but far more saints have been poor people. So the Church does not condemn wealth as such but simply warns of its dangers and at the same time urges those with more of this world's goods to be mindful of their needy brothers and sisters.

Worship

In Revelation 19:10 it is written: "And I fell down before his feet to worship him. And he said to me, 'Thou must not do that. I am a fellow servant of thine and of thy brethren who give the testimony of Jesus. Worship God!'" If an angel from heaven says, "Thou must not do that," why must we bow down and worship our pope? — *Ramiro Rueda, South Gate, Calif.*

Worship is the reverence due only to God. To give it to anyone else would be seriously sinful. Like the angel, the pope is only a servant. Indeed, one of his titles is "Servant of the Servants of God." But because the pope is the vicar of Christ on earth and the successor of St. Peter, we do show him respect for his office. Respect is shown in many ways. In the United States we show respect for the flag by saluting it and we show respect for people by shaking hands. In England, when one is presented to the queen, a man bows low and a woman curtsies. This is not worship but respect for the office. In Arab lands the deep bow (salaam) is a sign of respect, so also in Oriental cultures. Thus, when a person bows to the pope, it is a sign of politeness and respect, not of worship.